Maritime Professions

International Studies in Maritime Sociology

Series Editors

Agnieszka Kołodziej-Durnaś, Frank Sowa,
and Marie C. Grasmeier

VOLUME 2

The titles published in this series are listed at *brill.com/isms*

Maritime Professions

Issues and Perspectives

Edited by

Agnieszka Kołodziej-Durnaś, Frank Sowa
and Marie C. Grasmeier

TUTA SUB AEGIDE PALLAS · 1683 ·

BRILL

LEIDEN | BOSTON

Cover illustrations: (top left) Fishing Spiekeroog, year: 2014, source: copyright by Frank Sowa; (top right) Contship, year: no date, source: copyright by Marie C. Grasmeier; (bottom left) Stevedores, year: no date, source: copyright by Marie C. Grasmeier; (bottom right) Ship Norddeich, year: 2011, source: copyright by Frank Sowa.

Library of Congress Cataloging-in-Publication Data

Names: Kołodziej-Durnaś, Agnieszka, editor. | Sowa, Frank, editor. | Grasmeier, Marie C., editor.
Title: Maritime professions : issues and perspectives / edited by Agnieszka Kołodziej-Durnaś, Frank Sowa and Marie C. Grasmeier.
Description: Leiden ; Boston : Brill, [2023] | Series: International studies in maritime sociology, 2667-0798 ; volume 2 | Includes bibliographical references and index.
Identifiers: LCCN 2022058793 (print) | LCCN 2022058794 (ebook) | ISBN 9789004518858 (hardback) | ISBN 9789004518841 (ebook)
Subjects: LCSH: Marine resources. | Fishers. | Sailors. | Aquaculture.
Classification: LCC HC92 .M374 2023 (print) | LCC HC92 (ebook) | DDC 333.91–dc23/eng/20230104
LC record available at https://lccn.loc.gov/2022058793
LC ebook record available at https://lccn.loc.gov/2022058794

Typeface for the Latin, Greek, and Cyrillic scripts: "Brill". See and download: brill.com/brill-typeface.

ISSN 2667-0798
ISBN 978-90-04-51885-8 (hardback)
ISBN 978-90-04-51884-1 (e-book)

This book is printed on acid-free paper and produced in a sustainable manner.

Contents

PART 3
Micro-Sociological Approaches

Tables and Figures

Tables

Figures

Notes on Contributors

Marco Alberio
is Professor of Sociology (economic and labour processes) in the Department of Sociology and Business Law at Alma Mater Università di Bologna (UNIBO), Italy. His current position is the result of an international career path across Europe and North America. He has been Professor in Canada for more than eight years before being also appointed at UNIBO: one year at Sainte-Anne University (Nova Scotia) and seven at the University of Québec (UQAR - Lévis). He is holder of a Canada Research Chair (CRC) in social innovation (2016-2022) at UQAR. He is editor of the Canadian Journal of Non profit and Social Economy Research/Revue canadienne de re-cherche sur les OSBL et l'économie sociale. He has been doing research in the field of maritime sociology since several years, studying more specifically the career paths in the Canadian fishing industry, as well as the impacts of global and climate change on coastal fishing (indigenous and non-indigenous) communities. He also does research in Europe (Italy, Switzerland, France etc.), and elsewhere (e.g., Brazil, Colombia, Mexico).

Linda Beck
currently works as a research assistant at the Institute of Sociology at the University of Göttingen. She holds a M.A. in Sociology. For her doctoral project she is conducting research on ethnic fragmentation and solidarity among workers in the German construction sector.

Roland Dobrzeniecki-Łukasiewicz
PhD; sociologist, associate professor at Warsaw Management University in Warsaw, Lecturer at Vistula University in Warsaw. Coordinator of family foster care in Family Support Center. His professional and personal interests cover the issues of Polish immigration in Europe and its relationship to transnational homelessness and social rejection (cyber rejection, rejection of prisoners, religion aspects of rejects inclusion, evangelization through art). Methodology of migration studies- blog, web page and other immigrant data resources. Methodology of quality research, Visual Grounded Theory, Visual data, Sociology of politics and Maritime sociology.

Marie C. Grasmeier
currently works as a research assistant at the Institute of Sociology at the University of Göttingen. She holds a M.A. in Sociology. For her doctoral project she

is conducting research on ethnic fragmentation and solidarity among workers in the German construction sector.

Nuria Jiménez García

Phd in Social and Cultural Anthropology from the National University of Distance Education (UNED), Spain. She has just finished a postdoctoral stay in the Rural Development Postgraduate Program at the Autonomous Metropolitan University (UAM) of Mexico City, in which she developed the research "Gender, fishing and defense of natural resources. Strategies and struggle of fisherwomen for the rescue and conservation of the coastal lagoon system". This research arises from the proposition that the problem of fisherwomen today is one of the main emerging issues in fisheries and maritime anthropology and in studies of the new rurality, which has been little studied compared to other important issues that have focused on the greatest attention from the academy. This clear lack of studies on gender issues contributes to leaving rural women and women in fishing societies in a threshold of invisibility that favors their social fragility. Her main lines of research have been focused on feminist ethnography, rural women, resistance, use of spaces, gender and fishing, tourism and environmental management.

Agnieszka Kołodziej-Durnaś

is a sociologist and psychologist, professor at the University of Szczecin, Poland. She has published articles on maritime professions (e.g. in European Societies, Transformations in Business and Economics) and introduced Research Stream in Maritime Sociology to European Sociological Association conferences.

Iwona Królikowska

holds a PhD in social sciences in the field of sociology. She is a researcher and lecturer at the Naval Academy in Gdynia (AMW) and a career advisor and trainer cooperating with seafarers' training centers. Królikowska's advisory and research interests relate to the sociology of the sea, professional development and management in a multicultural environment. It also runs a children's and youth university promoting maritime culture.

Camilla Mevik

is a doctoral candidate in Social Anthropology at the Centre for the Studies of the Professions, at the Oslo Metropolitan University, in Norway, and an affiliate to the research project (Dis-)Assembling the life cycle of container ships: Global ethnographic explorations into maritime working lives, at the

Department of Social Anthropology of Oslo. Her PhD project is based on an extensive ethnography of the everyday organisation of work aboard a vessel, which she examines as an example of how highly racialized unequal social relations form an integral part of the maritime industry today in addition to the political scope of the maritime world. Mevik is a maritime ethnographer with many years of experience researching the maritime industry and maritime labour. She has carried out ethnographic research onboard a Scandinavian-crewed vessel engaged with the oil-and gas segment of the maritime cluster as well as onboard a mixed nationality crewed gas tanker trading worldwide.

Astrid Męczkowska-Christiansen
is an associate professor at the Faculty of Humanities and Social Sciences of the Polish Naval Academy. Her research interests involve social, cultural and political contexts of education and development of the human. As a representative of critical current in social sciences her research interests (both theoretical and empirical) are focused on issues related to distribution of power, with its asymmetries, in various fields of educational and social practice. In her research she mostly employs post-structuralist methodological orientation, with a special attention to post-Foucauldian critical discourse analysis.

Birgit Pauksztat
is an Associate Professor at the Department of Business Studies at Uppsala University, Sweden. Her research interests include social networks, organizational behavior and employee well-being. Much of her work has focused on seafarers, addressing topics such as job demands, strategies for dealing with problems, interpersonal relationships, social support, and well-being. Her most recent work concerns seafarers' experiences during the COVID-19 pandemic. Her work has been published in, among others, Social Networks, International Journal of Human Resource Management, Maritime Policy & Management, Marine Policy and Safety Science.

Shaun Ruggunan
is an associate professor of human resources management at the University of KwaZulu-Natal, in South Africa. His research focuses on maritime labour markets with a focus on seafarers in the global shipping industry. Shaun has also published on management education, the sociology of professions and what it means to decolonise management studies in a South African context.

Ana Slišković
is Associate Professor of Psychology at University of Zadar, Croatia. She received her PhD in Psychology from University of Zagreb, Croatia, in 2010.

Her main research interests relate to occupational stress and work-related well-being. She contributed to the book Maritime Psychology (editor: Malcolm MacLachlan, Springer, 2017) by the chapter on occupational stress in seafaring. Her latest paper in this field focuses on seafarers' well-being in the context of Covid 19 pandemic (WORK, 2020).

Frank Sowa
is Professor of Sociology at Nuremberg Institute of Technology, Germany. He received his PhD from the Friedrich-Alexander-University Erlangen–Nuremberg in 2013. His main research interests are poverty, social welfare and social policy as well as culture studies, identity politics in Greenland and sociology of social problems. One of his latest works is 'The transformation of work in welfare state organizations: New public management and the institutional diffusion of Ideas' (together with Ronald Staples and Stefan Zapfel, Routledge, 2018).

Ya Wen
is an assistant professor in the department of social work, school of marine culture and law, Shanghai Ocean University in China. Her main research interests are children's welfare, social policy and environmental social work.

Wen Zhang
is an associate professor in the department of social work, school of marine Culture and Law, Shanghai Ocean University in China. Her main research interests are ocean sociology and environmental anthropology. She is the author of "Disembedding 'Nature': Environmental and Social Change of a Pastoral Area in Inner Mongolia since 1949" (2016), and the Chinese translator of "Becoming Salmon: Aquaculture and the Domestication of a Fish" (2021).

Introduction: Maritime Professions as a Field of Social Research

Marie C. Grasmeier, Agnieszka Kołodziej-Durnaś and Frank Sowa

1 Introduction to this Volume

On a global scale, more than 40 million people make their living working directly at sea as fishers, seafarers, in aquaculture or seabed-mining, or related occupations such as dockworkers, shipbuilding, logistics, maritime administration, secondary branches of shipping, marine tourism and other maritime professions. Moreover, the world as we know it today would be inconceivable without the maritime economy and the people who work in such maritime professions (Kołodziej, 2022). Significant social developments such as industrialisation or globalisation are historically and currently closely entangled with the phenomenon that the Polish maritime sociologist Ludwik Janiszewski named 'marinization' ('marynizacja') (Janiszewski, 1988; see also: Kołodziej & Kołodziej-Durnaś, 2022). With this concept, Janiszewski refers to a development of increasing importance for human life and society, an increasing entanglement of the terrestrial with the maritime realm (Kołodziej, 2019; Bryniewicz, 2004).

Since ancient times, the work of the maritime professions has connected societies through maritime trade and extended the circulation of material goods and people, but also of narratives, beliefs, ideas, languages, species, diseases, violence, and cultures, to the entire world known at the time (Braudel, 1972). Global maritime trade and the maritime professions that carried it out were also a necessary prerequisite for the later development of industrialisation and capitalism, in that in many cases they only made possible what Karl Marx called 'primitive accumulation' through economic exploitation of the colonies of the European empires (Campling & Colás 2021, p. 42–45; Grasmeier, 2021). Thus, according to many researchers, the transatlantic, so-called 'triangular trade' contributed a considerable part to the growth of social wealth in the imperialist centres, which was necessary for industrialisation, but also, through the displacement of enslaved people and indentured labourers as well as the transport of migrants, to the development of the population structure in large parts of the world such as the Americas, Australia and Africa. Thus, not only the world economy but also global societal structures such as racism (Gilroy, 1993), the development of modern gender relations (Federici, 2004) and class configurations (Limebaugh & Rediker 2012; Aguilar 2003; 2014) are

 | DOI:10.1163/9789004518841_002

historically as well as currently closely linked to the practice of maritime occupations. Today, the shipping industry and overseas trade are a necessary condition for the existence of a fully developed world market (Campling & Colás, 2021, p. 216–218).

Often, maritime activities and professions played and still play pioneering roles in developments that later continue in other social fields (Campling & Colás, 2021, p. 163, 216). For instance, joint-stock companies developed with overseas trade, which required distribution of risk among a pool of shareholders due to the large sums of capital and long turnaround times needed at the time (Campling & Colás, 2021, p.26–30). Nowadays, as another instance, seafarers populate the first almost completely globalised labour market, which anticipated the transnationalisation of labour taking place now in many other areas, too (Aguilar 2003; Gerstenberger & Welke 2004, Ruggunan, 2016, p. 77–90).

Not only does the sea serve as a natural space as a precondition and means for economic and military activities, but its human use also changes it (Campling & Colas 2021, p. 41). For example, whaling was historically not only a significant factor for industrialisation by supplying raw materials for emerging technologies and an industry that provided employment for many people (Dolin, 2007). At the same time, it caused an immense change in the marine ecosystem through the near extinction of many species (Rocha, Clapham, & Ivashchenko, 2015) and, with the International Convention for the Regulation of Whaling, the establishment of the International Whaling Commission (IWC) and the resulting catch moratorium of 1982, became one of the first areas of international environmental governance (cf.: Fitzmaurice, 2017, Gambell, 1993, Kalland,1993, Young et al. 1994), even though whaling as a maritime profession still plays a role in some societies, e.g. in the Arctic or Japan (Caulfield, 1997, Freeman, 2000, Kalland & Moeran, 1992, Sowa 2014, van Ginkel, 2007).

Today, global fisheries represent a similar problem area. The overfishing of the world's oceans, which has been going on since the beginning of industrial fishing, is changing maritime ecosystems and threatening a significant source of food for the world's population. This is evident not only globally, but above all regionally in the competition between capitalist industrial fishing fleets of the global North and local coastal fisheries, for example in many African countries, which threatens to destroy the livelihoods of the latter and thus brings about fundamental upheavals in the coastal societies concerned (Bolster, 2012; Nauen, 2020).

However, the maritime professions and their history have not only such material societal, political, and ecological repercussions on humanity's life but also a significant influence on cultural meaning-making. Since they take place on the sea as the *Other* of land-society, they are largely removed from the general population's gaze and therefore lend themselves as a projective surface for longings, fantasies, and mythicisations (Foucault, 1986; Heimerdinger, 2005). Thus, narratives about the sea, much of which relate to the experiences of the lifeworlds of maritime professions, are a significant component of the cultural web of meaning in societies and an important factor shaping local cultural identities (Asmussen, 2022, Ellis, 1991, Izdebska & Kozłowska, 2022; Kołodziej, 2022; Kronfeld-Goharani, Mondré, & Werner, 2020; Pessel, 2022, Sowa, 2013, 2022; Warsewa, 2022). For example, many languages, such as English, as well as political and societal discourses, are full of maritime metaphors (see Mussolf, 2000). For instance, we speak of 'being all at sea' when we are not sure what to do in a certain situation; a person or a thing that is particularly important in a certain context and on which a lot depends is referred to as a 'mainstay' in reference to the eponymous element of ship's rigging; someone 'is on board' when they are in the picture about something, and someone new to an organisation receives an 'onboarding' in order to be 'on board'; the editor has the job to make all the chapters for this volume 'shipshape'. Such established linguistic images are the expression of centuries of human activities on and with the sea (see also Kim 2022).

A local example of the cultural significance of maritime professions is the discourses around the culture of migration of Filipino seafarers. Since early colonial times, the Philippines has become a nation of professional seafarers who supply the global market with maritime labour until today (Aguilar, 2003; 2011; 2012). Overseas Filipino workers, a significant proportion of whom are seafarers, are now an omnipresent social type in the everyday consciousness of the Philippine society, heavily charged with cultural meanings and playing an important role in economic, developmental and nationalist discourses (Aguilar, 1996; 1999; 2014; Fajardo, 2011).

Another instance is whaling in some coastal areas around the world where regional whaling cultures could be characterised by activities that had cultural or social significance during the production, distribution, or consumption of whale meat and construct regional and indigenous identities (Akimichi et al., 1988, Dahl, 2000, Firestone & Lilley, 2005, Kalland & Moeran, 1992, Sowa, 2014; 2015). Members of the maritime profession of whalers need to have knowledge of whale behaviour, whaling skills and technological competences. Furthermore, the commercial distribution of whale meat as well as a non-commercial culture of sharing it also have an impact on local people's beliefs and activities, e.g. the spiritual worldview of the human-animal relationship, the respect for whale souls and the exchange and invention of culinary whale recipes.

Concerning the knowledge of maritime professions, formal schooling and training are obviously important but are not the only knowledge bases when dealing with the ocean environment. Ethnographic research revealed that the wealth of knowledge of Icelandic skippers about the ecosystem did not come from a formal education but resulted from years of practical involvement with the environment (Pálsson, 1994; 2006). The skippers' extensive knowledge of the ecosystem comes during the course of fishing where they learn outdoors, acquiring a kind of tacit knowledge, hunches and intuition.

Not least because of these social relevancies, sociological research on maritime occupations is almost as old as sociology itself (Sowa & Kołodziej-Durnaś, 2015). Ferdinand Tönnies, who is considered one of the founding fathers of the sociological discipline, delivered empirical studies on seafarers' social situation in Schleswig-Holstein and a dockworkers' strike in Hamburg as early as the end of the 19th century (Assmussen, 2022). When sociology was established as a scientific discipline in Poland after the Second World War, and with it the sociology of the sea, the first empirical subjects were the occupational groups of deep-sea fishers in the 1960s and seafarers since the 1970s (Kołodziej, 2019, p. 162). Later, studies on dockworkers, shipbuilders (Kołodziej-Durnaś, 2019) or sex workers in port cities (Kozłowska, 2016) were added, just to name a few examples.

Sociologists in and from the Philippines are primarily concerned with the country's role as a labour supply country for the global labour market for seafarers. They study the cultural and socio-economic impact of labour migration on the domestic society (cf. Aguilar, 1996, 2014, Flores, 2015, Lorente, 2012, Ofreneo, 2015, Opiniano, 2004, Serquiña, 2016), the working conditions of Filipino seafarers in the global merchant fleets (cf. Acejo, 2021, Aguilar, 2003, Amante, 2003, 2015, Binghay, 2015) and their subjective coping strategies (cf. Aguilar, 2003, Dimayuga, 2008, Fajardo, 2011; Fernandez & Krootjes, 2007, Mendoza, 2015). Established, in 1995, the Seafarers' International Research Centre constitutes another important institution of sociological research on maritime professions on a global level. The centre's work focuses mainly on issues of working conditions and occupational health and safety of seafarers in the global merchant fleet and the effects of the global labour market (cf. Gekara & Sampson, 2021).

For some sociologist, the ship as a social space has also served as an exemplary case or a laboratory to study social systems in general. When Erving Goffman (1961) developed his conception as a total institution, he also used life on board ships as an object of study. However, the characterisation of ships as such institutions does not remain uncontested and initiated an important controversy among sociologists of maritime professions (Grasmeier, 2020, p. 22–24; Janiszewski, 1992, Kołodziej & Kołodziej-Durnaś, 2022, Grasmeier, Kołodziej-Durnaś, & Sowa, 2022).

2 On the Individual Articles

Yet, the study of maritime labour and occupations is still under-represented in the social sciences and humanities. With the present volume, we attempt to fill this gap by representing recent research on maritime professions drawing on a wide variety of disciplinary approaches and subject matters. From macro-structural reflections about maritime labour and employment, through empirical explorations of specific issues of maritime labour, reflections on gender and diversity in the maritime professions to the politics of ocean and coastal management, the volume attempts to grasp the diversity of the field and provide an introduction to key research questions of maritime social research. With a wide range of case studies from Asia, Latin America, Canada, and Europe, this collection of maritime social research hopes to reflect the discipline's international character. The book is divided into three parts. The first one comprises the studies of macro-sociological and meso-sociological approach to professions.

In the first chapter, **Shaun Ruggunan** indicates that the sea is surprisingly rarely studied by sociologists and sociology. He thinks maritime sociology is necessary but not easy to establish as a new sub-discipline and popularised worldwide. He postulates to theorise the sea as a social space via the perspective of industrial sociology and discusses two professional categories: dockworkers and seafarers. His contribution consists of emphasising the Black trade union movement's role, and the dockworkers' strikes in the historical struggle against Apartheid in South Africa. Further, he analyses capital and labour restructuring processes under the condition of globalisation (by the example of the practice of 'Flags of Convenience' to seek cheaper workforce and generally cut the transport costs). From the perspective of critical industrial sociology, the author provides the reader with a comparison of traditional (national) employment of seafarers vs global (flag of convenience) maritime labour.

Camilla Mevik conducted ethnographic research including participant observation on an offshore supply vessel operating in a windmill field off the North Sea's German coast. She analyses seafarers' everyday practices of 'making a ship'. As constructing a windmill is a complex operation, representatives of many companies (e.g. charterers) and institutions are also involved in organising the work of the vessel's crew. In such circumstances, a ship is perceived by the charterer as merely a tool used (simply a part of 'global supply chain through logistics'), making it difficult for crew members to create the vision of their professional identity and the stability of working conditions. The author shows how seafarers are de-skilled and deprived of control of their work and how they attempt to reclaim it daily.

In their ethnographic study **Marie C. Grasmeier and Linda Beck** explore how seafarers in the global merchant fleet constructed occupational identities through symbolic boundary work processes. Their data stem from qualitative interviews with seafarers, ethnographic fieldwork on board a container ship, and autoethnographic data Marie C. Grasmeier had at her disposal due to her many years of professional experience in the industry. The authors use the theoretical lens of boundary-work, initially proposed by Frederik Barth (1969) and later popularised in sociology by Michel Lamont (1992, 2000) and others, combining it with Marxian theory to explore the connections of everyday boundary-work and the subjects experiences within globalised class-relations. Besides a strong tendency to draw boundaries between themselves and 'landlubbers' as outsiders to the occupational group, the seafarers studied by the authors employed background identities such as nationality, 'race', and gender in their occupational boundary-work. Seafaring is still understood as a masculine culture of work that expressed itself in regular observations of misogynist practices and instances of the patriarchal discourse of exclusion identified by Marie C. Grasmeier and Linda Beck (this volume) in everyday life. Moreover, despite being de facto members of a transnational occupational group, European seafarers widely understood their occupational identity in terms of whiteness, thereby symbolically excluding their colleagues from the global South from the community of practice. Besides the importance of such background identities, the ships crew's formal internal differentiation by ranks and departments also served as a boundary-work and identity construction field.

In the second part of the book another three chapters are presented which deal with gender issues at sea taking into account the relevance and importance of gender discourses in the field of maritime professions.

Astrid Męczkowska-Christiansen and Iwona Królikowska use the methods of Critical Discourse Analysis to investigate gendered discourses in the identity construction of women seafarers. They identify both discourses of exclusion (misogynistic discrimination) and openness (of the maritime labour market towards women). The data analysed include, among others, focus-group interviews, individual in-depth interviews, photos and reporting as well as information texts published by organisations and institutions operating in the maritime industry. The authors recall the history of women's presence at sea and present their data analysis. Males express a patriarchal discourse of exclusion to protect seafaring as a space of male dominance. Another discourse, the one of maritime career instrumentalisation, is mostly expressed from successful women seafarers' position. Finally, a discourse of openness of the labour market is mostly met in the texts of documents issued by maritime branch institutions and organisations.

In the next chapter, **Nuria Jiménez García,** explores the struggles of rural Mexican fisherwomen to work in a strongly male-dominated profession and to sustain their eco-system of a coastal lagoon. The women-fishers' cooperative Mujeres pescadoras del Manglar, located in Costa Chica, Oaxaca, started operating in 2016. Nuria Jiménez García analyses life in the cooperative from the perspective of maritime anthropology, gender studies and political ecology. Themes of her study are different ways of accessing natural resources as well as environmental racism in an area mainly inhabited by Afro-Mexicans. The cooperative is exceptional in that its members do not only care for profit but are engaged in socio-ecological issues, e.g. for ecological education, conservation of natural resources, biodiversity and gender equality.

Marco Alberio provides another chapter about gender relations in the fishing industry. He discusses the issue of the gendered division of labour in the fishing sector. The shortage of human resources in this branch makes it more open not only to technological but also social innovativeness. The author provides an analysis of the development of the industry in Canadian Quebec based on the data of national censuses 1986–2016 and detailed qualitative research. Women working in the fishing industry are most frequently employed as deckhands which is the lowest-paid occupation in this profession. The author shows that women are perceived as playing an important but invisible role in this branch. They are mainly involved in processing and marketing of maritime resources ashore. Even if they are not employed formally in the fishing business, women contribute reproductive work in the domestic sphere helping to organise their husbands' businesses, preparing food, doing accounting or assisting in repairs.

The third part of the book is devoted to studies with micro-sociological orientation dealing with the situation of crew members, seafarers and fishers.

Drawing on an increasing scientific interest in understanding the factors contributing to accidents in shipping and issues of health and well-being of crews, **Birgit Pauksztat** scrutinises the importance of social relations among crewmembers on board merchant vessels. While much of the existing state of research focuses on individuals, the author shifts the attention towards the social interactions among seafarers on board and their social interactions, as well as the factors shaping them. Moreover, she states that their consequences tend to be underestimated by social interactions typically being ignored in studies on fatigue and sleepiness. Here, social isolation is considered a mental health problem of individuals, and crewing decisions are made based on individuals' salary costs rather than efficient collaboration. In sum, it is not reflected in the majority of current research that, rather than a collection of individuals, it is 'the crew' who runs the ship. Accordingly, the author highlights the importance of crew members' social relations on board. Moreover, she identifies and analyses the social factors shaping social relations on board.

Ana Slišković examines the role individual personality traits, work motivation and job satisfaction play in seafarers' well-being. While previous research has focused mainly on physical aspects of occupational health and safety, mental health has only recently become the subject of both research and interest among maritime stakeholders. In this context, Ana Slišković asks about the importance of individual differences as a complement to a consideration of socio-demographic and work-related aspects. In her study, she used Diener's measures of well-being (Satisfaction with Life Scale, Scale of Positive and Negative Experience, and Flourishing Scale), Goldeberg's IPIP Big-Five factor markers, Work Extrinsic and Intrinsic Motivation Scale, and the newly developed Seafarer's Job satisfaction Scale, to determine the extent personality traits, work motivation and job satisfaction can explain different aspects of seafarers' subjective well-being. She shows that certain personality traits, self-determined motivation, and satisfaction with working conditions are significantly related to seafarers' well-being.

Setting sails on a course further East, we present **Wen Zhang and Ya Wen's** study on retired fishers' situation in China. Here, the authors compare two islands on the Chinese archipelago of Zhoushan. They conducted research among elderly former fishers living in these islands, finding that the retired fishers acquire insufficient social and psychological support. The majority of the respondents live alone or only with their spouses since their children migrated to the large cities. The former fishers feel marginalised and cheated by the society at large, forgotten during the process of modernisation although, at the same time, they recall their past as brilliant and great and express a kind of nostalgia for the sixties and seventies of the twentieth century, although fishing at that time was very dangerous (e.g. due to the lack of weather forecasts at these times). The authors explore the topic in the perspective of ocean sociology with respect to sociological imagination and the social changes in China and demand the development and improvement of marine social work.

Roland Dobrzeniecki-Łukasiewicz analyses the situation of families of Polish seafarers after the socio-political changes in 1989. The situation of seafarers in communist Poland was privileged in that they could visit the world outside the Iron Curtain and earned a part of their salary in Western currencies which meant access to foreign goods. However, this part of the salary paid in "real money" did not accrue for seafarers' pensions. Since the seafarers' families usually consumed these riches day-by-day, not considering investments in the future, they became poorer and poorer after the economic system changes starting in the 1990ies. The author shows how seafarers and especially fishers lost their jobs during the transition period, and both themselves and their wives were not able to quickly acquire new education and qualifications. These were the main causes of today's poor condition of many Polish families of former seafarers.

References

Acejo, I. (2021). The Experience of Being a Filipino Seafarer on a Multinationally Crewed Ship. In V. O. Gekara & H. Sampson (Eds.), *The World of the Seafarer* (pp. 99–111). Springer International Publishing. https://doi.org/10.1007/978-3-030-49825-2_9

Aguilar, F. (1996). The Dialectics of transnational Shame and National Identity. *Philippine Sociological Review* 44(1–4). 101–136.

Aguilar, F. (1999). The triumph of instrumental citizenship? Migrations, identities, and the nation-state in Southeast Asia. *Asian Studies Review* 23(3). 307–336.

Aguilar, F. (2003). Global migrations, old forms of labor, and new transborder class relations. *Japanese Journal of Southeast Asian Studies* 41(2). 137–161.

Aguilar, F. (2012). Manilamen and seafaring: engaging the maritime world beyond the Spanish realm. *Journal of Global History* 7(3), 364–388.

Aguilar, F. (2014). *Migration revolution: Philippine nationhood and class relations in a globalized age*. Singapore: NUS Press in association with Kyoto University Press, Japan

Akimichi, T., Asquith, P. J., Befu, H., Bestor, T. C., Braund, S. R., Freeman, M. M. R., Hardacre, H., Iwasaki, M., Kalland, A., Manderson, L., Moeran, B., & Takahashi, J. (1988). *Small-Type Coastal Whaling in Japan. Report of an International Workshop*. Occasional Publication No. 27. Edmonton: Boreal Institute for Northern Studies, Japan Social Sciences Association of Canada.

Amante, M. S. (2003). *Philippine global seafarers: A profile*. Cardiff: SIRC–Cardiff University. http://marinerscanaman.edu.ph/L4SS/images/2014/june/Amante%202003%20Philippine%20Global%20Seafarers%20SIRC%20Cardiff%2097%20pp.pdf

Amante, M. S. (2015). *Industrial democracy in the rough seas: The case of Philippine seafarers*. Members-Only Library.

Assmussen, J. (2022). Maritime identities in Western Baltic Port Cities. In: A. Kołodziej-Durnaś, F. Sowa, M.C. Grasmeier (eds). *Maritime Spaces and Society* (pp. 71–89). Leiden/Boston: Brill.

Barth, F. (1969). Introduction. In F. Barth (ed.). *Ethnic Groups and Boundaries: The Social Organisation of Culture Difference*. (pp. 9–38). Bergen, Oslo, Tromsö: Universitetsforlaget.

Binghay, V. C. (2005). *Ensuring occupational health and safety for overseas Filipino seafarers*. 8th ISLSSL Regional Congress, Taipei, Taiwan, Invited Paper, 149–164.

Bolster, W.J. (2012). *The Mortal Sea: Fishing the Atlantic in the Age of Sail.* Belknap Press.

Braudel, F. (1972). *The Mediterranean and the Mediterranean World in the Age of Philip II.* Collins.

Bryniewicz, W. (2004). *Geneza i dzieje socjologii morskiej.* Szczecin: Wydawnictwo Naukowe Uniwersytetu Szczecińskiego.

Campling, L., Colás, A (2021). *Capitalism and the Sea.* Verso

Caulfield, R. A. (1997). *Greenlanders, whales, and whaling: sustainability and self-determination in the Arctic.* Hanover: University Press of New England.

Dahl, J. (2000). Saqqaq. *An Inuit hunting community in the modern world.* Toronto: University of Toronto Press.

Dimayuga, R. (2008). The social identities of Filipino seafarers. *Asian and Pacific Migration Journal* 17(1). 79–90.

Dolin, Eric J. (2007). *Leviathan: the history of whaling in America.* New York: W.W. Norton & Company.

Ellis, R. (1991). *Men and Whales.* New York: Alfred A. Knopf.

Encinas-Franco, J. (2016). Overseas Filipino workers (OFWs) as heroes: Discursive origins of the "Bagong Bayani" in the era of labor export. *Humanities Diliman: A Philippine Journal of Humanities* 12(2).

Fajardo, K.B. (2011). *Filipino crosscurrents: oceanographies of seafaring, masculinities, and globalization.* Minneapolis, London: University of Minnesota Press.

Federici, S. (2004). *Caliban and the Witch. Women, the Body and Primitive Accumulation.* Brooklyn. Autonomedia.

Fernandez, B., & Krootjes, R. (2007). Seafarers—Invisible Part of the Filipino Diaspora in Europe: Scenarios from Onboard Research. In F. M. Hoegsholm (Ed.), *In de Olde Worlde: Views of Filipino Migrants in Europe* (pp. 58–82). Philippine Social Science Council and Philippine Migration Research Network. http://unesdoc.unesco.org/images/0015/001530/153056e.pdf

Firestone, J., & Lilley, J. (2005). Aboriginal Subsistence Whaling and the Right to Practice and Revitalize Cultural Traditions and Customs. *Journal of International Wildlife Law and Policy* 8, 177–219.

Fitzmaurice, M. (2017). *International Convention for the Regulation of Whaling.* United Nations. https://legal.un.org/avl/pdf/ha/icrw/icrw_e.pdf. Accessed on February 12, 2021.

Flores, V. B. (2015). Remittances of the Overseas Marine Service Workers To The Philippines: Implications To Good Governance. *Asia Pacific Journal of Education, Arts and Sciences* 2(2), 60–67.

Foucault, M. (1986). Of other spaces. *Diacritics* 16(1), 22–27.

Freeman, M. M. R. (2000). *Endangered peoples of the Arctic. Struggles to survive and thrive.* Westport, Conn.: Greenwood Press.

Gambell, R. (1993). International management of whales and whaling: an historical review of the regulation of commercial and aboriginal subsistence whaling. *Arctic* 46(2), 97–107.

Gekara, V. O., & Sampson, H. (Eds.). (2021). *The World of the Seafarer: Qualitative Accounts of Working in the Global Shipping Industry* (Vol. 9). Springer International Publishing. https://doi.org/10.1007/978-3-030-49825-2

Gerstenberger, H., Welke, U. (2004). *Arbeit auf See: zur Ökonomie und Ethnologie der Globalisierung*. [Work at Sea: on the Economy and Ethnology of Globalisation.] Münster: Westfälisches Dampfboot.

Gilroy, P. (1993). *The Black Atlantic*. Harvard University Press.

Grasmeier, M.C. (2020). Das Schiff als sozialer Ort. [The ship as a social space]. In U. Kronfeld-Goharani, A. Mondré, and F.J. Werner (eds). *Der Mensch und das Meer – wie Erzählungen unseren Umgang mit dem Ozean beeinflussen* (pp. 21–34). Kiel, Hamburg: Wachholtz.

Grasmeier, M.C. (2022). The ship as a postcolonial space. In A. Kołodziej-Durnaś, F. Sowa, M.C. Grasmeier (eds). *Maritime Spaces and Society* (pp. 202–219). Leiden/Boston: Brill.

Grasmeier, M. C., Kołodziej-Durnaś, A., & Sowa, F. (2022). Thinking Maritime Spaces Sociologically: An Introduction. In A. Kołodziej-Durnaś, F. Sowa, & M. C. Grasmeier (eds). *Maritime Spaces and Society* (pp. XIV–XXIX). Leiden/Boston: Brill.

Heimerdinger, T. (2005). *Der Seemann: Ein Berufsstand und seine kulturelle Inszenierung (1844–2003)*. [The Seaman: An Occupational Status Group and Its Cultural Production.]. Köln: Böhlau.

Izdebska, K., Kozłowska, U. (2022). Specificity of Maritime Culture on the Example of Urban Monuments and Anti-monuments. In: A. Kołodziej-Durnaś, F. Sowa, M.C. Grasmeier (eds). *Maritime Spaces and Society* (pp. 163–181). Leiden/Boston: Brill.

Janiszewski, L. (1988). Marynizacja. Przyczynek teoretyczny. *Roczniki Socjologii Morskiej* 4, 5–14.

Janiszewski, L. (1992) Statek morski jako instytucja totalna. *Przegląd krytyczny głównych stanowisk badawczych*. Szczecin: Wydawnictwo Naukowe Uniwersytetu Szczecińskiego.

Kalland, A. (1993). Management by Totemization: Whale Symbolism and the Anti-Whaling Campaign. *Arctic* 46(2), 124–133.

Kalland, A., & Moeran, B. (1992). *Japanese Whaling: End of an Era?* London: Curzon Press.

Kim, S.K. (2022). Toward Sea of Hybridisation: An East Asian Theoretical Exploration. In: A. Kołodziej-Durnaś, F. Sowa, M.C. Grasmeier (eds). *Maritime Spaces and Society* (pp. 25–45). Leiden/Boston: Brill.

Kołodziej, A. (2019). The Concept of Marinization by Ludwik Janiszewski. To Understand the Influence of the Sea. *Cultural Interaction Studies of Sea Port Cities* 20. 159–179.

Kołodziej, A. (2022). Maritime culture – ways of understanding, scope of influence, controversy. In A. Kołodziej-Durnaś, F. Sowa, M.C. Grasmeier (eds). *Maritime Spaces and Society* (pp. 129–144). Leiden/Boston: Brill.

Kołodziej, A., Kołodziej-Durnaś, A. (2022). Maritime sociology in the making. In A. Kołodziej-Durnaś, F. Sowa, M.C. Grasmeier (eds). *Maritime Spaces and Society* (pp. 3–24). Leiden/Boston: Brill.

Kołodziej-Durnaś, A. (2019). The Changing Maritime Industry Sector in Poland: Organizational Field and Organizational Culture. *Pomorstvo-Scientific Journal of Maritime Research* 33(2), 241–246.

Kozłowska, U. (2016). Ciemna strona miasta portowego. Kuplerstwo i sutenerstwo jako nieodłączny element prostytucji (lata sześćdziesiąte). [The dark side of the port city. Procurement and pimping as integral elements of prostitution (1960's)]. *Roczniki Socjologii Morskiej. Annuals of Marine Sociology* XXV, 37–43.

Kronfeld-Goharani, U., Mondré, A., and Werner, F. J. (2020). Einführung. In: Kronfeld-Goharani, U., Mondré, A., and Werner, F. J. (eds.). *Der Mensch und das Meer. Wie Erzählungen unseren Umgang mit dem Ozean beeinflussen* (pp. 9–17). Hamburg, Kiel: Wachholtz.

Lamont, M. (1992). *Money, Morals, and Manners: The Culture of the French and American Upper-Middle Class*. Morality and Society. Chicago: University of Chicago Press.

Lamont, M. (2000). *The Dignity of Working Men: Morality and the Boundaries of Race, Class, and Immigration*. New York: The Russel Sage Foundation.

Linebaugh, P., & Rediker, M. (2012). *The many-headed hydra: Sailors, slaves, commoners, and the hidden history of the revolutionary Atlantic*. Verso.

Lorente, B. P. (2012). The Making of "Workers of the World" Language and the Labor Brokerage State. In A. Duchêne & M. Heller (Eds.), *Language in Late Capitalism. Pride and Profit*. (pp. 183–206). Routledge.

Mendoza, V. M. (2015). Filipino Maritime Students and Seafarers: Defying Dominant Social Imaginaries. *Philippine Sociological Review* 63, 33–59.

Mussolf, A. (2000). Maritime journey metaphors in British and German public discourse: transport vessels of international communication? *German as a foreign language* 3/2000. http://www.gfl-journal.de/3-2000/musolff.pdf. Accessed on February 12, 2021

Nauen, C. E. (2020). Sozial gerecht und ökologisch nachhaltig? Widersprüchliche Narrative in der handwerklichen Fischerei. In: Kronfeld-Goharani, Ulrike, Mondré, Aletta, and Werner, Franziska J. (eds.). *Der Mensch und das Meer. Wie Erzählungen unseren Umgang mit dem Ozean beeinflussen* (pp. 141–157). Hamburg, Kiel: Wachholtz.

Ofreneo, R. E. (2015). Growth and employment in de-industrializing Philippines. *Journal of the Asia Pacific Economy* 20(1), 111–129. https://doi.org/10.1080/13547860.2014.974335

Opiniano, J. M. (2004). *Our future beside the exodus: Migration and development issues in the Philippines*. Friedrich-Ebert-Stiftung.

Pálsson, G. (1994). Enskilment at Sea. *Man* 29(4), 901–927.

Pálsson, G. (2006). Nature and Society in the Age of Postmodernity. In A. Biersack & J. B. Greenberg (Hrsg.), *Reimagining political ecology* (pp. 70–93). Durham: Duke University Press.

Pessel, W.K. (2022). When The Sea Comes to the City. The Case of Polish 'Port' Elblag. In: A. Kołodziej-Durnaś, F. Sowa, M.C. Grasmeier (eds). *Maritime Spaces and Society* (pp. 108–125). Leiden/Boston: Brill.

Rocha, R. C., Clapham, P. J., Ivashchenko, Y. (2015). Emptying the Oceans: A Summary of Industrial Whaling Catches in the 20th Century. *Marine Fisheries Review* 76(4), 37–48.

Ruggunan, S. (2016). *Waves of Change. Globalisation and Seafaring Labour Markets*. HSRC Press.

Serquiña, O. T. (2016). "The greatest workers of the world": Philippine labor out-migration and the politics of labeling in Gloria Macapagal-Arroyo's presidential rhetoric. *Philippine Political Science Journal* 37(3), 207–227. https://doi.org/10.1080/01154451.2016.1253822

Sowa, F. (2013). „Was bedeutet ein Wal für Sie?" – Divergenzen von Walperzeptionen in Deutschland, Japan und Grönland. *Forum Qualitative Sozialforschung/Forum: Qualitative Social Research* 14(1), Art. 10.

Sowa, F. (2014). Seaside Communities in Crisis: On the Construction of Collective Identity in a Japanese Whaling Town after the Moratorium. *Annuals of Marine Sociology/Roczniki Socjologii Morskiej* XXIII, 21–35.

Sowa, F. (2015). Kalaalimernit: the Greenlandic taste of local foods in a globalised world. *Polar Record* 51(3), 290–300.

Sowa, F., & Kołodziej-Durnaś, A. (2015). A Short Introductory Note on Maritime Sociology. In S. Lessenich (ed.). Routinen der Krise - Krise der Routinen. Verhandlungen des 37. Kongresses der Deutschen Gesellschaft für Soziologie in Trier 2014 (pp. 1564–1570).

van Ginkel, R. (2007). *Coastal Cultures: An Anthropology of Fishing and Whaling*. Apeldoorn-Antwerpen: Het Spinhuis.

Warsewa, G. (2022). Local culture in the process of transformation of port-cities. In: A. Kołodziej-Durnaś, F. Sowa, M.C. Grasmeier (eds). *Maritime Spaces and Society* (pp. 90–107). Leiden/Boston: Brill.

PART 1

Macro-Sociological and Organizational Approaches

CHAPTER 1

Seafarers and Dockworkers: Implications for Industrial Sociology

Shaun Ruggunan

1 Introduction

The aim of this chapter is to show how studies of seafaring and dockworker labour markets can enhance and contribute to a fuller picture of industrial sociology. Seafarers' labour restructuring in the merchant marine and dockworker organising are the two cases examined by the chapter. Industrial sociology has historically both in the global North and South focused overwhelmingly on terrestrial social issues. These include the analysis of labour markets, labour processes, organised labour, labour geographies, professional milieus of workers as well as understanding the trajectories of global capitalism. When these social phenomena are considered from a maritime perspective, they tend to emanate from maritime historians, maritime economists, and maritime scholars generally working outside of sociology. Whilst the empirical work done by maritime scholars has important implications for industrial sociology, the lack of a maritime sociological imagination in theory building from maritime cases often means that sociology and its subdiscipline of industrial sociology are poorer for it. This chapter argues that one way to reinvigorate industrial sociology is for it to consider the maritime social world not as a peripheral area of interest but one that is central to understanding trajectories of capitalism and organised labour in a globalising world.

2 Industrial Sociology

Sociology is broadly understood as the systematic study of social groups, social institutions and human social behaviour that collectively comprise society (Giddens & Sutton, 2017). Given this broad definition, a number of sub-areas of the discipline developed to understand specific aspects of human societies. One sub-area is that of industrial sociology or the sociology of work. Industrial sociology is concerned with understanding how work is organised, the dynamics of work organisations, how labour market institutions shape

 | DOI:10.1163/9789004518841_003

the organisation of work and the various ways in which work and labour markets intersect with other aspects of society such as social identities, social movements and economic well-being (Watson, 2008).

The industrial revolution's preoccupation with productivity and efforts to increase it via Taylorist and Fordist principles was a fertile ground for both industrial psychologists and industrial sociologists to try and understand the machinations of humans within formalised industrial work contexts. Industrial psychologists such as Elton Mayo were concerned with how to increase motivation levels of workers through more subtle means than Taylor's scientific management approach (Ransome, 2020). For industrial sociologists, however, the analysis was two pronged. First, it was at a macro-level and focused on how capital manufactured control and consent in the workplace. Harry Braverman's study on organising production, for example, remains a seminal account of managerial control, worker resistance, manufacturing consent of workers and the deployment of power in the industrial workplace (Previtali & Fagiani, 2015). Beynon's work also remains seminal in any account of understanding work in the industrial factory (Thompson & Ackroyd, 1995). Second, it focused on subjective experiences of work under capitalism. Themes of consent, control, autonomy and viewing the worker as more than a factor of production, provided a critique of scientific management approaches. As the discipline evolved, so did the ethnographic accounts of work in modern settings. For example, Burawoy's ethnography of work in Russian factories (Burawoy, 1996). As the West experienced a decline in its manufacturing industries, industrial sociologists turned towards the analysis of postindustrial workplaces with Bolton's work, for example, looking at emotional labour in the services industry in aviation and hospitality (Bolton, 2009). In countries of the global South such as South Africa, industrial sociologists were concerned with post-colonial labour markets, trade union organisation as a form of social movement unionism, as well as racialised forms of capitalism such as Apartheid and its impacts on workers (Webster & von Holdt, 2005).

Common to the trajectories of the discipline in both the global North and South is the emphasis on land-based labour. Some exceptions in this trajectory are the work by Goffman (1961) that examine the ship as a total institution. The work by Tönnies (1897) about the occupational lives of seafarers in Hamburg was also important but not widely known in the English-speaking world. Even these two seminal examples of early work using the maritime as an empirical cases are not widely known by industrial sociologists. The sea, as Cocco (2013, p. 5) contends, "remains generally a stranger to contemporary sociology". Maritime sociology may exist as a relatively new sub-discipline of sociology.

Recognition as such exists in Europe and parts of East Asia such as China and Korea under the label of Ocean Sociology (Feng and Weijun, 2010) (Creating a subdiscipline is not the same as acknowledging the centrality of the maritime world to theorising and thinking about sociology in general and industrial sociology specifically).

Sociological ignorance of the maritime world is ironic, given the profound role of the sea in shaping sociological phenomena. Our interaction with the sea has shaped the current shape of the world. This includes understandings of European hegemony through colonial exploit, the Atlantic slave trade, the economies of empire, iterations of global capitalism, and understanding how occupational hierarchies operate on ships. These profound ways in which the maritime has shaped the world and global industry is only a footnote in industrial sociology, however. Similarly, whilst the industrial revolution saw terrestrial spaces reconfigured with the shift to large-scale manufacturing and new technologies, concomitantly these technologies changed shipping and dockside organisation. These changes in shipping, however, are usually invisible in curricula in industrial sociology in its examination of the industrial revolution.

Yet the ways in which shipping and maritime labour shaped the global economy is central to the work of sociologists trying to understand how the social institutions of economy and work operate. As Cocco (2013, p.6) shows, sociologists have "a fascination with land as though social relations would only occur on land and not on waters". The terrestrial bias frames social relations at sea as temporal akin to being in a waiting room until the 'real' events take place on land. The sea in this sense is a conduit only (Cocco 2013, p.8) "never a social space in its own right". Crucial here is understanding the difference between the sea viewed as a utilitarian space for ships, food harvesting, a medium for internet cables and resource extraction, and the sea as 'a space for society' (Cocco, 2013, p.8). If we think about the ocean as a space for society, it prompts a range of heuristics about the world we live in (Hannigan, 2017).

At the same time, caution needs to apply to view the land and sea as binaries. Binaries are common in sociology, for example, urban versus rural sociology and structure versus agency debates. Like most binary thinking in social relations, it is not always useful. Instead, it is more nuanced and valuable to view these social spaces as mutually constituting, shaping and reshaping each other and social relations over time.

The following sections examine some of the ways in which the maritime world has together with the terrestrial world mutually constituted and shaped social relations that are important areas of study for industrial sociologists.

3 The Power of Maritime Labour to Transform Society: The Case of South Africa

Two types of maritime workers are central to understanding how maritime workers historically and currently are agents of globalisation and global labour solidarity. The first category is dockworkers or longshoremen (as they are known in the United States of America), and the second category is seafarers. The former category has received more attention from industrial sociologists than the latter. This is to be expected, given that dockworkers, in contrast to seafarers, are terrestrial-based and work at the nexus of ocean and land. A full appreciation, however of the role of these workers in global circuits of capital is missing in industrial sociology.

Dockworkers and their work in port cities are integral to understanding how global circuits of capitalism work. Yet this is often ignored in 'mainstream' sociology. Port cities are trans-local, they exist beyond their national identities, they are nodes of global capitalism and dockworkers, therefore, were and are central players in both shaping and subverting global capital's power in shaping the world.

Peter Cole's (2013; 2018) comparative work on dockworker power in San Francisco, United States and Durban, South Africa, as well as work done by Ruggunan (2016) on merchant marine seafarers, shows that more so than other categories of workers, maritime workers view themselves and their 'local struggles' in larger regional and global contexts. However, this does not necessarily translate into a deeper sense of of class-consciousness as demonstrated by Aguilar (2003) and Grasmeier (2019). It is tempting to view the global nature of the labour market for seafarers for example as one that lends its self to the Marxist axiom of 'workers of the world unite'. For seafarers, however, class consciousness may be temporary and trumped by other forms of worker identity such as nationality, gender and race. Aguilar (2003) argues that whilst globalisation does allow for 'alliances' to emerge, at the same time, it deepens nationalist tendencies amongst workers and even organised labour. More pessimistically, this translates into 'workers of the world compete'. However, this does not mean that seafarers and dockworkers are not able to organise themselves to advance their interests on a global stage.

Their ability to organise as labour despite the global nature of their occupations, sees both organised seafarers and dockworkers engage in social movement unionism. This form of unionism advocates for social and political issues as central to working-class struggles (Webster and von Holdt, 2005). For example, the struggle against South Africa's racist Apartheid system was supported and often led by organised labour nationally and globally. Over decades, dockworkers in the port cities of San Francisco and Durban deployed their power in support of racial justice in South Africa. The success of these campaigns was due to the central role of these workers in key nodes of the global economy.

The International Longshore and Warehouse Union (ILWU) has an eighty-year tradition of demonstrating solidarity with social justice issues globally (Cole, 2013). ILWU, as early as 1934, demonstrated its support for social justice issues beyond its national borders. In 1934, the union's members refused to load metals needed by the Italian fascist government to support its war efforts (Cole, 2018). The union would also not load ships with scrap iron that were destined for the Japanese expansionist war efforts in Asia. These forms of social justice actions continued into the 1970s with labour boycotts of ships from countries that had repressive governments (at the time). This included Pinochet's Chile, El Salvador, South Korea and South Africa (Cole, 2018).

In 1962, the ILWU led the first American boycott of ships carrying South African cargo by refusing to offload or service them. This anti-Apartheid militancy would continue to grow amongst American dockworker unions. Their actions represent the first cohesive attempt by organised labour outside South Africa to use their collective labour-power to protest and destabilise the apartheid state (Cole, 2013; 2018). Thousands of kilometres away, in the South African port city of Durban, dock workers would also be at the forefront of the anti-racist struggle against the repressive apartheid state. The militancy of these maritime workers is one of the best examples of social movement unionism. Durban's dockworkers were amongst the first group of workers to militantly challenge the apartheid state (Hemson, 1979).

Durban dockworkers, similar to their San Francisco counterparts, engaged quite early on in global solidarity on social justice issues. In 1935, Durban's dockworkers refused to service and load a ship (the Perla) with food supplies bound for Italian troops in Ethiopia (Cole, 2018). This shows that these workers were acutely aware of global events and their actions show that they would not support the European subjugation of an African country. Again, it demonstrates the wider class, social, and political consciousness that dockworkers have due to the unique nature of their jobs as agents of globalisation.

Throughout the 1950s and onwards, two maritime sites of anti-racist and anti-apartheid struggle would emerge in Durban and San Francisco respectively. Durban dockworkers would be the catalyst for militant labour struggle against apartheid. Their struggles would influence the larger (terrestrial) labour movement in South Africa. Historian David Hemson asserted "The strike of dockworkers in 1969 signalled the reawakening of black working class action [...]". South African industrial sociologists agree that the self-organisation of

Durban's dockworkers and their strike action reignited terrestrial workers to resist apartheid through strike and protest action (Cox & Hemson, 2008).

4 The 1973 Dockworker-led Durban Strikes and the Struggle Against Apartheid

Durban's maritime labour history and the way it has shaped the city's development and spearheaded the national and global anti-apartheid struggle remains largely understudied. Recent attempts by the Ethekwini municipality through the Ethekwini Maritime Cluster to position and brand the city as a port city have a uniquely ahistorical 21st-century focus on modernity and technology only. There is an amnesia that Durban has always been an important port city. Durban's dockworkers were able to exercise agency despite the constraints of a deeply oppressive apartheid state. They were able to elicit global solidarity through leveraging solidarities through their global circuits of maritime labour relationships.

South African scholars such as Cox & Hemson (2008) have documented the labour process and labour organising efforts of Durban's dockworkers. It is only recently that work by Peter Cole (2013; 2018) has connected these local maritime labour strategies to the national resurgence of the Black trade union movement in South Africa from 1973 onwards. Prior to this and indicative of a terrestrial bias in South African industrial sociology, most discussions of the 1973 Durban strikes attributes it to an almost spontaneous ahistorical act by the workers of the Coronation Brick and Tile factory in Durban. A recent analysis by Cole (2018) demonstrates the causes of the strikes by the Coronation Factory workers were catalysed by the militant labour action of Durban's dockworkers.

It is unlikely that, without the sustained history of dockworker labour militancy, the 1973 Durban strikes would have happened with the same levels of success. Dockworkers provided a 'model' of successful strike action. The outcome of the 1973 strikes was profound with the Apartheid state providing many concessions to Black workers. More importantly, the strikes provided a model for Black labour to strike across the country, resulting in a wave of sustained labour organising against the Apartheid state.

The value of examining how maritime workers fought against racism and white supremacy in two different countries shows us how workers can deploy solidarity as a strategy to form powerful and effective unions but also to achieve large social justice goals. That these struggles took place in what are essentially nodes of global capitalism, that is port cities, is all the more remarkable.

Port cities and the nature of the maritime industry and labour, especially shipping and dockworkers, meant that these workers were cosmopolitans exchanging and sharing ideas from around the world about politics and worker struggles, achievements and strategies. Both the accounts of Durban and San Francisco also underlie another point. If the maritime labour history and work of maritime workers are invisible in port cities, then we do not truly understand these cities and their larger place in the world.

A considerable part of industrial sociology is focused on organised labour strikes, yet, in industrial sociology, we often do not realise that the word 'strike' has its origins in the maritime world (Cole, 2018). To strike the sail meant to stop work on ships but eventually referred to work stoppages in general. Maritime workers such as seafarers and dockworkers are perhaps the oldest examples of workers at the nodes and centres of global capitalism. Understanding over time how their unique position in the labour market allows them to influence the trajectories of global capitalism and/or social justice struggles, rather than just be 'victims' of capitalism, challenges views that workers have little to no agency in a hyper-capitalist world. The race to the bottom need not be the only outcome for workers in global industries.

5 Seafarers, Trade Unions and Globalisation

This section examines the second group of maritime labour, merchant marine seafarers. Seafarers were the first global labour force, the first cosmopolitan workers and perhaps even the first storytellers of globalisation and global capitalism. Their working life identity was always constructed in relation to a wider, less parochial world than their terrestrial homes. It is not surprising, therefore, that their ideas of class identity would invoke ideas of a global working class, and the need for global labour solidarity as opposed to exclusively local identities.

Nonetheless, whilst this line of reasoning may seem to lead to the conclusion that seafarers always embody global identities, this is not necessarily the case. One of the contradictions of the global labour market for seafarers is that the global nature of the industry, actual work space and labour market, would intuitively imply that a form of global class consciousness would naturally occur. However, as Østreng (2001) shows that any tendency towards a seafarer global class identity and subsequent global labour solidarity is not the a necessary outcome. In her study of Norwegian and Filipino seafarers, Østreng shows that the meaning of what it is to be a seafarer very much depends on local contexts of the seafarers, such as their nationality and its attendant "values, traditions and public attitudes" (Østreng, 2001, p. 18). This challenges narratives of global workplaces and globalisation being a flattener of local identities by always creating cosmopolitan workers.

Surprisingly absent from industrial sociology theorising and curricula is the largest labour market restructuring event since the industrial revolution. That is the restructuring of the labour market for merchant marine seafarers since the 1970s. For a subdiscipline that establishes so much of its identity of the industrial revolution, this is a remarkable oversight. Perhaps the preoccupation with the industrial factory as a site of capitalist relations accounts for this preoccupation at the expense of understanding the ship also as a site of capitalist relations. The ship, after all, is literally a mobile form of fixed capital. I see the contribution of the restructuring of seafaring labour markets in the merchant marine offering the following four contributions to industrial sociology.

6 Understanding How Capital Deploys Its Accumulation Strategies Globally

The history of capitalism shows us that, when faced with crises of accumulation, capital restructures. Flags of convenience (FOC) shipping was perhaps the most global and accelerated response in any industry. The scale and scope of the restructuring was breathtaking. Within approximately eight years, both the industry and its labour market completely reconfigured (Ruggunan, 2016). It foreshadowed similar restructuring strategies in a range of other terrestrial industries.

Understanding the ways in which shipping capital restructured because of a myriad of crises offers industrial sociologists insight into the global scale of capitalist restructuring of industries. The scale and multifactorial influences of the case of shipping enlargens the lens of industrial sociology when examining the ways in which industries restructure. Shipping shows that the forces of capitalist restructuring are multifaceted and global. When faced with threats to its reproduction and survival, capital needs to find new strategies to accumulate profit in its future iterations. These strategies offer clues to those industrial sociologists studying terrestrial sectors faced with large-scale capitalist restructuring projects.

Precipitating the almost eight-year seafaring labour market restructuring event was a series of crises in accumulation strategies of shipping capital. Two major geopolitical oil crises in 1973 and 1979 saw a considerable increase in oil prices. Fuel, along with labour, are the two largest expenses of shipping companies, so the considerable increase in fuel prices strained the fiscus of shipping companies (Bloor & Sampson, 2009). At the same time, the volume of oil that needed to be transported as cargo declined significantly impacting on trade capacities. Given this reduction in the transport of oil, the shipbuilding industry found its supply and demand projections upended. Consequently, an oversupply of tankers and bulk carriers occurred at the peak of the recession in shipping. The banking industry also changed the way it financed shipping companies shifting more of the financing risk to ship owners (Bloor et al., 2013).

Wider global financial upheavals unsettled the industry as the global economy was transitioning from a regulated one to one characterised by uncertainty and flexibility. Shipping as an industry had to respond to these economic changes rapidly to survive profitably. The welfare state was in decline in the West. There was the unravelling of the family wage and a shift towards the individual wage. In short, the 'golden age' of labour rights, that allowed for a greater participation of workers in the societal wealth of the Global North in large parts of the western world. A new international division of labour was occurring with Fordist factories being relocated to the global South in search of cheaper labour markets. The decline in labour market security manifested in many forms, including the shift towards casualised and flexible labour markets and a steady race to the bottom for workers as global competition and whipsawing resulted in cheap wages and questionable working conditions (Ruggunan, 2016). Whilst terrestrial based industries would take up to or more than two decades to fully engage and profit from cheaper labour in the new international division of labour, shipping made the transition in less than a decade. Whilst the world's economies were always connected to some extent and global, the speed and pace at which neoliberal global capitalism spread from the late 1970s are unprecedented (Sampson, 2013).

In part, this acceleration was made possible by the development of new technologies in the 1970s such as the computer microchip, for example. New technologies and their impact on labour markets, work organisation and political economy is a central analytical lens of industrial sociologists. The understanding of how new technologies restructured the world's most global industry has much to offer to industrial sociology. New technologies also meant that ships could now run on cheaper grades of fuel oil, and automation of many aspects of seagoing vessels meant a reduction in the size of crews needed to work on vessels.

Containerisation was the other significant technological change that altered the industry and its supply chains in profound ways. It allowed for the use of intermodal standardised containers to transport goods. These containers can shift seamlessly unopened from one form of transportation to another. The handling of the containers can be fully automated. The invention of containerisation and its systems of support revolutionised the industry. In many ways it also compressed time and space in the industry. This occurred by reducing the amount of time taken to load and off load goods as well as the space needed to store goods. This impacted on turn around times of ships at docks, sailors leisure time and obviated the need for large numbers of dockworkers to manually handle goods.

7 Flag of Convenience Shipping as a Flexible Accumulation Strategy

Perhaps the most significant intervention by shipping capital to cut costs was a shift towards Flag of Convenience (FOC) Shipping. FOC shipping allows shipping capital to reconfigure geopolitical space as to benefit private companies. As a reaction to high ship-registration costs, regulatory labour laws and the high cost of seafaring labour in the traditional maritime nations, shipowners register their ships offshore, mostly in smaller countries of the Global South. Ships registered in these countries then fly the flags of these offshore registry nations. These states are paid a registration fee. As such, FOC registration provides a means for these countries to earn foreign income (International Transport Workers Federation, 2020)

In most cases, the shipowners can register their vessels to another country without physically leaving the country of ownership. For example, Liberia has FOC ship registration offices in the United States. Panama has an Internet site that shipowners can use to register their vessels (International Transport Workers Federation, 2020). Hence, there is no link between the state where the ship is owned and the state where the ship is registered. The flag of the state under FOC shipping no longer serves as a symbol of a nation-state authority but instead assumes what Barton (1999, p. 144) refers to as geo-economic and geopolitical significance. By taking advantage of the less regulated economies of the South, shipping companies have shifted the economic landscape of ship registration in order to reduce operating costs.

The criteria for FOC registry are easily obtainable. This may mean that the standards of operating vessels are lower or non-existent. Although Stopford (2007) indicates this is not always the case, analyses of merchant navy accidents indicate this is a distinct possibility. Global regulation of safety standards makes the non-compliance of these standards anomalous through monitoring by port state control inspections. Further, the country of registration allows ownership/control of its merchant vessels by non-citizens. From an employment perspective, FOC registers do not make any constraints on the nationality of the crew employed. The globe becomes a single market place from which to source seafarers.

The case of shipping is important for industrial sociology when thinking about other cases of capital and labour restructuring in the following ways:

- Shipping shows us that capitalism is global in scope and has always been and that globalisation is often a shorthand for global neoliberal capitalism.
- Global capitalism is not interested in fair or regulated labour markets and will seek to engage in a 'race to the bottom' for workers in terms of working conditions and wages.
- In its ever-increasing appetite for profit and market share, a capitalist enterprise will seek new labour markets, destroying existing labour markets and seeking new sources of cheaper labour.
- The cycle of creative destruction of labour markets is one that permeates other sectors and economy but is best demonstrated by the shipping industry.
- Capital will use new technologies as part of this creative destruction project. This may be used as crew reduction strategies and deskilling of seafarers through automation of ships.
- Currently, as vessels get larger and larger, the irony is that crews get smaller due to the technological capabilities of modern vessels.
- At the same time, smaller crews mean greater work intensification on board. The work design of seafarers includes larger scope of responsibilities, as well as longer hours of work. This inevitably leads to issues of burnout, fatigue, stress, sleep disorders and lack of engagement with work (Pauksztat,2017a,b; Bloor, 2011; Oldenburg and Jensen, 2019; Oldenburg et al, 2011)
- Yet, technology also serves as an enabler of workers' agency in organising against the vagaries of capitalism. Organised labour and workers use the internet, social media, GPS technologies, satellite, and cell phones as means of organising and holding ship-owners to account.
- The polycentric and global nature of shipping also reveals much about global supply chains of value and labour that industrial sociologists may find useful. At every point in the supply chain, capital endeavours to balance the strains between costs and quality of labour, the tensions between the demands of global capital and the agency of nation-states. Shipping is perhaps the first traditional industry to manifest these types of global supply and value chains. As such, it serves as a prototypical industry that capital in the extractive, technology, clothing and textile industries are emulating (Ruggunan, 2016, p. 138).

8 Seafaring Labour Markets

Part of the flexible accumulation strategies of shipping capital was to seek cheaper sources of seafaring labour. This meant abandoning the traditional seafaring labour markets of Europe and a shift towards 'new' global labour markets such as the Philippines, India and other South-East Asian countries. Historically, ships have always been multi-nationally crewed, but since 1973, there was a deliberate shift to source crews from what shipping capital in the Global North views as 'new labour supply countries (NLSC)' (Landon, 2020). Despite being called 'NLSC', these countries often have centuries old traditions of sailing (Aguilar 2012; Fajardo 2011). Often the labelling of these countries as 'new' is a manoeuvre by capital to construct these workers as inexperienced, needing to be skilled and not deserving of the same wage rates, ranks or respect compared to their European counterparts, who are viewed as 'traditional and 'real' seafarers. Even within a country like South Africa, black African seafarers are viewed as 'new' compared to white South African seafarers that are viewed as 'traditional authentic seafarers'. This despite black South Africans having a long centuries old tradition of seafaring along the Southern African coast (Ruggunan, 2016). The majority of the worlds' seafarers at rating levels come from these so called 'new' labour supply countries, with one in four of them being Filipino (International Transport Workers Federation, 2020). In making the shift to new labour markets, shipping capital helped shape seafaring labour markets in the following ways:

1. Destroyed seafaring markets of Western Europe, also influencing generational transfer of maritime skills and careers.
2. Produced new labour markets for seafaring global supply chains.
3. Shifted the nature of employment of contemporary merchant marine seafarers in significant ways.
4. However, given the nature of seafaring work, shipping capital unintentionally created a double-bind. It needed cheaper labour provided 'just-in-time' but also needed labour that also was appropriately accredited and trained to global regulatory standards. Skilled labour, even if cheaper from countries of the global South, still needed to be trained to global standards. The double-bind refers to wanting skilled labour on demand, which presented many challenges to the industry.

The table below shows the shift in the typology of traditional seafarers to FOC seafarers, and the fourth column shows how these changes are indicative of general trends in understanding work and labour markets beyond the maritime industry. The changes observed in the fourth columns were well established in the maritime industry from the early 1970s but little known by

TABLE 1.1 Distinction between traditional and global seafarers and trends in terrestrial labour markets

Characteristics	Traditional (National)	Global (Flag of Convenience)	Trends in labour markets for terrestrial workers
– Preferred working place	National owned fleet	Foreign owned ship	Virtual/transnational employers.
– Working conditions	National standards	International standards	Industry dependent ranging from no regulation to high regulation.
– Welfare and pay	Low pay, high welfare	High pay, no welfare	High Pay and Autonomy for high skills. Shift from family wage to individual wage. Race to bottom for low and unskilled.
– Crew pattern preference	Mostly but not always Homogenous	Multinational crews	Multinational/ increased competition amongst workers both locally and globally.
– Relation with a foreign company	Direct employment	Indirect employment	Global trend towards indirect employment.
– Relation with crew members	Experiments with flatter hierarchies, though short-lived.	Hierarchy	Hierarchy based on algorithmic control (rather than rank) and review of work. For example, reviews and ratings of freelancer work on job recruitment apps.
– Career development reference	National counterparts	Foreign counterparts/ Self-funded	Career development is mostly self-funded and directed.

SOURCE: ADAPTED FROM WU (2006, P. 41).

industrial sociologists. As I have shown in column four, the features of FOC labour markets have come to characterise many land-based labour markets over the last three decades.

Whilst shipping capital reshaped global labour markets from the 1970's as part of its new accumulation strategies, the hope by shipowners that this would mean passive acceptance by labour and regulatory bodies proved wrong. Filipino seafarers organised by the Associated Marine Officers and Seamens' Union of the Philippines (AMOSUP) became and still are a powerful seafaring union. They remain highly influential in both labour and shipping industry bargaining councils. The large numbers of Filipino seafarers mean that membership of the union is high at over 50,000, and the volume of fee-paying members means that the union is well resourced to serve its membership. It has also become an important and influential player within the International Transport Workers' Federation (ITF).

9 The International Transport Workers Federation (ITF)

The ITF is a global federation of national transport unions. Given the global and transnational work of seafarers, it is not feasible for national unions to represent and monitor multi-nationally crewed ships operating on FOC. The place of work for these seafarers is mobile and crosses national boundaries and national jurisdiction of labour legislation. Local or national negotiation of working conditions is not possible; neither would it be effective in such a global industry. Whilst other examples of transnational collective bargaining exist for land-based workers, what makes the ITF collective bargaining structures unique is that its outcomes have an "immediate, direct and significant real-world impact in terms of worker welfare and labour costs" (Lillie, 2004, p. 47). Shipping capital moved to FOC shipping as a means of circumventing national labour legislation governing wages and working conditions. The strategies to do this can offer insights to other transnational and global labour markets. First, it requires a measure of solidarity between high-wage capital-supplier countries and organised labour from mid to low wage labour supply countries (Lillie, 2004, p. 48). High wage capital countries have high levels of ship ownership but low levels of national seafarers whilst mid to low wage supply countries refer to countries that supply high levels of seafarers but have low levels of ship ownership (Lillie, 2004). For a short period of time in the ITF's campaign for a global wage rate, it became apparent that the high wage expectations of high wage capital supply countries of the global North would create friction with labour supply countries of the global South.

Accusations of imperialism and protectionism by unions of the global South were common and risked the opportunity for global labour solidarity. Indian and Filipino national seafaring unions argued that the high global wage rates set by the ITF did no favours for their memberships (Lillie, 2004). Shipowners could then just continue the practice of hiring seafarers from the traditional maritime nations of Europe whom they perceived as more skilled and experienced than the 'newer' seafaring supply countries despite a globally uniform credentialing system. If wages were high for all nationalities then nationalism, racism and subjective perceptions of which nationality/'race' made for better seafarers would decide the shape of labour markets. At the same time, unions from the global South recognised that fracturing the ITF would play into shipping capital's strategy of dividing labour. If wages were too low or negotiated on the basis of nationality, there would inevitably be a race to the bottom for all workers. Whipsawing would be inherent to the industry (Anderson, 2015; Ruggunan, 2016). Compounding this concern of unions from the new labour supply countries was that with the dissolution of the Soviet Union thousands of seafarers from the former Soviet bloc were entering the labour market and willing to work for cheaper than ITF wage rates. China's voluminous seafarer supply was also a potential threat in reducing global wage rates (Lillie, 2004).

The way forward was signalled by the Total Crewing Cost (TCC) concept. This means that the ITF rates negotiated with shipping employers through the employer forum, IMEC, are a 'total cost to company' package rather than a fixed 'hard' wage rate. Employers can decide how to structure the seafarer wage as long as it adds up to the approved TCC rate. So non-monetary benefits can make up part of this rate (such as leave for example) (Anderson, 2015). This allows flexibility for employers and does not allow for significant undercutting of global wages in the industry. It remains the only global industry where both wages and working conditions of ITF regulated ships have enjoyed an upward trend, whereas the opposite is true for most other global industries. From 2000, a formal global industry-level bargaining forum was established by the ITF (Lillie, 2004). Shipping capital realising it had to organise itself collectively to negotiate with the ITF established the International Maritime Employers' Council (IMEC). Labour had, in fact, precipitated the organisation of employers, rather than the other way around. More than 11,500 ships are covered by the ITF global wage and regulatory agreements (International Transport Workers Federation, 2020). An estimated 600,000 seafarers (across all types of vessels) are ITF members (International Transport Workers Federation, 2020). Approximately 150 ITF inspectors are employed to enforce and monitor ITF agreements at ports globally (International Transport Workers Federation, 2020). The average ITF wage rates for all skill levels of seafarers (from ratings to officers) outstrips the average wage rates for land-based jobs from 4% to 22% (depending on the country of comparison) (Lillie, 2004) As a global force of labour, the ITF has shown that global consensus-building despite the tensions of national labour differentials is possible.

The discussions of the ITF show that organised labour still represents a powerful global force in shaping labour markets, thus negating perceptions that organised labour both nationally and globally cannot influence capitalist accumulation strategies. That there is no decline in unionised seafarers' wages points to the agency of labour organisations in this sector to counter the pressure of shipping capital to reduce wages. This, then, implies that there is no inevitable 'race to the bottom' for workers in a global labour market provided certain conditions are in place. Whilst the 'race to the bottom' thesis dominates much of the labour studies and industrial sociology literature, the case of the ITF and global shipping shows that dominant explanations of the thesis are somewhat oversimplifying and misleading. For example, Silver, a labour scholar (2003, p. 5), demonstrates in her work that whilst capital has relocated to locations where labour is cheaper, this tends to be very industry-specific and is, therefore, less 'unidirectional' than the literature suggests. Where these relocations have taken place, working classes from regions where capital leaves become weakened, sometimes destroyed, but, as Silver (2003) points out, new working classes and working-class organisations are formed in the new host locations of capital.

10 Future Directions and Conclusion

This chapter has shown how dockworkers have acted as forces of global labour solidarity and social justice. They were critical in demonstrating a global awareness of working-class consciousness by engaging in boycotts of ships from or going to countries that were viewed as human rights pariahs. In Durban, in 1973, dockworkers were instrumental in re-catalysing the broader Black South African labour movement in its struggle against Apartheid. The case of the restructuring of shipping capital and seafaring labour markets shows how both capital and labour react and strategies to new regimes of capitalist restructuring and accumulation.

There are three further aspects that the case of seafaring labour can contribute to industrial sociology that can be fruitful for industrial sociologists to explore. First is the theorising of workers' identity. Merchant marine ships and their labour markets are melting pots of different identities. These include racial, ethnic and national but also regional (for example: historically, seafarers plying the Atlantic routes developed distinctive work identities from those servicing the Pacific). The theorising of the intersection between hierarchy, rank, gender, identity and globalisation amongst seafarers would contribute significantly to the field (as suggested by various authors in this volume). The ship as a site of work is in many ways the perfect 'laboratory' to observe how identities are leveraged, negotiated, formed and mobilised by workers.

Second, sailors were the first cosmopolitan workers even before the current era of globalisation. The ways in which cosmopolitanism was formed and deployed is little studied by industrial sociologists who tend to have fetishised globalisation as a recent phenomenon when, in fact, the historical record shows that sailors often existed in a space outside national borders.

Third, the global regulation and enforcing of seafarer qualifications in the merchant marine through the Standards of Training, certification and Watchkeeping for seafarers (STCW) system is instructive in understanding how global professions can be regulated. Added to this are the challenges in quality assurance of global accreditation as well as the process of credentialing serving as a proxy for exclusion and inclusion in labour markets.

Fourth, the unique conditions and the site of work have significant impacts on sailors mental and emotional well-being. There is a strong tradition in industrial sociology of work in occupational health and safety. This tradition continues by examining the occupational health and safety of seafarers, yet their publication tends to be outside traditional sociology of health journals, and more in specialist maritime or occupational health journals (cf.: Odenburg, Jensen, & Wegener, 2013; Oldenburg & Jensen, 2019a). Whilst the work exists, the framing of the work within a sociology of health perspective is not as explicit. Extrapolating from studies done by those working in maritime health may be useful to understand the ways in which global occupations that require extended periods of working away from 'home' impact on mental and emotional well being. What is the relationship between these occupations and accident rates, for example? How may this work be useful to understand similar kinds of workers such as migrants? How can sociologist develop ways to mitigate against the alienation and exclusion experience by itinerant and global workers? Work on agility and resilience may be useful, even helping us understand how a future wave of space exploration workers will cope on the potential settlement on Mars, for example.

Fifth, given the large and complex formal and informal networks that sailors develop over their careers, how can we understand and theorise complex social networks that are not always possible through understanding terrestrial networks only. This may involve dissolving the binary between land and sea from a social relations position as we make visible the trajectories of these social networks across land and sea.

References

Aguilar, F.V. Jr. (2003). Global Migrations, Old Forms of Labor, and New Transborder Class Relations. *Japanese Journal of Southeast Asian Studies* 41(2), pp. 137–161

Anderson, J. (2015). Towards resonant places: reflections on the organizing strategy of the International Transport Workers' Federation. *Space and Polity* 19(1), 47–61.

Bloor, M., & Sampson, H. (2009). Regulatory enforcement of labour standards in an outsourcing globalized industry: the case of the shipping industry. *Work, employment and society*, 23(4), 711–726.

Bloor, Michael (2011); An Essay on 'Health Capital' and the Faustian Bargains Struck by Workers in the Globalised Shipping Industry: The Health Capital of Seafarers. *Sociology of Health & Illness* 33(7): 973–986

Bloor, M., Sampson, H., Baker, S., Walters, D., Dahlgren, K., Wadsworth, E., & James, P. (2013). Room for manoeuvre? Regulatory compliance in the global shipping industry. *Social & Legal Studies*, 22(2), 171–189.

Bolton, S. (2009). Getting to the heart of the emotional labour process: a reply to Brook. *Work, employment and society*, 23(3), 549–560.

Burawoy, M. (1996). From capitalism to capitalism via socialism: The odyssey of a Marxist ethnographer, 1975–1995. *International Labor and Working-Class History*, 50(1). doi:10.1017/S0147547900013223

Burawoy, M. (2000). *Uncertain transition: Ethnographies of change in the postsocialist world.* Maryland: Rowman & Littlefield Publishers.

Cocco, E. (2013). Theoretical Implications of Maritime Sociology. *Roczniki Socjologii Morskiej. Annuals of Marine Sociology*, 22(1), 5–17.

Cole, P. (2018). *Dockworker power: race and activism in Durban and the San Francisco Bay Area.* Chicago: University of Illinois Press.

Cole, P. (2013). No justice, no ships get loaded: political boycotts on the San Francisco Bay and Durban waterfronts. *International Review of Social History*, 58(2), 185–217.

Cox, K., & Hemson, D. (2008). Mamdani and the politics of migrant labor in South Africa: Durban dockworkers and the difference that geography makes. *Political Geography*, 27(2), 194–212.

Feng, C and Weijun, W (2017) A Review of Overseas Studies on Marine Sociology: Comparison with China. *Journal of Ocean University of China (Social Science Edition)* 5 (1) 9–18

Goffman, E. (1961). *Asylums: essays on the social situation of mental patients and other inmates.* Garden City: Anchor Books.

International Transport Workers Federation, (2020). FOCs. Retrieved from https://www.itfseafarers.org/en/focs/about-the-foc-campaign

Gerstenberger, H./ Welke, U. (2004). *Arbeit auf See: zur Ökonomie und Ethnologie der Globalisierung.* [Work at Sea: on the Economy and Ethnology of Globalisation.]. Münster: Westfälisches Dampfboot

Giddens, A., & Sutton, P. (2017). *Essential concepts in sociology.* New Jersey: John Wiley & Sons.

Grasmeier, M.C. (2019b). *Race and Class at the High Seas. Intersectional Aspects of the Construction of Occupational Identities among Seafarers on International Merchant Ships.* Presentation at the Conference „Class without Consciousness – The Politics of Fragmented Class Identites“ in Florence. https://www.researchgate.net/publication/336881194_Race_and_Class_at_the_High_Seas_Intersectional_Aspects_of_the_Construction_of_Occupational_Identities_among_Seafarers_on_International_Merchant_Ships

Grasmeier, M.C. (forthcoming 2021). Rassismus und Klasse auf hoher See. [Race and Class at the High Seas]. *Berliner Journal für Soziologie.* Special Issue „Sozialer Raum, Klasskultur und politische Konfliktlinien – Zur Analyse fragmentierter Klassengesellschaften. Accpeted by the editors.

Landon, B. (2020). *Who Governs the Sea? An Analysis of the Regime Complex in International Shipping.* City University of New York, New York.

Oldenburg, M., Jensen, H.-J., & Wegner, R (2013). Burnout Syndrome in Seafarers in the Merchant Marine Service. *International Archives of Occupational and Environmental Health* 86(4): 407–416

Oldenburg, M. and Jensen, H.-J. (2019a). Stress and Strain among Merchant Seafarers Differs across the Three Voyage Episodes of Port Stay, River Passage and Sea Passage. *PLOS ONE* 14(6): e0217904

Oldenburg, M. & Jensen, H.-J. (2019b). Cross-Sectional Study about the Activities for Various Occupational Groups on Board during Different Voyage Stages. *Journal of Occupational Medicine and Toxicology* 14(1). https://occup-med.biomedcentral.com/articles/10.1186/s12995-019-0233-1, accessed September 13, 2019

Østreng, D. (2001). *Sailors-Cosmopolitans or Locals. Occupational Identity of Sailors on Ships in International Trade,* Oslo Summer School in Comparative Social Science, University of Oslo

Pauksztat, B. (2017a). Effects of Job Demands and Social Interactions on Fatigue in Short Sea Cargo Shipping. *Maritime Policy & Management* 44(5), 623–640

Pauksztat, B. (2017b). 'Only Work and Sleep': Seafarers' Perceptions of Job Demands of Short Sea Cargo Shipping Lines and Their Effects on Work and Life on Board. *Maritime Policy & Management* 44(7), 899–915

Previtali, F., & Fagiani, C. (2015). Deskilling and degradation of labour in contemporary capitalism: the continuing relevance of Braverman. *Work Organisation, Labour and Globalisation,* 9(1), 76–91.

Ransome, P. (2019). *Sociology and the future of work: contemporary discourses and debates.* London: Routledge.

Ruggunan, S. (2016). *Waves of change: globalisation and seafaring labour markets.* Pretoria HSRC Press.

Silver, B. (2003). *Forces of labor: workers' movements and globalization since 1870*. Cambridge: Cambridge University Press.

Sampson, H. (2013). *International seafarers and transnationalism in the twenty-first century*. Manchester: Manchester University Press.

Thompson, P., & Ackroyd, S. (1995). All quiet on the workplace front? A critique of recent trends in British industrial sociology. *Sociology*, 29(4), 615–633.

Tönnies, F. (1897). Hafenarbeiter und Seeleute in Hamburg vor dem Strike 1896/97. *Archiv für soziale Gesetzgebung und Statistik*, 2(10), 173–238.

Watson, T. (2008). *Sociology, Work, and Industry*. London: Routledge.

Webster, E., & von Holdt, K. (2005). *Beyond the Apartheid Workplace: Studies in Transition*. Scotsville: University of KwaZulu-Natal Press.

Wu, B., Lai, K., & Cheng, T. (2006). Emergence of 'new professionalism among Chinese seafarers: empirical evidence and policy implications. *Maritime Management and Policy*, 33(1), 35–48.

CHAPTER 2

'Making a Ship': Maritime Labour Regime(s) and Alienation in Norwegian Offshore Production

Camilla Mevik

1 Introduction

During work on a windmill field located off the German coast, the vessel alternated between the port of Ijmuiden and the windmill site located offshore. After a waiting period of five days at the port, the vessel was ordered out again to the site by the charterer. News travelled quickly to the different departments on board, and soon the vessel came to life again. The sound of the engines was heard throughout the vessel as the men on deck worked quickly to remove the gangway connecting the vessel to port. Soon after, the river pilot came on board, and the vessel started moving. On that particular day, there was quite a lot of traffic on the outskirts of the pier. A ferry was getting ready for departure, and altogether seven or eight vessels were passing by. Due to these circumstances, the captain appeared stressed as the river pilot rushed the vessel out. The captain ordered the other officers to opposite ends of the bridge to keep an eye out as we passed through the pier. The stress level increased as the captain said to the rest: "dette er et tulleopplegg", translated to "this is a ridiculous arrangement", while cursing out loud. The ships' young second officer told me later that same day that the captain's behaviour was a response to the lack of control he had felt as the river pilot ordered the vessel to move. As the port became more and more distant, and after the river pilot had disembarked, the vessel received an email from the charterer. It read, "Your services are no longer required".

As the vessel turned around and made its way back to the port, one of the officers was particularly bothered. "They move us around like cattle", he said. It was especially the sentence "Your services are no longer required" that the crew highlighted as we talked about the sudden change of plans. Later that day, however, in a conversation with the motorman apprentice, he told me that the email had in fact been more detailed. Due to bad weather forecast, the charterer had ordered the vessel back to port. Nonetheless, the lengthy conversations among the seafarers regarding the cancelled trip to the field site did not include the weather forecast. During dinner that afternoon, the crew was

 DOI:10.1163/9789004518841_004

still talking about what had happened. “That’s why they pay us; to go out, to go back, to go out, to go back”, the captain remarked humorously. The following night the vessel was ordered, once again, to depart from the port.

2 Seawork as Fieldwork

This chapter explores how seafarers relate to labour by focusing on the meaning they ascribe to different work-related tasks and issues on board. The data used are based on four months of fieldwork on board an Anchor Handling Tug Supply Vessel [AHTSV] working within the Norwegian maritime offshore industry. This type of vessel is specially designed for anchor handling and towing offshore platforms, barges and production modules/vessels, forming part of the Norwegian Maritime cluster. There were two shifts on board the vessel, respectively with a different work rotation of four weeks, overlapping each other. The two shifts consisted of sixteen crewmembers in different roles and positions. On board the different positions were captain, chief officer, second officer, bosun, able seamen, deck apprentice, chief engineer, first engineer, second engineer, electrician, steward, and engine apprentice and engine cadet. The fieldwork is based on a continuous engagement with the two shifts on board. In age, the crew varied significantly. The apprentices on board were in their early twenties while other crewmembers were close to retirement, and a few had even passed the age of retirement.[1] Geographically, the crew came from diverse areas although it was conspicuous how nearly every member of the crew, on both shifts, lived along the Norwegian coast in smaller places as opposed to bigger cities. Recruits to the maritime industry have traditionally been over represented by smaller places: rural areas, and places that already had familiarity and traditions of fishing and/or relations to the coast (Bjørklund & Jensen, 1989, p. 67–72). The demography on board resonated well with this recruitment pattern. The method of active social engagement with my informants led me to study life on board in relation to other contexts, expanding beyond the labour situation. Such contexts evolved around the relationship the crewmembers had with each other, the social environment on board and their daily conversations. I did so through constant data collection whilst on board. I documented work schedules, work routines, informal talks between crewmembers, and meetings on board; I documented complaints the men had about work as well as the joys they expressed. Engaging in their everyday life

1 Currently at the age of 60

on board permitted me to take part in their "life-worlds" (Wikan, 2012), as their life was not solely confined to the context of work off shore but stood in relation to external factors such as relations to friends and family on shore.

Interaction and, consequently, data collection was done through participating in the daily activities on board. A typical day started at eight in the morning with breakfast. After breakfast, the crew dispersed to their respective departments. The steward worked in the galley, the engineers had their base one level below deck in the control room, the able seamen[2] gathered a level up from the engineers in the dirty mess[3] and, ultimately, the officers were on the bridge. After breakfast, I would move down to the able seamen who routinely would gather around a table in the dirty mess planning the activities for the day. Sometimes I would join them in their work for the whole day and sometimes I would participate for a period. From the dirty mess I would spend time with the engineers and from there move upwards to the bridge. Together with the engineers, I participated in daily routines such as inspection rounds, maintenance of machines and spent time discussing topics related to work and life on board.

Participation with crew in their daily life therefore forms the background for the data I have collected through fieldwork. The majority of my empirical findings have been revealed through informal talks with and among the crew-members. As my work focuses on labour, a topic of great concern among the crew on board, data collection was ever present as the crew spent much time discussing topics concerning work. As a participant observer, I both listened and asked questions every day to every member of the crew, which very often took the form of informal talks in plenum.

3 Rationale

I argue that labour, whilst undeniably related to questions of wage, benefit, personal qualities and so on, should also be studied in the light of those processes of meaning the workers ascribe to labour. I argue that, by approaching the complex social arrangements that arise in the offshore labour organisation, one can better understand how labour is constantly under negotiation and hence peoples' different attitudes towards labour. I open this chapter with

2 Deck-workers

3 Also called "duty mess". A place where the seafarers have coffee, breaks, or breaks in general, without taking off dirty clothes

a description of email correspondence between the vessel and the charterer[4] to highlight two central points as I draw on Tanya Murray Li's understanding of labour regimes as "assemblages of elements that set the conditions under which people work" (Murray Li, 2017, p. 247). First, I argue that working for a contractor, e.g. a charterer and under the formalised modules and standardised tasks set by the shore-based company are examples of one particular labour regime where alienation from the labour process occurs. This, I argue takes place as the seafarers are subjected to orders given by the charterer, shifting the hierarchical shipboard organisation as the crew experience little to no power to influence decisions. From the shore-based company, seafarers are equally subjected to similar processes through standardisation and formalisation of work, e.g. standardised schemas for keeping track of accidents, near misses, and environmental measures taken on board, among others. This is information available for future charterers and also in compliance with international regulations. Second, I analyse the informal, socially contingent and collectively informed decisions seafarers make when it comes to the day-to-day organisation of labour as a second labour regime.

Returning, then, to the opening vignette, synchronously with the perceived push for power the charterer has over the vessel, the seafarers demonstrate dissatisfaction. With lengthy conversations about the sudden change of plans, comparison to cattle and the humorous remark by the captain of following the charts' orders are telling examples of how seafarers perceive their professional position vis-à-vis the chart and onshore company. Where the first labour regime points to the formal organisation of labour at sea, the latter points to the informal. Mostly, the informal organisation dealt with tasks such as maintenance: cleaning the interior and exterior of the vessel, picking rust, welding, painting, conducting safety rounds and other odd jobs. It was primarily with the deck workers and engineers that maintenance was a dominant task. On the other hand, however, two different companies chartered the vessel on separate occasions, which, as the opening vignette demonstrate, caused tension on board when it came to the organisation of labour.

Therefore, two conflicting labour-organising principles arise as a result as the seafarers are forced to template their desire to labour autonomously against the ever-increasing dependencies ashore and with the charterer. In light of this, I ask; *what constitutes autonomous labour on board a ship considering the presence of these particular labour regimes*. The chapter examines the influence of the presence of the charterer and the onshore organisation on the

4 A charterer either hires a ship from a shipowner to of transport a certain quantity of commodities from port A to B (voyage charter) or hires a ship for a certain period (time charter).

labour organisation. It makes the argument that this presence, through formalised, bureaucratic organisation of labour, exercises a great impact on how the seafarers organise their working day through engaging with work tackling autonomy and level(s) of control. Simultaneously, I address seafarers' strategies to create autonomy through routine labour.

In the first section, I discuss the first labour regime, working for the charterer and being under scrutiny from the shore-based company, through the theoretical lens of autonomy. In the second section, I discuss the different perspectives the crewmembers have towards labour, building an argument primarily on their own definitions of meaningful labour. Following that, I will discuss how perceptions of meaningful labour contrast the formalised labour structure of the vessel.

4 The Charterer

I will briefly explain the type of work the vessel was chartered to do on both locations. From there, I will illustrate how the relationship between the vessel and its contractor, the charterer, generated tensions between the seafarers and their sense of autonomy in the labour process. The majority of the seafarers were unaware of what the vessel had been chartered to do from month to month. There are webpages[5] available with an overview of both contracts and vessels, but very few crewmembers made use of this information. When they came on board after four weeks off, they would meet a familiar place, returning to the vessel they already knew. However, returning offshore was also unfamiliar for many, as contractors from different third parties chartered the vessel, from one rotation to the next, ordering different operations. In addition to performing the mandatory qualifications of each position on board, e.g. second officer or chief steward, and the proceeding skills they have accumulated through both formal education and experience at sea, different charterers and, therefore, different labour situations took place throughout fieldwork, with specific labour tasks.

Work aboard a ship is complex. One reason is the arbitrary nature of the shipping industry. One month, the vessel could be located in harsh weather in the North Sea whereas the succeeding month the vessel could be at a port along the French coastline. Some vessels are chartered under long-term

5 One I frequently used was Westshore Shipbrokers AS. It contains information about available contracts, which vessels are available, together with information on positions, the specifics of the vessel, and so on.

contracts that undoubtedly provide seafarers with a certain degree of work-related predictability. However, the majority of offshore vessels are chartered on short-term contracts, or for particular operations. Additionally, major oil and gas companies can also charter from a "pool" of available vessels through the arrangement of the spot-marked, essentially a day-by-day way of contracting vessels. Such arbitrary working conditions, changing scenery and location, the type of work the vessel engages with in addition to frequent changes of charterer had implications for the seafarers' attitude to work. Concretely, they made a separation between working *for the ship* and working *for a contractor*. I will return to the thoughts the seafarers had of working *for the ship*. As the crew faced different work situations from one rotation to the next, loyalty and commitment were primarily found between the seafarers and not to the charterer. Whenever the crewmembers discussed the specifics of the job, they would refer to it as "operation", and the company in charge was called, without exceptions, "the chart". The crew used the English language, not the Norwegian when talking about the chart. As the fieldwork unfolded, I participated in two different operations under two different charts. The first two months were spent in German waters and the following two in the North Sea.

In Germany, the vessel had been hired to assist in the building of a windmill park for the first two months, and then to do a rig move, starting out off a British port, using *heading control*,[6] after the rig had been successfully moved to the proper location. The company in charge of the windmill project was subsidised by the German state, which had set out to invest large sums in renewable energy. On location in German waters, the extent of this investment became apparent: rows on rows of soon-to-be windmills in a vast quadrangular area with no land in sight and multiple vessels involved in building the park. The central element of the operation revolved around a *jack-up*[7] rig in charge of beating a base construction of what would eventually become the base for a windmill about thirty meters below sea level, leaving about half of the construction above the surface. The actual windmill would later be positioned on top. To do this, they utilised a hydraulic *pile hammer*.[8] When the bottom of the windmill was placed on the location, the hammer was put on top of the windmill-bottom, and the operation commenced. It

6 Heading Control System with dynamic positioning function automatically controls a vessels' heading by controlling the ships' rudders.

7 A jack-up rig, or a self-elevating unit, is a type of mobile platform that consists of a buoyant hull fitted with several movable legs, capable of raising its hull over the surface of the sea

8 Mechanical device used to drive poles into the soil to provide foundation support. In this case, they create the foundation for windmills.

was a time-consuming operation that, on average, took close to six hours to complete. The underwater sonic pressure caused by pile driving had negative, potentially fatal, consequences for nearby marine life, and German state authorities had therefore prohibited pile driving in German waters if measurements minimising the sound pressure were not implemented.

As a result, new technology in soundproofing had been elaborated in the form of what my interlocutors called a *bubble curtain*. The vessel had been chartered for the purpose of this soundproofing. The operation consisted in placing a hose, filled with finely drilled holes, and weighed down by chains in the shape of an ellipsis around the jack-up rig before commencing the piling. Then, by using eleven compressors on deck, they would continuously pump air through the hose, creating a sound-isolating *bubble curtain* around the area of the base construction.

The second operation started out off a British port where the vessel, in collaboration with a second vessel, was connected to the rig they had been chartered to move by using the powerful winches on deck. Heading control consisted of maintaining the position of the rig whilst other vessels were involved in underwater operations connecting it to pipelines. The rig was a *floating production, storage and offloading*[9] installation. I will not go into detail on the specifics of the two operations. However, I aim to demonstrate how the seafarers experienced decreased autonomy in relation to the chart.

The hierarchical structure is further complicated as multiple vessels are involved in an operation. What this implies for the seafarers is a far more intricate mode of communication than otherwise required, although working for and together with other vessels and for different companies and projects is a rather standard procedure and not an exception.[10] Nevertheless, it became apparent that for the seafarers on board, this form of organising work challenged their sense of autonomy. During the operation in Germany, autonomy was especially challenged among the deck workers, whereas during the second operation in the North Sea, the officers experienced similar tendencies.

During the two months in German waters, two European representatives in charge of the *bubble curtain* were on board. As they were in charge of the equipment on deck, they had the authority to give orders to the deck workers.

9 A Floating Production Storage and Offloading (FPSO) installation is a floating facility, usually based on a (converted) oil tanker hull. It is equipped with hydrocarbon processing equipment for separation and treatment of crude oil, water and gases, arriving on board from sub-sea oil well via flexible pipelines.

10 Vessels working within the petrol segment are usually chartered/on-hire in for operations. The extent of thc operations, however, varies.

Orders from the charterer would normally go via the representatives to the bridge with notice to start laying out the *bubble curtain* around the jack-up rig. Via VHF, they would then instruct the movement of the vessel to the officers on duty. The deck workers would assist out on deck, but they rarely handled the equipment. As one of the representatives told me in front of the deck workers, "Why should others watch my equipment? If something happens, there's nothing we can do about it". Able seaman Mark, who had been listening to our conversation, tried to confront the representative. "If there's a leakage, we [deck workers] can …". He only managed to get in a couple of works before the representative interrupted him, "We never have leakages", he replied. The conversation between the two men continued for about fifteen minutes, mainly revolving around the equipment on deck and ended as Mark said, rather sarcastically, "You know more about this than me". As the representative left, the other deck workers were alone in the dirty-mess and came up with a nickname for him. Behind, his back they referred to him as "Adolf".

Working for a charterer seemed to imply that there were different considerations concerning the day-to-day organisation of labour. This was mainly manifested through a fine-meshed structure where orders were taken, as with this particular operation, from the charterer. The men on board met in the hallways, in the dirty-mess or in the galley questioning each other: "Have you heard anything", "What's the latest news", while at the same time being collectively aware that they had no control over the decision-making. Orders came from the chart via email or by VHF from the vessel in charge directly to the bridge. Alternatively, as during the operation in Germany, orders came from the European representatives. Such orders would often centre on commands regarding the vessel's position. During the operation in the North Sea, the vessel had to maintain the position of the FPSO, which, the navigational officers on the bridge expressed, prevented them from doing other more sought-after tasks. This was especially voiced as the North Sea job description, *heading control*, meant that the navigational officers steered the vessel using the dynamic position system.[11] The sought-after task, they shared, was anchor handling related operations. The main difference between the two operations, I was told, was that, during anchor handling, they would steer the vessel manually. They regarded this type of labour as far more demanding, in reference to acquired skills. As one officer so tellingly highlighted when he talked of anchor handling, "More action". The lack of "action" was a frequent topic on the bridge. Many of the officers could spend their entire watch on the bridge simply monitoring the

11 A computer controlled-system to automatically maintain a vessel's position and heading by using its own propellers and rudders.

ships' dynamic position system. Effectively, this meant watching the system operate automatically for hours on end with the sole purpose of maintaining the automatically pre-set position to the FPSO. During *heading control*, these were some of the conflicting interests the officers revealed regarding both the type of operation and their relation to the chart.

The same operation prevented the able seamen[12] from moving freely out on deck since a powerful wire connected the winches to the FPSO. They also voiced similar tensions as the navigational officers. Located in a double bind (Bateson, 1972), the attitude towards the chart did not reflect displeasure for the job they were hired to do, but rather an experienced disconnect with how the work was organised. Additionally, working for a charterer was a considerable part of offshore activities. As such, without charterers, there would be no contracts for the vessels either, placing seafarers in a conflicting position.

5 Big Fish / Small Fish

One officer on board used a comparison between a big fish and a small fish to explain the vessels' position in this kind of operation. "Boats[13] are not prioritised, they don't mean anything, we are small fish", referring to the major oil companies that hire them. As the job to any commercial vessels are, largely, to serve as tools to hiring charterers, it nonetheless affected how the seafarers perceived themselves in relationship with the chart. As the vessels' function to the chart was that of a tool, I observed how the seafarers came to think of their own labour as potentially replaceable by the chart. This view stems from the imbalance the seafarers felt took place whenever working under a charterer. Both in Germany and the North Sea, the type of work the vessel had been hired to do depended on very specific weather conditions. In Germany, measurements of wave periods affected whether or not the vessel could work and in the North Sea, weather was decisive for the positioning of the FPSO. Faced with such specific conditions meant that, very often, tasks and messages from the chart were revoked, changed or cancelled.

A common reaction from the seafarers in such situations was to comment on how the charterer ran the operation. Again, the metaphor of the vessel as merely a tool for the chart was raised among many. On numerous occasions, the officers attempted to contact the chart by VHF without them replying,

12 Deck worker, abbreviated to AB.

13 The officer explicitly said «boats» as opposed to the more fitting description of the vessel as a «ship»

which led the seafarers to gossip about the people in charge of the operations in a derogatory manner. In a conversation with Ronald, the second officer, the communication they had with the chart revealed some tensions; "We only tell the chart the absolute minimum", he proclaimed one afternoon on the bridge. The context for this conversation was that during the night, the European representatives had requested the vessel to move the *bubble curtain* as they thought it lay crooked. This request took some hours to complete. The next morning, however, in the mandatory daily progress report, sent out to the chart from the vessel, this information was omitted. In fact, for the officers, such actions were not out of the ordinary. As they had little control over the flux of incoming information, from company and charterer respectively, being in charge of the information that came from the vessel, was controllable.

The relationship with the chart is an interesting example of the "technocratic management of movement that has become a driving force of trade" (Cowen, 2016, p. 4) and the interconnectedness with the global supply chain through logistics (Alimahomed-Wilson & Ness, 2018). On the one hand, the vessel is a fixed structure; it does not change from one rotation to the next, perhaps not for fifteen to twenty years, which is the expected life cycle for these vessels. On the other, echoing Richard Sennet, the vessel is also an institution that, through its entanglement with these intricate global supply chains is "continually being torn apart and reorganised" (Sennet, 2001, p. 17).

6 The Shore-based Company

The chart is an example of a labour regime that challenges the autonomy of the seafarers, as they have little to no power to influence the decisions. This took place explicitly through orders and communication, revealing the power asymmetry between the seafarers on the one hand and, on the other, the charterer in charge. Power asymmetry is, however, not found solely between the seafarers and the chart. The shipping company, although geographically distant from the vessel, had developed detailed instructions concerning tasks on board. Formalisation and standardisation of ship-work were implemented for the whole fleet in a software programme named Star Information System (SIS),[14] which provide the offshore industry modules ranging from maintenance to safety issues. These instructions were sent to the bridge by email on a weekly, sometimes more frequent, basis. From the bridge, the officers then

14 http://www.sismarine.com

distributed the tasks to the different departments. The STAR-jobs, as seafarers referred to them, varied both in quantity and scale and the crew had a flexible relationship to them. They tried to incorporate the tasks into their daily rhythm rather than doing them all at once. Despite the crew's flexible relationship to the STAR-jobs, they nevertheless structured labour on board and thus had the potential to set off conflict when viewed in relation to the question of autonomy.

In addition to the actual organisation and incorporation of STAR-jobs into daily routines, they also carried the potential to bring out the question of autonomy in situations that challenged the experience and competence the crew claimed to possess. Such a situation also took place during my fieldwork. The shore-based company ordered the chief officer to make the deck workers sign a paper of competence to use an angle grinder. Rather than provoke a reaction from the deck workers, whom this permission paper affected, they did not react at all. As I talked to the chief officer about whether or not he thought this was important, he confessed that he viewed it as "a way [for the company] to cover their own ass". Additionally, he told me that the deck workers were aware of this and that he did not feel uncomfortable telling his colleagues to sign the paper. However, it was evident that the disregard for the permission paper I encountered among the crewmembers clearly signalled that they did not take it seriously.

Furthermore, the seafarers were subjected to register incidents on board through "Registered unwanted event", RUH,[15] forms. The general perception among the crew was that these forms were a "show for the gallery" to show to potential charts. The idea behind the RUH forms, I was told, was to demonstrate the vessel's commitment to safety through constant reporting safety issues. The problem, however, as the crew saw it, was that they felt they had to invent problems to comply with the standards set by the shipping company. This provoked many of the seafarers immensely, and they often complained about them. "With fourteen years of experience, now I have to show that I know how to handle the equipment on board?" was a rhetorical question that came up. During a mandatory Safety and Environment Board meeting, VMU,[16] on the bridge, the officers read the reports, written on small pamphlet-like sheets, aloud. In total, there were three[17] reports during this particular meeting. The first event had taken place in the gym when one of the seafarers had lost a

15 Registrert uønsket hendelse – registered unwanted event.

16 Verne- og miljø utvalg – Safety and environment board.

17 In this chapter, I address two of the reports. The third report was a request to reorganise and re-decorate the gym on board.

used package of snuff on the treadmill. This was a minor event. The extent to which the crew felt obliged to produce RUH's is illustrative in this specific case. On their last rotation, they had only delivered one. Consequently, the management ashore had told them to produce more. Hence, the snuff on the treadmill was an incident the crew thought would fit well as an RUH incident. The officer read aloud from the card: "There has been an observation of a used package of snuff in the gymnasium [...] This is unsanitary and might affect the well-being on board". The officer reading was obviously uncomfortable and attempted to ridicule the cards by both mumbling and lifting his eyebrows whilst reading.

Obviously, there are differences in the subjects addressed in the RUH cards. The incident with the snuff did not provoke thoughts of de-skilling in line with the previous example of competence certification of equipment such as an angle grinder. Instead, the incident with the snuff was an example of the level of coercion these cards represented for the crew, as they would not have written the report willingly. The next report, however, is an example of the former, namely the sense of de-skilling these cards activated. Helen Sampson and Bin Wu (2003) view de-skilling, together with benefits the industry has achieved. Examples they highlight are "less work, more leisure time, less stress, and increased safety" (Sampson & Wu, 2003, p. 151). The aforementioned external demands, e.g. the chart, STAR-jobs and, ultimately, RUH-schemes all point to processes Sampson and Wu could characterise as potential de-skilling-processes. They depend on technological aid as well as communication with the shore company and chart and the formalised organisation of work tasks. However, de-skilling may very well be connected to a subjective experience regarding labour and not solely a result of automation and technology. The next incident is an example of how the subjective experience of own labour, when confronted with such formalised procedures, can generate a feeling of de-skilling. As the officer finished reading the card regarding the misplaced snuff, the next card was about the organisation of labour on deck. An observation report had been written concerning misplaced equipment on deck, which was directed at the ships' bosun. Again, every member of the crew participated in these meetings,[18] and as the officer finished reading the card, the bosun said aloud that he did not agree with the description of an unorganised deck as portrayed in the RUH. He was clearly offended over the observation.

What appeared to be the problem for the bosun was the lack of solidarity the others demonstrated as the observation was read. Indeed, they did show sympathy for the bosun and collectively showed that they did not think of him

18 Exceptions were made, however, for members who worked during the night and were sleeping at the time of the meeting.

unorganised. However, the emphasis was that these cards are part of the work organisation on board. The officer stuttered to the rest: "we have to write *something* on these cards". By referring to the demands set by the company, the officer tried to trivialise the function of the RUH's. However, to the bosun, it felt this observation would "stick" to his name. The captain interrupted after some time as the wording among the crew had centred around the bosun and his position on deck. Erik Henningsen[19] has argued that the principle of equality has been perceived as a "natural" condition of what is comprehended, he argues, as the dominant social order of the Norwegian society (Henningsen, 2001, p. 126). As the situation became tense, the captain intervened. He did so through an emphasis on such a principle of equality. He intended to remove the personal focus on the bosun whilst simultaneously contending the importance of a well-organised, secure organisation of the vessel for every seafarer. The principle of "equality as peers" the crew followed was challenged when the company became present in the work organisation, through RUH's.

After the meeting, the seafarers dispersed, and I found the bosun sitting in the recreational room near the mess hall with the second engineer. He was furious. When he stood up during the meeting to defend himself against such "utter nonsense", as he put it, the other, younger, officer replied, "They have to write something [on the RUH's]". In other words, the same logic as with the snuff incident was decisive for the RUH reporting regarding misplaced equipment as well. They had to fill out such cards. For the bosun, however, this observation was severe since every card were recorded and sent to the company. His reaction indicated that he had been made suspicious to management and, given the protocol system, this observation would stick to his name.

7 Alienation and the Labour Process

For the remainder of this chapter, I turn to the second labour regime, the informal, socially contingent and collectively informed decisions seafarers make when it comes to the day-to-day organisation of labour. I will show how the seafarers actively negotiated routine labour to reclaim control and autonomy in their daily work. An overarching topic through the many issues raised by the crew on board was the question of how to organise work on a daily basis. This included personal and collective strategies submitting to the formalised tasks on board, including mandatory tasks such as inspection rounds, weekly

19 While the object for Henningsen's work is athletes and public figures, he leads his argumentation along the lines of values of equality and personal qualities that others seek.

samples of fuel and water in the engine and weekly cleaning routines of the vessel.

There were many similarities between the two shifts that worked on the vessel during my fieldwork. Both shifts experienced the same work description, both in Germany and in the North Sea. Additionally, both shifts had the same routines and tasks that consequently, and not so surprisingly, made the two shifts share much of the same ideas and thoughts on labour organisation and shared attitudes to labour offshore.

Beynon and Blackburn (1972), in their now classic account of labour and alienation, have argued that given the small degree of control workers exercise over decisions, their position can be seen as one that embodies alienation (Beynon & Blackburn, 1972, p. 5). Whereas Beynon and Blackburn couple the degree of control directly with the question of alienation, other contributions to the field attend to alienation differently. James Carrier, for instance, attends to alienation as the degree of people's separation from the processes, relations and objects of production (Carrier, 1992, p. 539). It is my contention, nevertheless, that more discussion is needed in order to make explicit my assumption concerning the multifaceted processes of labour, especially under the specific conditions of offshore labour. In the example above of a particular labour regime, then, what measures do the seafarers take to counter the loss of control and building autonomy in their labour? Is it merely through studying degrees of control or separation from the labour process we are able to pinpoint how alienation occurs in the modern offshore fleet? I suggest that control and proper strategies to obtain a sense of work autonomy, both personal and collective, should be studied together. By viewing the three conditions articulated by Carrier, namely the separation from processes, relations, and objects of production, as relational to one another, the study of alienation becomes more fruitful. As such, I approach these complex arrangements through the friction arising between autonomy, on the one hand, and dependency [to the charterer and company] on the other.

The crew, as mentioned, varied in both age and experience. Nonetheless, they did seem to share specific views on labour. Mainly, they shared an understanding of what they perceived as meaningful labour. Their thoughts, despite some differences, revolved around the already mentioned distinction between working *for the ship* and working *for contractors*. Whereas working for the charterer, doing STAR jobs and writing RUH forms were examples of one particular labour regime, the views the seafarers had of meaningful labour were coupled to working *for the ship*.

Among the seafarers, a common perception of work was shared as piecemeal tasks that concurred with certain activities where they experienced a high degree of autonomy by deciding how to work. In the following section, I will demonstrate different strategies that were pursued by the crew to allocate meaning to their daily labour through the crewmembers Peter, Martin and Bob. Even if the strategies they portrayed were personal, they had in common that they were all arranged around autonomous tasks. In other words, the application of how the seafarers subjectively created meaning was an important element in both constructing ownership of their labour input as well as restraining the degree of alienation.

8 Evaluating Labour

During the operation in Germany, the vessel alternated between the port and the offshore position at the windmill field due to the very specific weather conditions that the operation required, namely that the wave period did not exceed five seconds. The periods spent at port varied in length. On some occasions, the vessel barely made it in before receiving notice from the chart of good weather reports and thus setting the course for the field again. On other occasions, the vessel waited, at the most, a week at the port.

The workday, for those on the day shift, would typically start after breakfast. At around eight o'clock, the crew dispersed to their respective departments. The able seamen would start their day with coffee down in the dirty-mess if time allowed them to do so. Usually, I found them sitting around their table, making plans for the day. Both bosuns,[20] Peter and Martin, had thoughts on what constituted valuable labour on board the vessel. Both of them organised the daily work tasks with this in mind. Martin was explicit when he first introduced me to his idea of meaningful labour when he initiated a conversation about how he enjoyed his position as bosun on board. When in port, he confessed, "There's little work to be done", but he made a point of distinguishing between meaningful and meaningless work. For example, he did not see the use in "inventing" tasks for the sole purpose of keeping the crew busy. For that reason, he said he would never send his colleagues to the storage space only to check its content: "it's pointless", he said, shrugging his shoulders whilst sitting comfortably in his chair. His colleague, Bob, also sitting in the dirty mess, commented that he enjoyed "finding work for himself". On slow days, when the remainder of the crew enjoyed the idleness on board, I found Bob in various parts of the vessel, self-employed, waxing the floor in the ship's hospital,

20 They worked on an opposite rotation. Nevertheless, I found similarities in how they organised labour.

dusting or doing other everyday activities. Peter, on the other hand, did not use the word "meaningful" when talking about the day-to-day organisation of work. He would, however, emphasise the importance of "doing a good job", "not to do something you'll later be ashamed of", and, ultimately, his idea of 'making a ship'.

Peter was not as preoccupied as Bob with upholding a busy schedule, but nonetheless, he prided himself in doing a "proper job". For the able seamen, the workday would generally start around eight-thirty in the morning and maintenance was a central part of their work on a day-to-day basis. Cleaning was an activity that took place frequently. As Peter, the young apprentice Phil, and I finished our coffee, we put on our overalls, helmet and protective footwear and headed out on the deck. Peter fetched buckets and industrial soap for us to clean the deck and Phil and I cleaned while Peter was in charge of the hose. We started cleaning just below the bridge and made our way down to the main deck. Phil rather enjoyed this type of maintenance, "you can see it gets clean", he professed with a strict grip around his broom. "Sometimes, we have to clean places where it's already clean or places where you don't even see the difference". As we moved from one deck to the next, the deck really transformed. The green and white paint had bright reflections as the sun appeared from behind the clouds. At ten o'clock, we left our equipment out on deck and went once again for coffee in the dirty mess. In the company of two other able seamen and the engineers, we took a sought-after break.

9 The Strategic Element of Pauses

The functions of pauses are often formulated in relation to relaxation. Snow and Brisset (1986) state that pauses have different functions:

> The most far-reaching consequence of pauses is that they are essential in establishing a rhythm in one's personal and social existence. The fact that rhythm is ubiquitous in all life forms may belie its importance. At the very least, we feel that pausing provides the contrast, emphasis, and energy that aid in developing and sustaining meaning in any area' (Snow & Brisset, 1986, p. 12).

Apart from the daily meals aboard, two breaks were especially important. The entire crew took breaks at ten and three every day in the daytime.[21] As Snow

21 The only times the crew did not sit down at these hours were when they were doing specific labour tasks that could not be interrupted. For example, if they were in the middle of

and Brisset argue, these breaks had a rhythmic function insofar as it clearly marked a time to sit down and they were repeated every day. In addition, it was a time where the crew could contemplate their work in a more subjective manner. Often, it was during the breaks that the crew reflected over work. As the breaks had been more or less institutionalised on board, they did form part of the workday, and, therefore, enmeshed in the labour structure. However, the breaks were more than just a legitimate reason to stop working. On many occasions, they stretched out in time and on other occasions, the crew sat down for breaks at other hours. This is important for two reasons. Firstly, aboard a ship, the separation between work and leisure is not clear-cut. Reminiscent of a total institution (Goffman, 1961), the ship is both a social space where people live together for periods and, concurrently, a formally administrated place of work. Secondly, there is an element of freedom in these pauses. Essentially, they represent a space where the seafarers are actively deciding to stop work. As such, I found that the crewmembers engaged in empty labour during idle periods on board. As a definition, I follow Roland Paulsen's articulation that "empty labour is everything you do at work that is not your work" (Paulsen, 2014, p. 5). Aboard the vessel, then, where labour is highly standardised and regulated, working *for the ship* constituted labour where the crew could decide the pace and rhythm of work and, as a result, such tasks often ended in lengthy breaks. Hence, certain routines, e.g. chipping rust, painting, maintenance, odd jobs, represented a different labour regime for the seafarers. Mainly, it represented labour where the crew, although working, could decide not to work.

During breaks, the crew talked about whatever came into their heads: gossip about work, small talk, hobbies, and so on. Nevertheless, the status of the oil industry was a recurring topic during their breaks. The crew talked about the decline in the petrol industry and their feelings towards the policies in the industry. "It should be as in Brazil and Australia, fixed by law that work on the Norwegian continental shelf has to be performed by Norwegians", one of the engineers sitting in the dirty-mess mumbled from across the table. "We might be expensive, but so what", Peter contested whilst adding; "we have to have enough to live". With this comment, he revived an argument common for Norwegian seafarers. The crewmembers were convinced that if there was a count of the hours they worked that the result would reveal that they were in fact not that expensive. The conversation turned to Statoil[22] and the belief

moving the vessel, finishing tasks that took more time than expected or complying with orders from the charterer.

22 Statoil is the largest Norwegian oil-and-gas company. The Norwegian state is the capital shareholder. In May 2018, Statoil changed its name to Equinor, marking a strategic shift towards becoming a broader energy company.

the crewmembers shared that it was they who initially started the process of disposing of the Norwegian maritime workforce. "Just imagine, Statoil being the first [to promote foreign workers]", another engineer said. This sparked a vivid discussion of "carrots"[23] being offered from the Ship Owners Association and hidden envelopes finding new owners. There was consensus among the crew that the constant re-flagging of fleets lead to equal actions by other companies.

Discussions such as the one described above were not out of the ordinary. Quite the contrary, they were told, retold and shared amongst the crew, and clearly marked a distinct separation between "us" and "them". This did not only refer to the company, i.e. management, but to the industry as a whole. As time passed, the chief engineer, having misplaced his keys to a storage room, interrupted the crewmembers. As Peter handed them to him, he got up from his chair, clearly signalling that the men should head out on deck again. It took about three additional hours to complete cleaning the deck after the break, but the deck was indeed noticeable cleaner, and the fresh air was revitalising. After this, the deck workers did not find additional tasks for the day. I asked the young apprentice, Phil, what he thought his working hours consisted of, and his answer resonated well with the emphasis on autonomy as piecemeal tasks where the crew themselves decided how and when to work: "I get up at eight and get off at five. We finish at five. We do have routines. You get up at around eight; it's standard. Then you sit in the dirty-mess until about eight-thirty and talk nonsense. Then you would go out [on deck] and, yes. We do have routines on the cranes, routines on this and that, things we would check. We go around the vessel and see to [it] that everything is in order. If we're not working [an operation], we drink a lot of coffee".

The clear separation between working [operation] and having time to drink coffee, points to two things. Firstly, it strengthens the view shared by the crew of working for the chart as something different from doing routines. Especially, as Phil stresses routines when talking about what his working hours primarily consists of, the focus is on how the crew organises labour. Secondly, it points to the value found in empty labour. Drinking coffee whilst "on the clock" is a result of the crew's ability to appropriate time through specific labour tasks. Respectively, this takes place because of subjective processes where the crew feel they have the power to decide what to do. More importantly, this power enables for recreation during the working hours through visions of 'making a ship' and meaningful labour. As the crew comply with the social norms regarding how to organise labour, they stand freely to choose to stop working as well.

23 Suggesting a "rigged" and "corrupted" industry.

Paulsen writes of time appropriation as coupled to acts of workplace resistance (Paulsen, 2014, p. 50–51). Moreover, Paulsen compares time appropriation to a broader understanding of sabotage echoing Pierre Dubois' thoughts as "sabotage primarily means working slowly and lowering the quality of what is produced" (Dubois, 1979, p. 103). Although the crew have opportunities to not work whilst working, the concept of empty labour strictly as a means of sabotage is not entirely fitting. Empty labour represented time where the crew could subjectively contemplate and create autonomy in the labour situation.

A general attitude among the crew was that labour was not measured in how busy or overworked they were but, rather, that the work they did was well executed. Work that was based on an idea of meaningful labour, including Peter's thoughts on "good work", were dominant attitudes when it came to thoughts on valuable labour. As Carrier emphasised, a degree of control is found here in that it values the amount of collective knowledge the men have of the vessel (Carrier, 1992, p. 549), thus rendering them capable of assessing, on their own, which jobs to prioritise. In this manner, Peter's vision of 'making a ship' is realised.

Through specific routines, the crew managed to create their own rhythms on board, reinforcing their conception of themselves as valuable for the industry. A common feature for the routines highlighted by the crew was found in their emphasis on working *for the ship*. In this case, the crew decided both the pace of labour together with how to best execute given tasks. General maintenance resonated well with the attitude the crew demonstrated. Empty labour was, therefore, more of a strategy that defied the locked mechanisms brought forward by the charterer and company policies. As such, rather than resist work, the crew was actually strengthening its position vis-à-vis themselves as capable and competent workers.

10 Conclusion

In this chapter, I have investigated the multifaceted dimensions of alienation by contrasting two different labour regimes seafarers engage with in their daily labour offshore. I have argued that working for a contractor and under scrutiny from the shore-based company inherently created tensions concerning the organisation of offshore labour. When the crew were subjected to orders given by the charterer, the hierarchical organisation on board shifted, as the crew was unable to influence decisions. As it was the charterer who, ultimately, dictated the activities related to the operations, one seafarer compared the vessel to a tool when explaining this relationship. Additionally, as pointed out by the captain as he said, “That’s why they pay us”, further strengthens the idea that the crew perceived their relationship with the charterers as an uneven one. Secondly, through standardisation of mandatory tasks on board, the presence of the shore-based company brought about similar tensions. This is not to say that the seafarers were without opportunities to counter the powerlessness. Particularly, by examining the vessel as an institution that is continually being torn apart and reorganised, I turned to the seafarers’ response to breaks and routine. The ethnographic material in this chapter has especially highlighted the distinction the crew made of working *for the ship* as a vital part of promoting autonomy in labour on board. However, the material suggests that such bonds take place between and among the seafarers and do not extend to management. Tactics of resistance against charterer and company were collectively carried out through omitting information or responding with a lack of interest to specific tasks. This is at the core of the chapter. Through Martin’s emphasis on meaningful labour and Peter’s vision of making a ship, they create a defence against the rigid framework imposed by the first labour regime, and collectively, through time-appropriation and mundane tasks, labour autonomously. During routine labour, the crewmembers can structure their time according to what they prioritised as essential tasks. Further, breaks became an arena where the crew was in a position to challenge formal structures. When called out to the deck by the European representatives during a coffee break, one of the deck-workers said out loud, “They’ve [the representatives] been with us long enough to know this is our coffee break”. They turned down the volume of the VHF, ignored the message, and continued with their break.

References

Alimahomed-Wilson, J. & Ness, I. (Ed.) (2018). *Choke points. Logistics workers disrupting the global supply chain*. Pluto Press.

Bateson, G. (1972). *Steps to an ecology of mind*. Chicago: The University of Chicago Press.

Beynon, H., & Blackburn, R. M. (1972). *Perceptions of work. Variations within a factory*. Cambridge: Cambridge University Press.

Bjørklund, J. G., & Jensen, I. (1989). Norsk Sjøfart i det 20. århundre. In B. Berggreen, A. E. Christensen, & B. Kolltveit (Eds.), *Norsk Sjøfart*, Bind 2. Oslo: Dreyer

Cowen, D. (2014). *The deadly life of logistics. Mapping violence in global trade*. University of Minnesota Press

Carrier, J. G. (1992). Emerging alienation in production: A Maussian history. *Man, New series*, 27(3), 539–558.

Dubois, P. (1979). *Sabotage in industry*: Penguin books.

Goffman, E. (1961). *Asylums: Essays on the social institution of mental patients and other inmates.* Garden City new York: Anchor books.

Henningsen, E. (2001). Selvforvaltningens dilemmaer. Idrettshelten og fellesskapet. In M. Lien, H. Lidén, & H. Vike (Eds.), *Likhetens paradokser. Antropologiske undersøkelser i det moderne Norge.* Oslo: Universitetsforlaget.

Paulsen, R. (2014). *Empty labor. Idleness and workplace resistance.* Cambridge: Cambridge University Press.

Sampson, H., & Wu, B. (2003). Compressing time and constraining space: The contradictory effects of ICT and containerization on international shipping labour. *International Review of Social History*, 48(S11), 123–152.

Sennett, R. (2001). *Det fleksible mennesket : personlige konsekvenser av å arbeide i den nye kapitalismen* (V. Enebakk, Trans.). Bergen: Fagbokforl.

Snow, R. P., & Brisset, D. (1986). Pauses: Explorations in social rhythm. *Symbolic interaction*, 9(1), 1–18.

Wikan, U. (2012). *Resonance: Beyond the words.* Chicago: University of Chicago Press.

CHAPTER 3

Boundary-work, Occupational Identities and Class-experiences of Global Seafarers

Marie C. Grasmeier and Linda Beck

1 Introduction

In his contribution to this volume, Shaun Ruggunan has identified a need for research on the identity constructions of seafarers and other workers in transnational maritime professions. This chapter aims to address this research question by analysing how seafarers translate their experiences within class relations into everyday symbolic boundary-work (cf. Lamont & Molnár, 2002), thus producing socially and culturally significant differentiation within their occupational group.

The study is part of a broader research programme that seeks to understand how workers' identities and symbolic boundary-work at the micro-level relate to their societal situation and how class relations are expressed in such processes. By 'class', we refer to the actors' position in the production process determined by the nature of their source of income. Workers, in the sense of Marxian economic critique, are those who, in the absence of other revenue sources such as capital or landed property, are compelled to sell their labour-power to make a living (Marx & Engels, 1981, p. 1025–1026, 1956, p. 18–19).

How do workers translate their experiences in class society into the creation of various forms of "human differentiation" (Hirschauer, 2020)? What consequences do such processes of differentiation have for the individuals' chances to make a living in class societies? Our research project builds on several other works that address these questions (cf: Beck, 2022; Hürtgen, 2019, 2020; Purser, 2009, Sherman, 2005; Vallas, 2001).

With the triumph of neoliberalism and the talk of the "end of class society", the study of class relations as has largely fallen out of fashion (Dörre et al., 2013; Mayer-Ahuja, 2018). Especially in social anthropology where postmodern approaches became highly influential the notion of social totalities or systems in general has fallen into disrepute. Thus, following Weber's and Foucault's terminology, power relations tend to be conceptualised as micro-phenomena. A concept of power rooted in societal theory, as in Marx, is rejected as a "grand narrative" (Heyman, 2016; Stan, 2016).

 | DOI:10.1163/9789004518841_005

However, in the wake of the global financial crises after 2007 and the social dislocations they caused, as well as the rise of right-wing populist movements in many parts of the world, there is a renewed societal and scholarly interest in questions of material inequality and class relations (Beck & Westheuser, 2022; Mayer-Ahuja, 2018). With this study, we aim to contribute to these debates on the relevance of materialist theory in the social sciences.

As one of the first industries to be historically affected by globalisation processes and currently probably the one most globalised, the shipping industry with its global labour-market and nationally and racially constituted labour segments is particularly well suited for an analysis of workers' experiences with and in transnational class relations. As Shaun Ruggunan notes in this volume, ships in some ways offer laboratory-like conditions for the study of these social phenomena.

2 Theoretical Framework

2.1 *Symbolic Boundaries*

To answer the questions outlined above, it is necessary to advance a methodological-theoretical perspective which allows to examine the construction of difference and group boundaries at the micro-level. The most prominent example of such a perspective is probably the approach of "doing difference" (Fenstermaker & West, 2002). The authors ask how people produce symbolic orders of difference and identity in their everyday micro-interactions. A central assumption is that depending on the context of interaction, social differentiations such as gender or ethnicity can be charged with different meanings and vary in their relevance. Acknowledging for the flexibility of processes of differentiation is a central strength of this ethnomethodological tradition. However, the authors decouple the analysis from cross-situational social structures. They implicate that the social order is newly created in every situation (West & Fenstermaker, 1995a,b). However, this seems not plausible since social differences are relevant to society as a whole, and their generality transcends the concrete situational contexts.

An alternative heuristic to study processes of social differentation is the perspective of boundary-work, reaching back to Frederik Barth, Michèle Lamont and Andreas Wimmer. The concept of boundary-work focusses on how individuals create socially and culturally meaningful groups by constructing symbolic boundaries in their everyday interaction. Like those following the approach of doing difference, researchers of symbolic boundaries treat the forms and relevance of different lines of social differentiation as an open empirical question (Wimmer, 2013, p. 207). In this respect, the boundary-work approach is quite similar to ethnomethodology. However, it has the advantage of overcoming its micro-bias (Wimmer, 2002, p. 28–31). More concretely, it refers to shared cultural resources and material conditions to grasp patterns of boundary-work transcending individual situations (Lamont, 1992, p. 6–7).

According to this perspective, actors do not spontaneously invent the meanings and symbols they mobilise in the construction of symbolic boundaries in the respective situation in everyday interaction. Instead, they draw on culturally shared images to make demarcation efforts plausible and fill them with concrete content. For example, in their racial boundary-work towards colleagues from the global South, European seafarers referred to current public discourses of immigration to Europe as well as traditional colonial ideologies about the inferiority of colonised subjects. Such repertoires are provided by "national historical and religious traditions and various sectors of cultural production and diffusion – intellectuals, the educational system, the church, the mass media" (Lamont, 2000, p. 7). Hence, their prevalence varies among social groups as for example between members of different nation-states, social milieus and classes or 'racial groups' (Lamont, 1992, p. 6–7, 135; 2000, p. 7).

In addition to cultural repertoires, Lamont identifies the material conditions in which people live and within which the respective boundary-work processes take place as a relevant background structure. "The macro-sociological context, whether political or economic in nature, is also crucial: individuals are located within organisations and institutions, they belong to groups with interests, and they form political forces" (Lamont & Fournier, 1992, p. 3). Elsewhere, Lamont cites the "[...] market positions of workers, their networks, and the level of criminality in the communities in which they live" (Lamont, 2000, p. 7) as examples for material relations. However, all these instances are concrete surface phenomena. The analysis remains in the "domain of the actual" (Banfield, 2004, p. 59) and does not touch the reasons for the presupposed facts.

2.2 *Extending Boundary-Work Theory by Marxian Class Analysis*

In our analysis, we will primarily follow Lamont's concept of symbolic boundary-work. However, we want to level two criticisms at the approach. The first of these criticisms is of social-theoretical nature. The second criticism relates to Lamont's empirical method of data collection and possible biases inherent in her methodological framework.

As indicated above, at times, the contextualisation of boundary-work within material relations remains superficial in its implementation. Lamont herself describes her approach as inductive (Lamont, 2000, p. 4; 2014, p. 816). Thus, she detects salient symbolic boundary processes among different social groups and, subsequently, interprets them with a 'cultural-materialist' framework (cf. Lamont, 1992, 2000).[1] Accordingly, the actors' motivations for their boundary-work cannot be determined in advance but stem from different sources, such as the need to interpret social realities, the pursuit of recognition or the aim to exclude some groups from access to resources (Lamont, 2014, p. 816; 1992, p. 11–12). Despite acknowledging different motivations for boundary-work processes, Lamont often implicitly assumes the pursuit of recognition and dignity as the central motive and ultimate reason (Vallas & Cummins, 2014, p. 237).

It is not our intention to question that actors pursue different ends when they draw lines of demarcation and create group boundaries. In the following, however, we will show how a more theory-guided approach can foster a deeper understanding of symbolic boundary-work. More concretely, we go "into the field with Marx" (Bernstein 2021). Going into the field with Marx according to Bernstein means two things: It implies to make use of Marxist concepts theorising capitalism more generally, as well as to "locate [the] object [of research] in a particular time and place within the histories of capitalism on a world scale" (Bernstein 2021, p.21). Accordingly, our analysis is guided by acknowledging the fact that social actors are embedded in capitalist class-relations that generate specific contradictions and the reflection of concrete positionings of actors within those relations.

Our thesis is that cultural phenomena, such as symbolic boundaries, can be interpreted – at least in part – as the ways actors process the 'deep structures' (Banfield, 2004, p. 59) they are embedded in and the daily experiences such structures generate. Or, put differently, they are "the forms of thought developed in response to, and in the effort to manage, [the] social relations [of production]" (Carter, 2008, p. 448).[2]

Extending the study of symbolic boundaries by Marxian analysis of social class promises to gain a better understanding of the societal conditions under which boundary-work occurs. To provide a materialist interpretation for meaning-orientations, it is necessary to make the structural conditions

1 An example of such a 'materialist' explanation can be found in Lamont's comparative study on the boundary-work of middle-class individuals in the USA and France. Here, the greater importance of socioeconomic boundaries among members of the American middle class compared to French respondents, is explained by the higher permeability of the stratification system in the USA, which strengthens "the belief in the importance of mobility and achievement" (Lamont, 1992, p. 145).

2 This statement of Carter's (2008) refers to racism. We apply the argument to the more general processes of group formation and identity constructions.

and corresponding experiences of actors more concrete as it is often done in the boundary-work approach. It should be stressed, however, that seeing class experiences as a central factor structuring boundary-work does not imply the existence of strong class identities. Instead, it is contingent how structural social relations and experiences are transformed into identities and boundary-work (Bernstein, 2021, p. 28; Chibber 2022). For example, previous research has shown that, sometimes, workers interpret their lived experience of intensified inequalities and the rise of precarious work in the neoliberal era as increased exploitation driven by an antagonistic class, while, in other occasions, they refer to increased ethnic competition to comprehend their social realities, each with different implications for possible group formations (cf. Dörre et al., 2018; Goes, 2015, Hürtgen, 2020, Vallas, 2001, Beck & Westheuser, 2022).

3 Methods

The primary data analysed in this chapter stems from interviews and participant observation collected by Marie Grasmeier as part of her doctoral research project on the occupational culture and occupational identities of global seafarers (cf. Grasmeier, 2020c).

In addition to the inadequate social-theoretical embedding of boundary-work theory discussed above, our second point of criticism is that Lamont based her research programme exclusively on interview data. In their further developments of the approach, various scholars have called for a methodological extension to include an ethnographic approach and have implemented this in various projects. Since symbolic boundary-work takes place in everyday practice and is highly context-dependent in its concrete forms, it is to be expected that it assumes different forms in the actual everyday world of work than in an interview situation (cf. Burawoy, 2019, p. 50). Accordingly, we assume with the authors cited here that in both situations, different boundaries can become relevant in different ways and that actors draw on different cultural repertoires to construct boundaries (Vallas, 2001, p. 10). "[...] because [Lamont's] approach limits the analysis to the aggregation of data drawn from randomly sampled individuals, it becomes all but impossible to capture the very relational processes with which boundary theory ought to be most concerned" (Vallas & Cummins, 2014, p. 237). Through ethnography, researchers can contextualise and thus concretise the abstractions interviewees make from their concrete everyday-life practice in their narratives (Sherman, 2005, p. 133).

In addition to an ethnographic research trip on a merchant ship lasting about two months, during which Marie participated in the everyday work of the crew in the role of a deck cadet, she drew on everyday observations that she was able to make during her nautical training and her subsequent employment in the industry for several years as a maritime school teacher and cargo superintendent, in the sense of an analytical auto-ethnographic approach (cf.: Anderson, 2006). Thus, the data presented here are based on voyages on a total of six ships with a total duration of about 14 months.

Marie conducted interviews both during fieldwork on board and ashore with seafarers she recruited through personal contacts. These interviews were largely unstructured narrative interviews in which it was up to the interviewees to set the relevance of their narrative. Besides, acquainted seafarers provided her with observations and diary entries about their daily work on board. To supplement these primary data, the article draws on secondary data collected in a non-systematic literature review from interviews published in existing research reports on seafarers' everyday work and life.

The data analysis was based on a form of thematic analysis common in ethnography, in which relevant themes were identified through an iterative-inductive procedure by open coding, which were, then, elaborated and differentiated in further coding steps (cf. O'Reilly, 2012, p. 181–207). To complement and deepen the analysis, Marie also participated in an ethnopsychoanalytic interpretation workshop to facilitate the emotional and critical distancing from the data (Grasmeier, 2017). Such distancing techniques are particularly important under the conditions of "insider ethnography" (Vernooj, 2017).

4 The Political Economy of Maritime Labour

As Shaun Ruggunan details in this volume, shipping was one of the first globalised industries in history and is arguably the most globalised today. This is particularly true of the maritime labour market. This pioneering role of shipping was also made possible by the peculiarity that, unlike in most other industries, its fixed capital is mobile, and the industry is, thus, little tied to a specific location. By registering under Flags of Convenience in so-called open ship registers, which make no stipulations about the nationality of crews, shipowners have a global labour market available to crew their vessels (Ruggunan, this volume).

Since the value of labour-power, which consists in the cost of its reproduction, often differs significantly between different countries and regions of the world (Marx, 1887, ch. 22; Bonacich, 1972), and the working class in different countries faces different legal and political conditions to defend its interests

(Aguilar, 2003, p. 150–152; Castells, 1975), shipowners can thereby significantly reduce the share of variable capital in the operating costs of a ship. While this share was around 40–50% before 1973, it could be reduced to values between 24% and 30% through flagging out (Ruggunan, 2016, p. 83). The exploration and development of ever new, low-cost labour resources in the world is thus becoming one of the most important weapons in the competition between shipping capitals.

It is not only a matter of searching the world for the cheapest possible labour in terms of absolute costs but also of finding the right workers for the respective capitalist interests of utilisation in the sense of 'race management' (Roediger & Esch, 2009, p. 7). Thus, ship owners recruit seafarers for the lower ranks mostly from labour supply countries in the global South, such as the Philippines, while hiring senior officers from their home country or other countries in the global North.

This racial segmentation of the labour-market goes hand in hand with an ideology of intercultural management, claiming that some workers are better suited to lead and others to follow (Grasmeier, 2022). This idea is usually justified with Geert Hofstede's 'cultural theory' (Fougère & Moulettes, 2005, 2007). Thus, the racially specific working capacity is said to have its cause in different 'power distance indices' of different 'cultures' (cf. Theotokas et al., 2007, p. 10), and in the 'collectivist' character of the Asian and the 'individualist' of 'Western culture' (cf. Russo, Popović, & Tomić, 2014, p. 175). A more plausible explanation for the popularity of multinational crews, however, is that of a 'strategy of divide and rule' (Campling & Colás, 2021, p. 153). While, on the one hand, ship managers can use the low-cost labour of workers from the Global South, they assume European senior officers to be more loyal to them in running the business. As we will see below, this accounting for people's racism works out well, in that they often identify more with their home capital than with their colleagues of foreign origin.

Accordingly, the globalisation of the maritime labour market was also accompanied by a relapse into authoritarian forms of human resource management, the overcoming of which had been on the agenda also in shipping since the 1960s (Grasmeier, 2020a). This "despotic factory regime" (Burawoy, 1985, p. 122–128) refers to the structures of steep formal hierarchies and strict disciplinary practices that were enforced in the course of industrialisation and modelled on organisational forms of naval shipping, intending to subsume seafarers as wage labourers under the rule of capital (Gerstenberger, 2001, Welke, 1997).

The development described above is an example to study how capital's search for new strategies of accumulation through a constant political, cultural and structural production, renewal and elimination of class fractions and subclasses not only homogenises the world in its subjection to the constraints of the market but, at the same time, produces ever new cultural lines of differentiations (cf. Bohrer, 2019, p. 189–190; Carbonella and Kasmir, 2015, p. 42; Chibber, 2013, p. 140–145; Mayer-Ahuja, 2018; Roediger & Esch, 2009).

5 External Boundary-work: Seafarers and Landlubbers

One first salient line of demarcation that Marie encountered was the boundary between the seafarers' community of practice as a professional in-group and outsiders as an out-group. In the narratives of the seafarers, this demarcation was mainly characterised by the feeling of not being understood by outsiders in their professional role and not receiving enough recognition for their work. A Filipino deck officer whom I asked for an interview agreed with the words: "It's also a chance. It's a chance for us to express ourselves. [...] Because most people only think it is a good life in the ship" (observation note). A Polish ship's officer told Marie during their sea watch together:

> He told me that many people ashore just could not imagine life at sea. They believed that seafarers did nothing on board. The thing with the foreign countries, too, is not what it seems to people ashore most of the times. He told me that he had been to Cuba. Initially, he had planned to do sightseeing in Havana. But after his watch, which lasted for six hours, he had just gone to sleep and had no more chance to go ashore. During his next watch, the ship already left the harbour. [...] He also mentioned the songs about the sea that, for instance, shanty-choirs perform. They were always produced and sung by people who had not gone to sea themselves. For instance, members of yacht clubs in his home place sang about the hardships of life at sea while they sail as a pastime (Observation note).

Here, the image that people ashore have of seafarers and seafaring because they do not know seafaring serves as a cultural repertoire seafarers appropriate negatively by distinguishing themselves from it. They construct the cultural symbolic boundary between those who know what life at sea is like and those who do not and develop ideological ideas accordingly.

Such feelings of not being understood and lack of recognition are also expressed by members of other professions on land (Beck & Westheuser, 2022). However, they become particularly plausible against the backdrop of typical interactions with outsiders in the seafarers' professional lives, such as representatives of shore-based management, charterers, port employees, government officials, etc. Such interactions are generally characterised by conflicting interests, in the negotiation of which seafarers are usually in an inferior position (Sampson et al., 2016, Knudsen, 2009, 2005, Gerstenberger & Welke, 2004). These clashes of interests are often fought through with remarkable brutality towards seafarers, which we will illustrate with the following example.

In her capacity as a cargo superintendent, Marie had the task of coordinating the loading of a general cargo ship. Due to the conditions in the port and the difficult cargo, the process was delayed considerably. The management started to exert pressure in order not to lose any more time. At some point, they gave the instruction that the crew should use the work breaks of the stevedores to open and close the hatches. Since the entire deck crew was needed during the loading operation, this would have meant depriving the seafarers of their only chance to take breaks during the very long working days of at least 16 hours. Therefore, the ship's chief officer refused to implement the order and insisted on handling the hatches during regular working hours. When Marie informed her client, who worked for the ship's management, about the Chief Officer's stance, he gave her the following instruction: "If he does not want to comply, tell him that there are enough others who are willing to do his job!" (observation note).

Against the backdrop of such forms of interaction in the workplace, the seafarers mentioned above complain that people on land do not understand the reality of their lives and do not properly recognise how they suffered from the hardships of their jobs, as Helen Sampson et al. (2016) and Fabienne Knudsen (2009, 2005) also note. Hence, in their complaints, seafarers do not address the antagonistic class relationship, consisting in capital's drive for the profitable exploitation of purchased labour-power versus labour's interest in its protection and reproduction. Instead, they interpret the pressure exercised on them as an intercultural misunderstanding between seafarers and land-dwellers (see also Mevik, this volume). In everyday life, people do not directly experience the abstract relationship, but concrete interlocutors of flesh and blood, which they identify with the experiential effects of class relations (Kalb, 2013. p. 14p.). The processing of their class experiences consists of an identitarian othering of the landlubbers, to whom seafarers ascribe the inability to understand and the lack of concern. We interpret this symbolic distinction towards landlubbers as an expression of the seafarers' resignation in the face of naturalised class-relations (see also Chibber, 2022). Because the general material damage brought about by their position within the class structure is taken for granted, workers are left with nothing else then scandalising excessive forms of domination as the violation of their dignity.

The distinction between the 'knowledgeable' and the 'ignorant' as an element of boundary-work in the construction of maritime occupational identity sometimes culminated in the notion of a secret knowledge accessible exclusively to seafarers. This theme was particularly pointed in stories about ghosts and other supernatural phenomena reported by seafarers on board. Paul Chapman (1992, p. 120) interprets such superstitions among seafarers as cultural baggage of seafarers from the global South. In contrast, Marie observed that this topic was, firstly, addressed by both Germans and Filipinos and, secondly, explicitly named by the seafarers themselves as a cultural difference between seafarers and non-seafarers or scientists: "You only understand that if you are a sailor!" (German captain, observation note). "You are a scientist, so you cannot believe. But we are seamen, we do!" (Filipino AB, observation note). Therefore, we interpret this talk about superstition as a cultural distinction with which seafarers signify the difference between insiders and outsiders (in this sense also Kołodziej, 2022).

However, the notion of somehow privileged access to knowledge due to sea-going experience was also brought up by seafarers in the everyday context of the practical labour process and the negotiation of individual competence. They repeatedly named "experience" explicitly as a quality that distinguishes good seafarers and sometimes valued it more highly than rational arguments, for example, when they tried to decide disagreements about technical issues on the basis of which of the discussants had been at sea longer (field observation).

Since industrialisation, there has been a tendency to "deskill day-to-day life" (Giddens, 1991, p. 242) in favour of external expert systems (Braverman, 1975; Giddens, 1990, p. 83pp.). The emphasis on exclusive experience in the narratives of occupational identity can be read as a reaction to this experience of being degraded to "cargo attendants" (Gerstenberger & Welke, 2004, p. 212, our translation) felt by seafarers who were formerly "semi-autonomous employees" (Wright, 1980, p. 182). The experience of having been at sea and knowing life there cannot be taken away from them as long as the profession exists.

In the light of this wide-spread boundary-work of seafarers in respect to 'landlubbers', one could assume a strong occupational identity encompassing the different social groups employed on the ship. In the following, however, we will see that this is not the case and that seafarers proved to be highly fragmented along lines of race, gender and functional roles.

6 Race and Gender: Background Identities

Occupational identities are always constructed in the context of so-called non-work identities. For example, many professions are culturally linked to gender and considered "men's" or "women's" professions. Those background identities serve as cultural repertoires for occupational boundary-work. They provide the primary framework constructing occupational identities, both in terms of self-attributions and ascriptions to others (Ramarajan & Reid, 2013; Ridgeway, 2009). 'Race' and gender were the background identities most salient in our data. In the following, we will, therefore, examine the significance of these two relations of difference for the symbolic distinctions in the construction of occupational identities.

6.1 *'Race'*

'Race' already plays a significant structural role in creating differentiation among seafarers. Seafarers from the global South mainly occupy the lower positions in the formal hierarchy on board, while seafarers from the global North hold the leading positions. Similarly, there are significant differences in working conditions in terms of pay, job security and the duration of on-board contracts (Markkula, 2011, p. 300–301).

In her field research, Marie was able to observe how seafarers referred to nationality and 'race' in various ways to mark identities and differences. There were the opposing tendencies of both racist demarcations of one's collective and the universalist move to emphasise the commonality of the transnational occupational group over differences in nationality and 'race'. First, we will dwell on the exclusionary tendencies.

At the very beginning of her seafaring career, when Marie asked an apprentice ship's mechanic about the professions that existed on board a ship, he replied: "Captain, officers, engineers and ship's mechanics". When asked about the other crew members, he said: "They are Filipinos. "What kind of job do they have?" "They are just Filipinos" (field observation). This seaman ascribes an occupational identity only to *white* or German seafarers, defining the others only by their national belonging (for a more detailed interpretation, see Grasmeier, 2022). As in the case of this ship's mechanic, maritime scholars note that when European seafarers speak of "seafarers" in general terms, they often only mean their own group of Europeans. The others "[…] are not seafarers, but 'foreigners'" (Gerstenberger & Welke, 2004, p. 308, our translation). They symbolically exclude the others from the community of practice in the sense of a "boundary contraction" (Wimmer, 2013, p. 55–56).

Another form of boundary-work by European seafarers was cultivating a racialising discourse of incompetence. In everyday conversations on board and in industry contexts ashore, they repeatedly told individual anecdotes exemplifying the incompetence of Filipino colleagues. Time and again, European seafarers reported on some Filipino colleagues who had made this or that mistake or did not know this or that. "The motormen do not know the difference between pressure and temperature. He [sic] remembers the columns on the control sheet where he has to put something. He can't deal with a changed sheet" (German engineer, quoted in Gerstenberger & Welke, 2004, p. 142, our translation).

However, some seafarers also reflect on the problematic nature of such generalisations: "I have never worked with Filipinos, but you arrive at this school and everybody tells another weird story where they let the Filipinos come across worse and worse. So now I have a bunch of prejudices people just passed down to me" (German cadet, quoted in Brenker et al., 2017, p. 371).

During her internships and fieldwork visits, Marie could observe how European seafarers, when they noticed a mistake, commented on it with remarks like "those Filipinos" instead of complaining about "those deckhands", for example. They framed nationality or 'race' as the reason for the fault. The fact that the seafarers executing the work were mostly Filipinos and their supervisors, who had to oversee the work, were European, confirmed this perception by itself. There was simply no control group of Europeans with which the Filipinos' performance could have been compared (Gerstenberger & Welke, 2004, p. 143–144). It is striking how much this rhetoric of *white* officers about their Filipino subordinates resembled the rhetoric with which the engineers spoke about manual operatives in an American paper mill studied by Steven Vallas (cf.: Vallas, 2001). In the latter case, however, the engineers and workers were of the same nationality and the rhetoric of incompetence, therefore, came across as social verticalism instead of racism.

Fabienne Knudsen (2004, p. 35) made similar observations. Through the constant repetition of such narratives, knowledge about the foreign group, which is taken for granted and not questioned, is reproduced and solidified within the "we" group. This body of knowledge then serves as a cultural repertoire for the boundary-work. Moreover, in Lamont's words, the symbolic boundary solidifies into a social boundary in that even those in charge, who usually come from seafaring themselves, make decisions about staffing certain positions and promoting seafarers against the backdrop of such generally shared industry knowledge (cf. Lamont, 1992, p. 1; Vallas, 2001, p. 12).

The racialised discourse of incompetence not only served to differentiate the workers from the out-group but was also used to discipline workers belonging to their own collective. For example, a German captain called down a group of German ratings by threatening them: "What the hell was that? I will now call the owner. Then he'll send here a couple of crackfeet,[3] but really black ones! They are still better than you are! (field observation). This disciplining through

3 German original: "*Knackfüße*". The term stems from the German dialect of the Ruhr-Area and usually means a stupid person one does not like to be around with (http://www.ruhrge

comparison with colleagues of other origins could only work on the condition that their fundamental inferiority was already assumed as general knowledge shared by those being disciplined.

Closely linked to this racialised discourse of incompetence are ideas about the cultural inferiority of the racialised others.

> We Germans really made an effort and the Filipinos, whose task it actually was, they sometimes did a really sloppy job, wishy-washy. They just wanted to get over with it quickly and be done. I noticed that really often. And then there is their attitude concerning working time (German cadet, quoted in Brenker et al., 2017, p. 372).
>
> I should say the Poles are better than the Filipinos because they are N. Europeans, they are as hardworking as we are; in quite a different way than the Filipinos. Filipinos may have all sorts of certificates but they can't live up to them. Not at all (Danish sefarer, quoted in Knudsen, 2004, p. 64).

After a failed safety drill, a chief engineer said of the Filipino crew: "If there is a real fire, you can completely forget about the wogs. We, the Germans, are then the ones to save the ship. […]. If things get serious, they'll all run and will be sitting in the lifeboat" (observation note). In this case, it also becomes clear that the engineer identified more with the compatriot capital whose ship he saw himself on a mission to save than with his Filipino colleagues. Due to their cultural characteristics, the latter appear as a threat to what he assumes to be the common interest of the German shipowner and the German seafarers. In his boundary-work, he shifted the contradiction of interests from class to race (Grasmeier, 2020a).

With their racist judgements, the seafarers quoted above turned their own subjugation to the ends of capital utilisation into a positive self-image. With their racist attributions, they affirmed the constraints to which they are subjected, made this subjection a badge of honour for themselves and accused the racially marked of violating its norms by accusing them of a lack of work ethic and discipline, cowardice, incompetence and/or a lack of identification with their work (Hürtgen, 2020, p. 27).

Another aspect of racial boundary-work was experienced seafarers' efforts to swear newcomers to the industry into belonging to the "white club" (Ignatiev, 1997), demanding racial solidarity among the *whites*. The chief engineer's

bietssprache.de/lexikon/knackfuss.html). However, this captain used to use the term as a racist slur,synonymously with, e.g. "*wogs*".

lecture on the Filipinos' poor work ethic, quoted above, which he, together with the captain, gave to Marie during her training on board a container ship, must also be seen in this context. Racial boundary-work is part of an unofficial curriculum in the practical training of seafarers on board.

The ideology of intercultural management, with its idea of principle incompatibility and gradual similarities between different 'cultures', also served as a cultural repertoire for boundary-work: "So, it's easier to connect with Eastern Europeans than with the Filipinos [...]. Somehow, culturally, one is more in tune with each other; one has more in common „(interview transcript, German cadet, our translation).

Besides, macro-level discourses about the immigration of labour as a threat to the prosperity of native workers, as they have been conducted in many countries of the global North in connection with labour migration from the periphery since the post-war period, served as cultural repertoires for these forms of racial boundary-work. In this sense, European seafarers constructed the ship, regardless of its flag or the location of management, as an extension of their home country and their colleagues from the global South as 'foreigners' (see below, section 7) or 'guest workers' (Grasmeier, 2022; Markkula, 2011, p. 301). Moreover, European seafarers repeatedly cited inherited colonial ideologies about the colonised subjects, constructing the latter as culturally and characteristically backwards and, therefore, to be civilised by the whites (Grasmeier, 2022).

Besides these strategies to create ethnically segregated factions within the occupational group, many seafarers also explicitly emphasised a universal occupational identity across nationality boundaries and saw themselves as members of a transnational occupational group. When Marie asked how everyday life on a ship with an international crew differed from that of a nationally homogeneous crew, a Filipino officer replied:

> Not so much. It has not so much to do with the nationalities because every individual is different. The main difference is language. Sometimes that is not so easy. But in the end, it is not such a big problem, because all seafarers have the same idea about this profession. So we usually know what someone wants to say and what to do, even if we do not understand every word (observation note).

Therefore, the question raised by Dorte Østreng (2001) as to whether global seafarers are "cosmopolitans or locals" cannot be answered as unambiguously as the author attempts by referring to nationally different occupational identities. According to Østreng, locally different, primordial occupational identities and attitudes to work between Norwegians and Filipinos led to the division of crews along ethnic lines. However, as Marie's observations show, it was much more context-dependent which of these registers – cosmopolitan or local identification – seafarers employed.

In most cases, the racialising interactions that emphasised difference were directed by Germans against Filipinos. Whether racist attitudes are less common among Filipino seafarers than among Germans, as Fabienne Knudsen (2004, p. 16) also observed in the relationship between Danish and Filipino seafarers, or whether it is a bias based on the researcher's social positioning as a *white* German (cf. Gerstenberger & Welke 2004, p. 36), cannot be clearly decided on the basis of the data available. However, different tendencies in the attitudes of the seafarers from the respective groups are plausible due to the existing power asymmetry, in which the Germans represent the dominant group. Although the racial divide of the occupational group contradicts their long-term interest as workers by making organisation on the basis of a common class position and a struggle for better working conditions difficult or impossible, from a short-term perspective, Europeans, as the dominant group, have an interest in maintaining social closure along the colour line and monopolising access to the higher paid positions of the hierarchy (Burawoy, 1981, p. 291). Accordingly, everyday racism can be interpreted as a strategy to defend their position as a racially defined labour aristocracy in a "caste arrangement" (Bonacich, 1972, p. 555) by excluding the others from their segment of the labour force (Hürtgen, 2020, p. 25–26). An everyday discourse repeatedly emphasising the inferiority and incompetence of Asian colleagues relegates the latter to their places in the lower positions of the hierarchy. At the same time, European seafarers underpin their claim to their status as the elite of the occupational group and, thus, to the more qualified and higher paid jobs (Knudsen, 2004, p. 35; cf. Hürtgen, 2019, p. 102).

The premise for such demarcation efforts is that the global competition for jobs appears to the seafarers as a competition between racialised fractions of their class. The above cited threat by the Captain to replace the crew by another ethnic group shows how such fears are actively mobilised to extract higher work effort.[4] Here, the competition no longer appears primarily as one between all seafarers seeking work but between Germans, Filipinos, Russians, Indonesians and Thais. The workers project their damage, stemming from the transnational comparison of the usefulness of the different fractions of

4 For others, such a replacement has not remained a mere threat. A Filipino rating told the story of how on one of his former ships, the crew was sent home one day to the next due to misconduct and replaced by one from Thaliand (interview transcript).

workers by and for capital, onto the racialised others and promote their exclusion (Hürtgen, 2020, p. 26). Stefanie Hürtgen explains this "xenophobic culturalisation" as an expression of resignation in the face of the constraints of the transnational labour regime. Because the material opposition between the different labour segments created by capital seems unchangable, workers try to pursue the success of their own collective against the others (Hürtgen, 2020, p. 26–28; see also Chibber 2022).

In contrast, the Filipino seafarers, in the same sense, had an interest in overcoming the racialisation of access to the higher and better-paid jobs and thus their exclusion. Instead, they were interested in the free competition of all those participating in the labour market. This interest plausibilises their tendency towards a universalist attitude and practices of boundary-blurring (Wimmer, 2013, p. 61–63) in their symbolic boundary-work. They downplayed the importance of the racialised boundary in favour of an identity as members of a transnational occupational group. This interpretation is also in line with Michèle Lamont's observations in her comparative observations of white and black workers in the USA (Lamont, 2000, p. 83–86).

6.2 *Gender*

Women are often perceived as exceptional in the occupational group, which is initially based on the small number of female employees in nautical-technical branches of shipping. However, some women seafarers perceived their unique position as a devaluation of their occupational identity. One female nautical officer describes this perceived stigmatisation with the metaphor of a "handicap". The occasion was that a male colleague previously pointed out to her in an enthusiastic manner that a female pilot had come on board:

> [The male colleague said] something à la "*Did you see the pilot?*" and in commendatory tone: "*The lady was the main pilot!*" I find this appreciative tone so terrible. This "*Wow, despite her handicap of being female, she can do such a job*". Even though it may be true that being female in seafaring (and probably many other areas as well) is a kind of handicap. That is not natural, though, but created by the very people who say such things (email communication, our translation).

The reason for this perception of one's gender identity as a devaluation of occupational identity is that a sexist ideology prevails within the industry, which Astrid Męczkowska-Christiansen and Iwona Krolikowska (in this volume) call the "Patriarchal Discourse of Exclusion". This discourse ties into cultural repertoires that construct seafaring as a masculine social space and connote occupational culture with hegemonically male values and norms (Kitada, 2021, 2010, p. 75; Heimerdinger, 2005, p. 196–198; Acejo & Abila, 2016, p. 123–125, see also Alberio, this volume). The image of the "seaman" (Heimerdinger, 2005) is traditionally associated with the type of military masculinity, both in traditional discourses in the global North and in labour supply countries such as the Philippines (Acejo & Abila, 2016, p. 124; Fajardo, 2011, p. 77–86; McKay, 2007; Sampson, 2021, p. 91). At the same time, at least in the global North, there is a traditional ideology of gender binary that ascribes to women the status of the "fair sex" (Męczkowska-Christiansen & Królikowska, 2019, p. 118–119), which, in a way, constitutes the counter-image to the "strong sailor" (Heimerdinger, 2005, p. 196). Even though such notions are increasingly challenged after decades of successful struggles by feminist movements, they are still available as cultural repertoires. In a survey of experienced Polish seafarers, about one-third saw the presence of women on board as a potential source of problems. Almost half considered them unsuitable as deck ratings because of their gender and more than one-fifth as officers (Kołodziej & Kołodziej-Durnaś, 2015, p. 169). In a Romanian maritime university, about eleven per cent of male students in the first year and 18 per cent in the last year of training felt that women on board were detrimental to the working climate (Dragomir, Bătrînca, & Surugiu, 2012, p. 13). No corresponding quantitative data exist from other countries. However, the results of qualitative surveys give rise to concerns that the situation is not significantly different there.

Even if such ideologies do not necessarily translate one-to-one into subjective identities, they serve as cultural repertoires for the boundary work with which seafarers construct their own and their colleagues' occupational identities. The concrete exclusion of women from the community of practice occurs both materially through gatekeeping and symbolically through the non-recognition of their occupational identity (Męczkowska-Christiansen & Krolikowska in this volume). For example, there are still shipping companies that do not hire seafarers as a matter of principle (Kitada, 2021, p. 68, Męczkowska-Christiansen & Krolikowska in this volume).

Symbolic exclusion often takes the form of "marginalizing interactions" in everyday work. The organisational researcher Deneen Hatmaker uses this term to describe forms of boundary-work that divert attention from occupational identity by emphasising the gender identity of the interlocutor (Hatmaker, 2013, p. 386). This is how the female ship's officer perceived the situation in the above quote. Sometimes, those patterns of interaction consist of male seafarers quite explicitly questioning the suitability of their female colleagues for the job: "I just heard: what have they sent me here! This woman can't even catch a mooring properly! We have to work for a month for her?" (Polish cadet, quoted in Królikowska & Męczkowska-Christiansen, 2018, p. 85, our translation).

It is much more difficult for women seafarers to assert their occupational identity than for their male colleagues. In the face of such notions of their principled unsuitability, women have to repeatedly prove that they are suited for the profession despite their gender (Męczkowska-Christiansen & Królikowska, 2019, p. 117, Acejo & Abila, 2016, p. 132–133). Such marginalisations are not only expressed in the explicit negation of women's suitability for the profession but can also implicitly be part of everyday interaction between male and female seafarers. On a ship on which she sailed as a cadet, Marie observed that the captain regularly addressed his first officer as "girl" (field observation).

The following quote from a former Polish seafarer shows how such symbolic devaluations of women seafarers' occupational identities can also lead to material exclusion: "I don't have the strength to struggle like that: first to find a job and then on the ship. It is a nice job, but not for me. It is a waste of life" (Królikowska & Męczkowska-Christiansen, 2018, p. 84, our translation).

The philosopher Kate Manne (2018) distinguishes between the concepts of "sexism" and "misogyny". She understands sexism as the dominant ideology of the gender binary, which asserts the primordial difference between the sexes and ascribes specific naturalised characteristics (ibid., p. 78). It is thus a false abstraction subsuming individuals under the status of "male" or "female" and seeking to derive their subjectivity from this subsumption (cf. Hegel, 1966). Misogyny, on the other hand, encompasses the concrete practices and structures, the boundary-work, which asserts this abstraction on people, enforces it against them by relegating them to their designated places in the symbolic order and thereby specifically establishes them as gendered subjects (Manne, 2018, p. 78–84). Following on from these considerations, it is appropriate to speak of *misogynistic boundary-work* in the forms of interaction outlined above.

However, the objection is justified that such practices need not be exclusively directed against women, as the term "misogyny" suggests. Misogynous boundary-work can also serve to discipline male subjects, as in the following case. On a ship, a male trainee who had not been on board that long was not getting on as well with the work as his female colleague. The bosun then addressed him: "Look, she can do this much better than you, and she is only a girl" (field observation). While the bosun directs his rebuke at the male intern, he reproduces the sexist notion of maritime occupational identity and thus marginalises the female cadet as well.

Misogynous boundary-work does not only take place on board ships but already in maritime educational institutions. For example, a professor at a German maritime university used to tell female students during his lectures in public: "If God had wanted you to go to sea, he would have painted the sea pink!" (field observation). The sociologist and master mariner Momoko Kitada reports similar experiences from a Japanese maritime university (Kitada, 2010, p. 8). The seafarers interviewed by Królikowska & Męczkowska-Christiansen (2018) did not report any specific experiences of discrimination in the maritime school, but they also criticised the lack of support from their teachers (ibid., p. 81).

We derive our understanding of the described interactions as efforts to exclude women from the professional group not only from our interpretation. It is also supported by empirical data. For example, a male Polish captain stated in an interview: "[...] leave us the space of the ship and this profession. Do not enter there! It's [a] male asylum! (quoted in Męczkowska-Christiansen & Królikowska, 2019, p. 122). In a German maritime school, two male students were outraged by the application of a woman professor: "It's bad enough that we have to put up with them on board. Now they are supposed to teach us as well" (field observation).

Misogynistic attitudes are not exclusive to male seafarers, as the following quote shows: "I know that I will never let any baba [woman] to get on board my ship! (female Polish captain, quoted in Męczkowska-Christiansen & Królikowska, 2019, p. 122).

Following these empirical accounts, the question arises as to how to explain the need to defend a professional field such as seafaring as a masculine space. Amy Denissen and Abigail Sagui (2015) argue in their study of the construction industry that members of occupations with rather low social prestige seek a symbolic enhancement of their occupational identity by distinguishing their occupation from women's work. If one does not receive sufficient social recognition for one's work, then at least for being a man, since masculinity has a higher social value than femininity. Building one's occupational identity around masculinity can then be interpreted as an attempt to change the normative status order of social groups in a way that is favourable to one's own position (see also Wimmer, 2013, p. 57–58). The presence of women is a threat to such a strategy against which misogyny can serve as a defence (Denissen & Saguy, 2015, p. 383–385; cf. also Purser, 2009, p. 120).

Women seafarers' responses to such practices of misogynistic exclusion vary, ranging from efforts to conform to the masculine occupational culture and "man up" to emphasising their female identity as a special quality of their suitability as seafarers (Kitada, 2010). Most common, however, according to a review of the research, seem to be strategies of "assimilation" (Wimmer, 2013, p. 59–60), in which seafarers adopt the hegemonically masculine identity norm and try to prove their compliance (cf. also: Kitada, 2021, p. 70–71). "They know that I'm not a sweet blonde but that I can roll up my sleeves and work hard. [...]" (Polish chief officer, quoted in Męczkowska-Christiansen & Królikowska, 2019, p. 120). In a shore-based company in the shipping industry, a female captain, when asked about her status as a woman in the profession, used to respond, "what do you want? I work as a seaman here!" (field observation).

As we noted earlier in this section, symbolic exclusions do not necessarily remain at the level of the symbolic but can sometimes have harsh material consequences for the opportunities of the actors. For example, the widespread forms of sexism and misogynistic boundary-works can significantly structure seafarers' agency in the workplace, as the following examples show.

A German trainee had a conflict with her German captain on a ship. The latter then tried to ruin her standing on board by accusing her of having a sexual relationship with the second officer. "Yes. That's the wound par excellence, as a woman on board. If someone wants to be hurtful and, I don't know, negative to you, as a woman, the biggest weakness is simply to invent a relationship" (interview transcript, German cadet). The captain used a gendered moral double standard as a cultural repertoire to delegitimise the female cadet. She could only hold her own because the male crew stood by her. "Well, I'm glad that I had a good standing within the crew, the whole team. Otherwise, it would have been my death on board" (ibid.). As the only woman on board, she depended on the solidarity of her male colleagues. Other seawomen were less fortunate in similar situations. "I ended up leaving the ship for health reasons. And the rest of the crew looked on. Nobody helped me. [...] I was alone" (Polish cadet, quoted in Królikowska & Męczkowska-Christiansen, 2018, p. 85, our translation).

In another case, a German cadet recounted that she was sexually harassed by her German officers and marginalised in her professional role. The rest of the crew consisted of Filipino and one German rating. In this case, the group formation ran across the racialised divide and the crew's vertical differentiation in that the German woman, together with the male Filipinos, allied as marginalised groups against the white German men. The opposing group here consisted of the German officers and the German deckhand.

7 Vertical Differentiation

Besides the external distinction between themselves as members of the occupational group and landlubbers, the seafarers drew internal symbolic boundaries not only on the basis of the background identities 'race' and 'gender'. The ship's crew's vertical internal differentiation into different functions and hierarchical levels played an equally important role. One deck rating, for example, characterised the difference between the two status groups on the basis of their participation in physical labour and the associated impositions:

> We are not officer, so we follow the rules here, what they want us to do in the deck [...] You lose your power, your energy. [...] But for the officer, is no problemo. Cause only and plotting, and bla bla bla bla! But for us, for the ratings, ah! Different thing (interview transcript, able seafarer, Philippines).

As the seafarer quoted here already indicates with his characterisation of his job as "follow the rules", a quasi-military discipline prevailed on the ships researched, at least on the level of symbolic representation by the seafarers. This admittedly contradicts the actual practical demands of the labour process. If seafarers really limited their performance to following orders, without thinking along when necessary and taking their own initiative, hardly any merchant ship could ever reach her port of destination safely. However, it seemed important to the seafarers to maintain the appearance of an order of unconditional obedience (field observation). This expressed itself above all in everyday practices of discipline. Small things were often enough to challenge superiors to assert their authority in everyday life symbolically. On board one of the ships, for example, Marie was reprimanded by the captain during her sea watch to sit up straight: "You are cadet. You should sit properly!" (field observation). The captain justified his instruction not with any practical requirement but with Marie's position in the hierarchy. On another ship, a bosun felt his authority threatened by the fact that a cadet had sat down in the mess hall in the seat usually reserved for him. He responded by having both cadets memorise the rule:

> He practised, yes, how can you say that, he practised subservience with us. For example, he said: „Where are you not allowed to sit?" „Yes, on your chair, of course". And: „Yes, and why are you not allowed to sit there?" „Yes, because it's your chair." [...] I mean, that's what he did to adult people, you know?! (interview transcript, German cadet, our translation).

The seafarers trained and internalised this practice of unconditional discipline through such everyday routines. Thus, the principle of command and obedience became firmly inscribed in the seafarers' habitus in the form of a "fear of authority", as two seafarers put it in a group interview. For example, some seafarers displayed a form of anticipatory submission by having their hair cut short in a military fashion before going on duty on the ship so as not to arouse the displeasure of their superiors (field observation).

As cultural repertoires for vertical boundary work and the description of their lifeworld in self-narratives, the seafarers mobilised various collective symbols that they repeatedly cited implicitly or metaphorically. On the one hand, they often claimed the idea of the ship as a total institution, a concept Erving Goffman (1961) developed mainly to describe disciplinary institutions such as psychiatric hospitals, prisons, military barracks or boarding schools. Contrary to a common assertion in maritime studies, it is true that ships are not such institutions in a structural sense. Nevertheless, images from the total institution's semantic field represented a significant cultural repertoire for corresponding boundary processes when seafarers identified with the roles of staff and inmates of such institutions (Grasmeier, 2020b, p. 22–24).

In one interview, two German junior officers referred to a shipping company whose ships they considered to have unacceptable working conditions as a "floating boot camp" (observation note). Seafarers employed such symbolic references to the semantic field of the total institutions not only to moralistically criticise conditions in their job, as in the previous example, but also to assert their position within the strict hierarchy. During her field trip and other voyages, Marie also observed how seafarers sometimes staged situations in their everyday working lives in which the participants appeared in the roles of staff and inmates of a total institution, for example when superiors spent their working hours emphatically thoroughly supervising and controlling the work of their subordinates while even accepting disruptions in the labour process for this purpose (field observation). The everyday disciplinary practices mentioned above also point that way.

Another semantic field in the seafarers' vertical boundary-work was the motif of infantilisation, the identification of superiors and subordinates with adults and children. A German captain commented to Marie about his Filipino crew when there had been a conflict between some seafarers that he did not understand: "Sometimes, the foreigners are like children!" (field observation). Due to the racialised formal hierarchy on board, it is not possible here, as in most cases, to distinguish whether it is boundary work in terms of vertical hierarchy or in terms of race in the concrete empirical case. Implicitly, the captain also referred to the colonial discourses mentioned above in connection with racial boundary-work, which infantilised the colonised subjects. A German cadet expressed similarly:

> Well, a ship is actually a big kindergarten, you know? My first officer also told me, he had a lot more experience [...]. So on the two ships where I was now, there it was, in any case, that you had to be more behind the people than it is, for example with us here, ashore, when we go to work here, you know? So as far as the quality of the work and so on (interview transcript, German cadet, our translation).

He compared the work on the multinationally crewed ship with that in a German factory, noting that the ship's crew required much more guidance and control over their work. In this sense, he identified them with the inmates of a kindergarten. Thereby, he also invoked the racialised discourse of the incompetence of non-European seafarers.

However, the seafarers used the semantics of infantilisation not only in the context of colleagues of other origins and not only when they spoke as (prospective) superiors about the relationship with their subordinates. The motif also played a role in the characterisation of the upward hierarchical relationship. For example, a German ship officer wrote about the relationship with her captains: "I still differentiate between 'adults' and me – and with adults, you do not joke, you do not talk normally about this and that" (communication via email, our translation). A Filipino ship's cook said: "the captain is like a father" (interview transcript).

In the previous section, we deviated from the holy trinity of race, class, and gender by leaving out Class. The reason is that 'class' as an identity category has empirically if at all, occurred negatively, as something that can be overcome through social advancement and that is worth striving to overcome. The seafarers drew boundaries between one's own group and capitalists as 'people above' only in rare cases.

Nevertheless, the class relationship plays a significant role in the seafarers' symbolic boundary work, albeit a mediated one. Class and occupation are different forms of differentiation that cannot be directly translated into one another. Nevertheless, the differentiation in occupations is based on the class relation in that most of the seafarers are in what Erik Olin Wright calls a "contradictory class location" (1980, p. 179–183).

Their task is not only to perform a certain amount of labour but also to exercise domination within the organisation by being superior to other crew members (Sampson, 2021, p. 94). Thus, a bosun is not only responsible for making repairs, handling the lines when docking and casting off, and maintaining the ship at sea, but also for distributing work among the other deckhands and supervising and monitoring them. A captain not only navigates the ship but is also responsible to the shipowner for ensuring that the crew spend their labour as productively as possible and that the ship makes a profit (Campling & Colás, 2021, p. 144–145). The "character mask" (Marx, 1993, p. 100)[5] of capital interest is, so to speak, part of their occupational identity (cf. also: Roediger & Esch, 2009, p. 6). Accordingly, seafarers distinguish themselves from each other not

5 German: „Charaktermaske". We cite from the German edition of ‚Capital' because the English translation does not contain the notion of „character mask".

only along the background identities discussed above but also based on their occupational function in the hierarchy as superiors and subordinates, as officers and ratings, and construct corresponding "leader" and "follower identities" (DeRue & Ashford, 2010).

The seafarers' vertical boundary-work, which always refers to the racialisation of the hierarchy and compares the social system to a "kindergarten", for example, thus also ties back into the discourse of intercultural management discussed above, which assumes that the members of different racially defined labour segments each have particular aptitudes for certain positions in the hierarchy. These assumed 'cultural' differences are not merely symbolic attributions. They are materially imposed on the subjects. Firstly, we can expect that people who work in an organisation structured like a 'kindergarten' will live up to the expectation. Secondly, the racialised roles of leaders and followers are already priced into the vocational training system. For although most seafarers, regardless of their position, have broadly the same level of training,[6] which is largely standardised worldwide, its form differs significantly between the countries of the global North and the labour supply countries. While seafarers in the former are trained in modern management methods in the "new spirit of capitalism" (Boltanski & Chiapello, 2007) and a scientific mindset, in the latter, training institutions are dominated by a paramilitary drill aimed at producing "docile bodies" (Foucault, 1977, p. 135) through the practice of command and obedience (Campling & Colás, 2021, p. 144; Ching, 2017, p. 56–57, Acejo & Abila, 2016, p. 127–128). This is one of the ways in which 'culturally' differentiated collectives are produced, equipped with racialised labour capacities suitable for the respective labour market niche in demand (Grasmeier, 2020a). Then, the produced 'cultural' difference also appears not only as a potential source of 'misunderstandings'. At the same time, European officers also value this 'mentality', which they criticise elsewhere as incompetence, as a special disposition of their subordinates to be compliant.

> I have sailed with the Filipino stewards and they are generally easier to handle because you can as it were go and say that is how I want it done, end of discussion! (Danish seafarer, quoted in Knudsen, 2004, p. 47).

While, on the one hand, they deplore a lack of initiative and independent thinking on the part of racialised others as a source of disruption in operations

6 In 2002, 56% of Filipino seafarers held an academic degree (Fernandez and Krootjes, 2007, p. 60). We can assume that this share is higher nowadays. During Marie's field research, all seafarers she spoke to held an academic degree.

(Knudsen, 2004, p. 25–36; Gerstenberger & Welke, 2004, p. 134–145), many European officers prefer crews from the Global South as easier to lead than European subordinates (Kołodziej & Kołodziej-Durnaś, 2015, p. 162; Sampson, 2021, p. 91).

8 Conclusion

In this contribution, we have analysed the construction of identities and boundary-work of workers in the transnational context of seafaring. The presented cases paint a picture of profound fragmentation within the ship's crew. Seafarers drew rigid boundaries between crew members in different hierarchical functions. Moreover, Marie observed the expression of symbolic boundaries along the lines of gender and 'race'. Such group formations often also had a structural empirical core, namely the actual "fragmentation of the experience of wage-dependency" (Mayer-Ahuja, 2018, p.20, our translation). In that sense, they corresponded to the differentiation generated by shipowners between predominantly European officers in leading functions and Filipino ratings in executive positions. Likewise, the defence of the ship as a 'male' space reflected the empirical reality of an industry dominated by men. By building collective identities and solidarities along such internal lines of differentiation, crew members can be expected to contribute to the reproduction of the racialised hierarchy as well as to the ongoing exclusion of women from the occupational field. Thus, in several places, we have shown how boundary constructions may lead to material disadvantages for the symbolically excluded (see Lamont, Beljean, Claire, 2014; Vallas 2003, p. 386).

Even if, in some situations, seafarers pursued strategies of "boundary-blurring" (Wimmer 2013, p. 61–63) (as in the case of Filipino seafarers with regard to racialised boundaries), we did not find expressions of a collective identity based on common class experiences, nor did we find notions of a common opponent embodied by shipowners.

Yet we have argued that class relations played a crucial role in structuring the boundary-work of seafarers. In that sense, we interpreted seafarers' boundary construction as reactions to and means to come to terms with their 'lived experiences' in class society, such as their vulnerability inscribed in their condition as being wage-dependent and their experiences of domination (Wright, 1989, p. 288–289; Chibber, 2022, p. 63–64). Thus, relations of domination evoked different forms of boundary-work, even though they did not lead to the formation of class consciousness. For example, we have argued that forms boundary-work against 'landlubbers' become plausible against the backdrop of experienced pressures to intensify work exercised by 'outsiders'. On other occasions, relations of domination were processed through forms of vertical boundary-work directed against other seafarers. Moreover, we argued that the European seafarers' boundary-work along lines of 'race' must be understood in the context of the labour market competition between workers which is inherent to capitalism and had been fuelled by the shipowners' strategies of 'race management' for recruiting labour (see also Chibber, 2013, p. 117–119). Lastly, symbolic boundaries were mobilised to realise capital's interests when those seafarers in contradictory class locations expressed racist and sexist ideologies to discipline their subordinates. Hence, our study shows that we do not need to fall back on functionalist arguments to see how capitalism generates ever new forms of social differentiations among the wage-dependent parts of society.

Our attempt to offer a 'materialist' interpretation of symbolic boundaries does, however, not lead to the conclusion that seafarers drew boundaries exclusively to gain material benefits directly. Indeed, we have shown at several places that the ways how seafarers drew boundaries (such as demarcations from 'landlubbers' or women) can be interpreted as serving to "protect their dignity" (Lamont 2000, p.5). Also our claim is not that all forms boundary-work that can be found in social reality are expressions of class-relations. Thus, in other social contexts class relations may play a smaller role in structuring the boundary-work of actors. Lastly, we have demonstrated how seafarers relied on cultural repertoires, societal stereotypes, and discourses to fill their boundary-work with meanings. Hence, their boundary-work was significantly shaped by 'culture'. Nevertheless, seafarers' expression of widespread ideologies should not be interpreted as the result of some sort of ideological manipulation (see also Chibber, 2022). Our thesis is that seafarers made use of ideologies as part of their cultural 'tool kit' (Swidler, 1986) to defend their (short-term) material and symbolic interests (see also Carter, 2008, p. 450–451).

Our study raises the question of why seafarers did not express class identities. Ruggunan (this volume) shows that seafarers were, historically, the first segment of the working class to develop a cosmopolitan occupational identity and maritime transport workers – dockers and seafarers – have a long tradition of transnational class struggles, e.g. against the South-African apartheid-system (Ruggunan, this volume) or the fight against German Naz-faschism (cf. Nelles, 2001). Contrasting to this radical history of the maritime professions, our findings indicate that contemporary global seafarers are highly divided in different nationally and racially defined fractions and far away from developing a transnational class consciousness (see also Aguilar, 2003). Where solidarities exist, they are often confined to the 'own' national collective.

At several places, we have formulated the thesis that seafarers' lack of class identities is not only the result of the fragmentation of their experiences but symbolises their resignation vis-à-vis seemingly unchangeable structural conditions. Such an interpretation is in line with the works of others (Chibber 2022, p. 106–113; Hürtgen, 2020, p. 27; Mann, 1973, p. 29–31) and implies that class solidarity as well as the idea of the own class as a transformative actor must be built through collective class organisation (Chibber, 2022, p. 74).

References

Acejo, I. (2021). The Experience of Being a Filipino Seafarer on a Multinationally Crewed Ship. In V. O. Gekara & H. Sampson (Eds.), *The World of the Seafarer* (pp. 99–111). Springer International Publishing. https://doi.org/10.1007/978-3-030-49825-2_9

Acejo, I. L., & Abila, S. S. (2016). Rubbing out gender: Women and merchant ships. *Journal of Organizational Ethnography*, *5*(2), 123–138. https://doi.org/10.1108/JOE-01-2016-0004

Aguilar, F.V. Jr. (2003). Global Migrations, Old Forms of Labor, and New Transborder Class Relations. *Japanese Journal of Southeast Asian Studies* 41(2), 137–161

Anderson, L. (2006). Analytic Autoethnography. *Journal of Contemporary Ethnography*, *35*(4), 373–395. https://doi.org/10.1177/0891241605280449

Banfield, G. (2004). What's Really Wrong with Ethnography? *International Education Journal* 4(4), 53–63

Beck, L. (2022). Differenz und Gemeinsamkeit. Sichtweisen deutscher Bauarbeitender auf migrantische Kolleg*innen. Z - Zeitschrift für Marxistische Erneuerung, 132, 52–61.

Beck, L., and Westheuser, L. (2022). Verletzte Ansprüche. Zur Grammatik des politischen Bewusstseins von ArbeiterInnen. Berliner Journal für Soziologie, 32, 279–316.

Bernstein, H. (2021). Into the Field with Marx: Some Observations on Researching Class. In A. Mezzadri (Ed.), *Marx in the field* (pp. 17–30). Anthem Press.

Bohrer, A. J. (2019). *Marxism and intersectionality: Race, gender, class and sexuality under contemporary capitalism*. Transcript.

Boltanski, L., and Chiapello, E. (2007). *The New Spirit of Capitalism*. London, New York: Verso

Braverman, H. (1975). *Labor and monopoly capital: The degradation of work in the twentieth century*. Monthly Review Press.

Brenker, M., Möckel, S., Küper, M., Schmid, S., Spann, M., & Strohschneider, S. (2017). Challenges of multinational crewing: A qualitative study with cadets. *WMU Journal of Maritime Affairs*, *16*(3), 365–384. https://doi.org/10.1007/s13437-016-0117-5

Burawoy, M. (1981). The Capitalist State in South Africa. Marxist and Sociological Perspectives on Race and Class. *Political Power and Social Theory* 2, 279–335.

Burawoy, M. (1982). *Manufacturing Consent: Changes in the Labor Process under Monopoly Capitalism*. paperback ed. Chicago; London: University of Chicago Press

Burawoy, M. (1985). *The politics of production: Factory regimes under capitalism and socialism*. Verso.

Burawoy, M. (1998). The Extended Case Method. *Sociological Theory* 16(1), 4–33

Burawoy, M. (2019). Empiricism and its Fallacies. *Context*, *18*(1), 47–53. https://doi.org/10.1177/1536504219830677

Campling, L., and Colás, A. (2021). *Capitalism and the Sea*. New York: Verso

Carbonella, A., and Kasmir, S. (2015). Dispossession, disorganization and the anthropology of labor. *Anthropologies of Class Power, Practice and Inequality*, 41–52.

Carrier, J.G. (2015). The concept of class. *Anthropologies of Class Power, Practice and Inequality*, (pp. 28–40). Cambridge University Press

Carrier, J.G, and Kalb, D. (2015, eds). *Anthropologies of Class Power, Practice and Inequality*. Cambridge University Press

Carter, R. (2008). Marxism and Theories of Racism. In J. Bidet & E. Kouvélakis (Eds.), *Critical companion to contemporary Marxism* (pp. 431–452). Brill.

Castells, M. (1975). „Immigrant Workers and Class Struggles in Advanced Capitalism: The Western European Experience". *Politics & Society* 5(1):33–66. doi: 10.1177/003232927500500102.

Chapman, P.K. (1992). *Trouble on Board: The Plight of International Seafarers*. Illustrated Press

Chibber, V. (2013). *Postcolonial Theory and the Specter of Capital*. London, New York: Verso

Chibber, V. (2022). The Class Matrix. *Social Theory after the Cultural Turn*. Cambridge, London: Harvard University Press

Ching, Manny Isla (2017); Quasi-Military Training Experience, Academic Performance and Shipboard Training Competence: The PMMA Success Indicators of Maritime Education and Training. Master's Thesis, World Maritime University. http://commons.wmu.se/all_dissertations/596, accessed July 17, 2019

Denissen, Amy M./Saguy, Abigail C. (2014). Gendered Homophobia and the Contradictions of Workplace Discrimination for Women in the Building Trades. In *Gender & Society*, *28*(3), 381–403.

DeRue, S., & Ashford, S.J. (2010). Who Will Lead and Who Will Follow? A Social Process of Leadership Identity Construction in Organizations. *The Academy of Management Review*, *35*(4), 627–647.

Dörre, K., Bose, S., Lütten, J., Köster, J. (2018). Arbeiterbewegung von rechts? Motive und Grenzen einer imaginären Revolte. *Berliner Journal für Soziologie* 28, 55–89.

Dörre, K., Happ, A., Matuschek, I. (2013). Das Unbehagen am Kapitalismus und die LohnarbeiterInnen. In K. Dörre, A. Happ, I. Matuschek (eds.). *Das Gesellschaftsbild der LohnarbeiterInnen. Soziologische Untersuchungen in ost-und westdeutschen Industriebetrieben.* (pp. 9–28). Hamburg: VSA-Verlag

Dragomir, C., Bătrînca, G., and Surugiu, F. (2012). Motivation of Joining Women in the Maritime Sector. *Maritime Transport & Navigation Journal* 3(3), 1–16

Dragomir, C., and Surugiu, F. (2013). Seafarer Women. Perception of the Seafaring Career. In *Advances in Fiscal, Political and Law Sciences. Proceedings of the 2nd International Conference on Economics, Political and Law Science.* Vladimir Marascu-Klein, (ed). (Pp. 15–18). Brasov: WSEAS-Press. http://www.wseas.us/e-library/conferences/2013/Brasov/EPLS/EPLS-01.pdf, accessed November 17, 2019

Fajardo, K.B. (2011). *Filipino Crosscurrents: Oceanographies of Seafaring, Masculinities, and Globalization.* Minneapolis, London: University of Minnesota Press

Fenstermaker, S., and West, C. (2002). *Doing Gender, Doing Difference: Inequality, Power, and Institutional Change.* Psychology Press

Fernandez, B., and Krootjes, R. (2007). Seafarers – Invisible Part of the Filipino Diaspora in Europe: Scenarios from Onboard Research. In *In de Olde Worlde: Views of Filipino Migrants in Europe.* Filomenita Mongaya Hoegsholm, ed. (Pp. 58–82). Quezon City: Philippine Social Science Council and Philippine Migration Research Network. http://unesdoc.unesco.org/images/0015/001530/153056e.pdf

Foucault, M. (1977). *Discipline and Punish: The Birth of the Prison.* New York: Vintage Books

Foucault, M. (1986); Of Other Spaces. *Diacritics* 16(1), 22–27

Fougère, M., & Moulettes, A. (2005). *Cross-Cultural Management Discourse – Ideas of Democracy, Development, Modernity and Progress in Hofstede's Culture's Consequences.* 4th International Critical Management Studies Conference, Cambridge.

Fougère, M., and Moulettes, A. (2007). The Construction of the Modern West and the Backward Rest: Studying the Discourse of Hofstede's Culture's Consequences. *Journal of Multicultural Discourses* 2(1), 1–19

Gerstenberger, H. (2001). The Disciplining of German Seamen. *International Journal of Maritime History* 13(2), 37–50

Gerstenberger, H., and Welke, U. (2004). *Arbeit auf See: zur Ökonomie und Ethnologie der Globalisierung.* Münster: Westphälisches Dampfboot

Giddens, A. (1990). *The Consequences of Modernity.* Stanford: Stanford University Press

Giddens, A. (1991). *Modernity and Self-Identity. Self and Society in the Late Modern Age.* Cambridge: Polity Press

Goes, T.E. (2015). *Zwischen Disziplinierung und Gegenwehr: wie Prekarisierung sich auf Beschäftigte im Grosshandel auswirkt.* Frankfurt: Campus Verlag.

Goffman, E. (1961). *Asylums. Essays on the Social Situation of Mental Patients and Other Inmates.* Garden City: Doubleday & Company

Grasmeier, M.C. (2017). Vom Vermuten zum Verstehen. In *Ethnografie und Deutung: Gruppensupervision als Methode reflexiven Forschens.* J. Bonz, K. Eisch-Angus, M. Hamm, and A. Sülzle, eds. (pp. 319–331). Wiesbaden: Springer Fachmedien

Grasmeier, M.C. (2020a). *The 'Fear of Authority'.* Presentation held at the 16th EASA Biennial Conference EASA2020: "New anthropological horizons in and beyond Europe." doi:10.13140/RG.2.2.16293.52963

Grasmeier, M.C. (2020b). Das Schiff als sozialer Ort. [The ship as a social space]. In U. Kronfeld-Goharani, A. Mondré, and F.J. Werner (eds). *Der Mensch und das Meer – wie Erzählungen unseren Umgang mit dem Ozean beeinflussen* (pp. 21–34). Kiel, Hamburg: Wachholtz.

Grasmeier, M. C. (2020). *"That is my Profession". Occupational Culture and Occupational Identities of Seafarers in the Global Merchant Fleet.* [Unpublished dissertation]. Universität Bremen.

Grasmeier, M.C. (2022). The ship as a postcolonial space. In: A. Kołodziej-Durnaś, F. Sowa, M.C. Grasmeier (eds). *Maritime Spaces and Society.* International Studies in Maritime Sociology. Brill

Hatmaker, D.M. (2013). Engineering Identity: Gender and Professional Identity Negotiation among Women Engineers. *Gender, Work & Organization* 20(4), 382–396

Hegel, G.W.F. (1966). Who thinks abstractly? In W. Kaufmann (ed). *Hegel: Texts and Commentary.* (pp. 113–118). Garden City: Anchor Books

Heimerdinger, T. (2005). *Der Seemann: Ein Berufsstand und seine kulturelle Inszenierung (1844–2003).* Köln: Böhlau

Heinrich, M. (2012). *An Introduction to the Three Volumes of Karl Marx's Capital.* New York: Monthly Review Press

Heyman, J. (2016). Conclusion. In J. G. Carrier (Ed.), *After the crisis: Anthropological thought, neoliberalism and the aftermath* (pp. 175–189). Routledge.

Holvino, E. (2010). Intersections: The Simultaneity of Race, Gender and Class in Organization Studies: Simultaneity of Race, Gender and Class. *Gender, Work & Organization* 17(3), 248–277

Hürtgen, S. (2019). Konkurrenz und xenophobe Kulturalisierung im transnationalen Raum der Lohnarbeit. In C. Book, N. Huke, S. Klauke, and O. Tietje (eds). *Alltägliche Grenzziehungen. Das Konzept der "imperialen Lebensweise", Externalisierung und exklusive Solidarität.* Münster: Westphälisches Dampfboot.

Hürtgen, S. (2020). Labour-process-related Racism in Transnational European Production: Fragmenting Work meets Xenophobic Culturalisation among Workers. *Global Labour Journal* 11(1): 18–33

Ignatiev, N. (1997). *The Point Is Not To Interpret Whiteness But To Abolish It.* Presentation held at the conference "The Making and Unmaking of Whiteness" Berkeley, California, April 11–13, 1997.

Jenkins, R. (2004); *Social Identity.* London; New York: Routledge

Kalb, D. (2013). *Regimes of Value and Worthlessness: Two Stories I Know, plus a Marxian Reflection.* Working Paper, 147. Max Plank Institute for Social Anthropology Working Papers. Halle/Saale: Max Plank Institute for Social Anthropology. https://www.eth.mpg.de/pubs/wps/pdf/mpi-eth-working-paper-0147, accessed November 24, 2019

Kitada, M. (2010). *Women Seafarers and Their Identities.* Cardiff University (United Kingdom). http://www.sirc.cf.ac.uk/Uploads/Thesis/Kitada.pdf, accessed September 28, 2017

Kitada, M. (2021). Women Seafarers: An Analysis of Barriers to Their Employment. In V. O. Gekara & H. Sampson (Eds.), *The World of the Seafarer* (pp. 65–76). Springer International Publishing. https://doi.org/10.1007/978-3-030-49825-2_6

Knudsen, F. (2004). Working and Leisure Relations between Danes and Filipinos on Board Danish Vessels. Arbejds- og Maritimmedicinsk Publikationsserie nr. 9. Esbjerg: Forskningsenheden for Maritim Medicin.

Knudsen, F. (2005). Seamanship and Anthropoship: Reflecting on Practice, vol.11. Arbejdsmedicinsk Afdeling, Sydvestjysk Sygehus

Knudsen, F. (2009). Paperwork at the Service of Safety? Workers' Reluctance against Written Procedures Exemplified by the Concept of 'Seamanship.' *Safety Science* 47(2), 295–303

Kołodziej, A., and Kołodziej-Durnaś, A. (2015). Diversity and Social Trust: Polish Seafarers in Multicultural Crews. *European Societies* 17(2), 158–175

Kołodziej, A. (2022). Maritime culture - ways of understanding, scope of influence, controversy. In A. Kołodziej-Durnaś, F. Sowa, M.C. Grasmeier (eds). *Maritime Spaces and Society*. International Studies in Maritime Sociology. Brill

Królikowska, I., & Męczkowska-Christiansen, A. (2018). Edukacyjne Doświadczenia Kobiet-marynarzy W Kontekście Praktyk Morskich. [Educational Experiences of Female Seafarers in the Context of Maritime Apprenticeship]. *"Colloquium" Pedagogika. Nauki of Polityce I Administracji*, *32*(4), 71–88.

Lamont, M. (1992). *Money, Morals, and Manners: The Culture of the French and American Upper-Middle Class. Morality and Society*. Chicago: University of Chicago Press

Lamont, M. (2000). *The Dignity of Working Men: Morality and the Boundaries of Race, Class, and Immigration*. New York: The Russel Sage Foundation

Lamont, M. (2014); Reflections Inspired by Ethnic Boundary Making: Institutions, Power, Networks by Andreas Wimmer. *Ethnic and Racial Studies* 37(5), 814–819

Lamont, M., Beljean, S., and Clair, M. (2014). What Is Missing? Cultural Processes and Causal Pathways to Inequality. *Socio-Economic Review* 12(3), 573–608

Lamont, M., & Fournier, M. (1992). Introduction. In M. Lamont & M. Fournier (Eds.), *Cultivating Differences. Symbolic Boundaries and the Making of Inequality.* The University of Chicago Press.

Lamont, M., and Molnár, V. (2002). The Study of Boundaries in the Social Sciences. *Annual Review of Sociology* 28(1), 167–195

Mann, Michael. (1973). *Consciousness and Action among the Western Working Class.* London/Basingstoke: The Macmillan Press

Marx, K. (1887); *Capital: A Critique of Political Economy*, (Vol. 1). Moscow: Progress Publishers

Marx, K. (1993). *Das Kapital. Kritik der politischen Ökonomie. 1. Band: Der Produktionsprozess des Kapitals*. (Bd. 23). Berlin: Dietz-Verlag.

Marx, K., Engels, F. (1956). *Capital: A critique of political economy* (Vol. 2). Moscow: Progress Publishers.

Marx, K., Engels, F. (1981). *Capital: A critique of political economy* (Vol. 3). London: New Left Review.

McKay, S.C. (2007). Filipino Sea Men: Constructing Masculinities in an Ethnic Labour Niche. *Journal of Ethnic and Migration Studies* 33(4), 617–633

Mayer-Ahuja, N. (2018): Klasse. Vom Elefant im Raum zum Schlüssel politischer Mobilisierung?, *Zeitschrift Marxistische Erneuerung* 116, 15–25

Męczkowska -Christiansen, A., & Królikowska, I. (2019). Perspectives on Women at Sea in the Light of Female Seafarers' Experience. Challenges for Maritime Education. *"Colloquium" Pedagogika. Nauki of Polityce I Administracji, 36*(4), 113–128. https://doi .org/10.34813/15coll2019

Nelles, D. (2001). *Widerstand und internationale Solidarität: Die Internationale Transportarbeiter-Föderation (ITF) im Widerstand gegen den Nationalsozialismus*. Klartext.

O'Reilly, K. (2012). *Ethnographic methods* (2nd ed). Routledge.

Østreng, D. (2001). *Sailors-Cosmopolitans or Locals. Occupational Identity of Sailors on Ships in International Trade*, Oslo Summer School in Comparative Social Science, University of Oslo

Østreng, D. (2001). *Does Togetherness Make Friends: Stereotypes and Intergroup Contact on Multiethnic-Crewed Ships*. Vestfold College Publication Series/Paper. Tønsberg

Purser, G. (2009). The Dignity of Job-Seeking Men: Boundary Work among Immigrant Day Laborers. *Journal of Contemporary Ethnography, 38*(1), 117–139. https://doi .org/10.1177/0891241607311867

Ramarajan, L., and Reid, E. (2013). Shattering the Myth of Separate Worlds: Negotiating Nonwork Identities at Work. *Academy of Management Review* 38(4), 621–644

Ridgeway, C.L. (2009). Framed Before We Know It: How Gender Shapes Social Relations. *Gender & Society* 23(2), 145–160

Roediger, D., & Esch, E. (2009). One symptom of originality: Race and the management of labour in the history of the United States. *Historical Materialism, 17*(4), 3–43.

Sampson, H. (2013). *International Seafarers and Transnationalism in the Twenty-First Century*. Manchester, New York: Manchester University Press

Sampson, H. (2021). The Rhythms of Shipboard Life: Work, Hierarchy, Occupational Culture and Multinational Crews. In V. O. Gekara & H. Sampson (Eds.), *The World of the Seafarer* (pp. 87–98). Springer International Publishing. https://doi .org/10.1007/978-3-030-49825-2_8

Sampson, H., Acejo, I., Ellis, N., Tang, L., and Turgo, N. (2016). *The Relationships between Seafarers and Shore-Side Personnel: An Outline Report Based on Research Undertaken in the Period 2012–2016*. Cardiff: Seafarers International Research Centre. http://www.sirc.cf.ac.uk/Uploads/Publications/The%20relationships%20between%20seafarers%20and%20shore-side%20personnel.pdf, accessed December 4, 2018

Sherman, R.l (2005). Producing the Superior Self: Strategic Comparison and Symbolic Boundaries among Luxury Hotel Workers. *Ethnography* 6(2), 131–158

Stan, S. (2016). Looking for a place to stand: Theory, field and holism in contemporary anthropology. In J. G. Carrier (Ed.), *After the crisis: Anthropological thought, neoliberalism and the aftermath* (pp. 114–132). Routledge.

Swidler, A. (1986). Culture in Action: Symbols and Strategies. *American Sociological Review*, *51*(2), 273. https://doi.org/10.2307/2095521

Vallas, S.P. (2001). Symbolic Boundaries and the New Division of Labor: Engineers, Workers and the Restructuring of Factory Life. *Research in Social Stratification and Mobility* 18, 3–37

Vallas, S.P. (2003). Rediscovering the Color Line Within Work Organizations. The 'Knitting of Racial Groups' Revisited. *Work & Occupation* 30(4): 379–400. DOI: 10.1177/0730888403256454

Vallas, S.P., and Cummins, E. (2014). Relational Models of Organizational Inequalities: Emerging Approaches and Conceptual Dilemmas. *American Behavioral Scientist* 58(2): 228–255

Vernooij, E. (2017). Navigating multipositionality in 'insider'ethnography. *Medicine Anthropology Theory*, *4*(2), 34–49.

Welke, U. (1997). *Der Kapitän: die Erfindung einer Herrschaftsform* [The Captain: Invention of a Form of Rule.]. Münster: Westfälisches Dampfboot

West, C., and Fenstermaker, S. (1995a). Doing Difference. *Gender & Society* 9(1), 8–37

West, C., and Fenstermaker, S. (1995b). REPLY: (Re) Doing Difference. *Gender & Society* 9(4), 506–513

Wimmer, A. (2002). *Nationalist Exclusion and Ethnic Conflict. Shadows of Modernity*. Cambridge: Cambridge University Press

Wimmer, A. (2013). *Ethnic Boundary Making. Institutions, Power, Networks*. New York: Oxford University Press

Wright, E. O. (1980). Class and Occupation. *Theory and Society*, *9*(1), 177–214.

Wright, E.O.. (1989). Rethinking, Once Again, the Concept of Class Structure. In *The Debate on Classes*, E. O. Wright (pp. 269–348). London/ New York: Verso.

PART 2

Gender Issues

CHAPTER 4

The Role of Discursive Contexts in Constructing the Identity of Women at Sea: Towards Informal Dimensions of Maritime Adult Education

Astrid Męczkowska-Christiansen and Iwona Królikowska

The chapter focuses on problems female seafarers encounter regarding professional identity construction. This subject is analysed in the context of the influence of *power-knowledge discourses* prevalent in the maritime labour sector. The results of critical discourse analyses (CDA) are presented and cover various cultural articulations of employment at sea as the domain of women's professional activity. Consequently, three types of discourses were identified: 1) *a discourse of the openness of a labour market* with neoliberal-economic provenance, that valorises women's employment in maritime professions, 2) *patriarchal discourse of exclusion*, of mostly an exclusionary and depreciating nature, and 3) *discourse of maritime career instrumentalisation*, where maritime employment is meant to be a temporary measure in order to increase the material status of seafaring women and their families. The dynamic structure of the professional identity of women employed at sea seems to form at the intersection of these three discourses. The process of the discursive construction of professional identities of female seafarers includes various strategies, such as *techniques of subjugation and technologies of the self* which, according to Foucault, relate to *subjectification* and *governmentality* as means for positioning female subjects in the maritime labour market as a domain of power relations.

The empirical research was multi-stage. Critical discourse analysis involved a secondary level analysis of empirical data collected with the use of biographical and phenomenographic approaches, in which both interviews, given by female seafarers (in-depth interviews and focus interviews), as well as texts (i.e. semiotic artefacts, Lemke 2003) that have been produced in the maritime culture, were used. The research subjects surveyed were Polish female crew-members of seagoing vessels. However, the data obtained during the interviews was embedded in the context of analyses carried out by international researchers. The results of the analyses were theorised in relation to both socialisation of the professional roles and informal aspects of adult education.

 | DOI:10.1163/9789004518841_006

1 Shedding Light on the Issue: Female Maritime Identities

The issue of employment of women in maritime professions has adopted numerous positions of articulations in recent years as expressed both from academic and business perspectives. The first highlighted area deals with this issue mainly with a focus on the specific situation of women in the maritime economy and at the same time their role as social actors, as portrayed taking into account the specificity of their experiences. Such research interest predominately involves the critical perspective of gender-oriented studies, which has often addressed the issues of structural inequalities related to the fulfilment of female gender roles in a male-dominated environment (Aggrey 2000; Guo & Liang, 2012; Pettersson et al., 2008; Stark, SJ, 1996; Kitada, Williams, Froholdt, 2015; Chia-Ling et al., 2017; Królikowska, Męczkowska-Christiansen, 2018, Królikowska, Męczkowska-Christiansen, 2019).[1] On the other hand, interest in the issue of female seafarers by the business community and by the governments of countries for which this sector contributes to the countries' well-being is particularly important. It is connected with the potential of this social group as a reservoir of insufficiently utilised human resources - a reservoir particularly valuable in a situation where employment forecasts in maritime economy indicate (on a global scale) a growing deficit of seafarers (Walker, 2015; WEF, 2015; IMO, 2018; ITF, 2017; ILO, 2019; Manpower Report, 2015). Judging by the interpretations of official (academic and business) discourses, we are currently not only faced with overcoming the stereotype of work at sea as a predominantly male occupation but drawing attention to the fact that the issue of working at sea is not gender-indifferent.

While the issue of female seafarers is culturally interesting, it is a relatively poorly explored research area of maritime culture and considered one of the 'cultural relics' of Western civilisation. This culture is predominantly one of strong patriarchal relations, with the dominant role of 'breadwinner ideology' being adopted by male crews. This is characterised by the inheritance of traditional (oftentimes ancient), cultural patterns from the seafaring field. In this sense, maritime culture can be studied as a kind of 'open-air museum of old rites', thereby drawing the attention of social researchers. For this reason, insights from research regarding roles played by females in the maritime industry are quite strongly focused on the issue of gender and highlight the

1 However, gender-oriented studies involving the problem of seafaring women, do not necessarily belong to the most recent academic achievements. They have been conducted since beginning of the 1970s. by such 'early' researchers as B. Greenhill and A. Giffard (1971); H. Henningsen (1981); B. Berggreen (1979; 1985).

polarisation of the positions occupied by women and men in their relationship with the sea.

This concerns the traditional perception of seafaring as a male profession, and therefore its exclusivity, is widely spoken of, and seafaring is generally regarded as being an exclusively masculine territory. The source of this belief is deeply rooted in Western culture and seems to also be associated with misogynistic attitudes, which have been evident for centuries in areas of official institutional discourse. For example, in the formal regulations of the British fleet under Admiral Nelson, the captain of a ship was 'not to carry any woman to sea' (Turley, 1999, p. 29). However, aside from official bans, there were prejudices in seafaring circles regarding not only women at sea, but even forbidding discussions about women (ibid). Women have been perceived to be cast in a different mould; considered to be 'made out of wood' in opposition to 'men of iron' (Creighton & Norling, 1996). However, as we will mention in more detail, women have always been present in seafaring culture, even on board ships, although not always in an official or public manner (Maenpaa, 2004, p. 145).

Even during *The Age of Sail*, the presence of women on ships was officially prohibited (Creighton, Norling, 1996; Norling, 2000) and was either hidden or took place unofficially. In Nelson's British Navy – where regulations forbidding women on board were extremely strict – some warrant officers, as well as specialist officers, took their wives to sea with them. The women often played roles of an unofficial nature of employment (Stark, 1996). This unofficial or covert nature of women's work on ships continued until the 19th century, which brought with it the development of emigrant shipping.[2] Contemporary historical and archaeological studies indicate that, through the ages, women accompanied and took care of their husbands, and even gave birth to children on board. Some women even enlisted (in disguise) to serve in Nelson's Navy (Slope, 2011). A similar situation occurred on merchant ships before the eighteenth century – when, surprisingly, many women ventured to the sea in roles such as cooks, washerwomen and servants (Cordingly, 2007). Women were also even present among pirates, although according to the 18th-century pirate code, 'No boy or woman should be allowed among the crew. If any man were found seducing any of the fairer sex and carried her to sea, disguised, he was to suffer death' (Turley, 1999, p. 96). The most well-known women in this context are Grace O'Malley, Elise Eskilsdotter, Lady Elizabeth Killigrew, Anne Dieu-le-Veut, Jacquotte Delahaye, Johanna Hård, Mary Read, and Anne Bonny (Klausmann, Meinzerin, Kuhn, 1997; Stanley, 1995). These female pirates were

2 This fact has fundamentally changed the role of women on board: since then women have been performing their occupational roles officially, but these have been low status roles.

disguised as men, and some of them were considered to be among the 'most dashing of pirates'. The latter two women in their behaviours combined the archetypal image of a 'whore' and the attitude of a 'faithful but passionate mate'; they were also regarded as 'women warriors' (Turley, 1991, pp. 97, 99). They were what could be called identity hybrids — on the one hand, practising mimicry allowing them to fit in to the specific masculine environment (where even bringing a woman on board was strictly prohibited), and on the other, to the archetypal image of being 'whores', who violated strict moral conventions. It is tempting to suggest they might have been rebels who expressed emancipatory resistance against social norms and conventions which subjectify women according to their traditionally defined roles.

When analysing historical sources, not only the presence of female seafarers is noticed, but also the importance of deep involvement of women in creating a context for the iron men on board. It is interesting to note the analyses of chronicles, literature, various documents and personal records showing the relationship between women and the sea mediated by the presence of a man. In maritime professions, for centuries, women have acted as guardians of men, people who took care of the home and family during their men's absence, and their basic virtues including the expectation of the man's return, in accordance with the motto: 'because it is for the man to be far away, and for the woman to wait faithfully'.[3] On the other hand, women associated with the sea were not only wives but also included lovers and prostitutes (Burton, 1999). They were presented as women who successfully emptied even the pockets of pirates (Turley, 1999, p. 29). Ignoring the existing bans, when in port, most ships' captains allowed prostitutes on board (Slope, 2011). The idea of having 'a woman in every port' - no matter whether casual lovers or quasi-professional prostitutes, is to this day the theme of sea shanties, vividly present in maritime pop-culture.

As mentioned earlier, the increase in the participation of women in maritime labour and women's involvement becoming more official progressed along with the development of passenger transport during the emigrant era (i.e. since the second half of the 19th century). Despite the relative popularity of their employment, women were denied professional roles assigned by an official contract of employment, a competitive salary and access to training. Their employment status was low, careers were restricted, and the tasks they performed were limited to 'traditional' female roles that women commonly

3 A quotation from the well-known Polish song entitled There is still a white sail there (1980). The lyrics perfectly illustrate how the stereotype of a woman whose relationship with the sea is mediated by the presence of a man has moved into popular culture.

performed in society. Employment of women was concentrated on passenger lines as well as strictly dependent on their marital status and life-cycle circumstances (Maenpaa, 2004, p. 145). Therefore, in this context, it would be difficult to talk about an increase in the proportion of employment of women at sea in terms of emancipation - simply, the traditional division of labour 'moved to the sea', where there was a strong polarisation of male roles (specialists, requiring qualifications, given a higher status)[4] and female roles (replacement roles, temporary, which do not require official rights, thus giving the possibility of a frequent rotation of female employees). Women were employed as cleaners, cooks, attendants, caretakers, nurses, or held 'supportive' and 'caring' roles stereotypically assigned to women. A condition for the employment of women at sea has often been the elimination of traditional attributes of femininity, such as physical attractiveness and the ability to procreate. For example, in the US Navy, since the end of the 1960s, the condition for employing women was that they had to have reached an appropriate age and hold a certain marital status – that is women, who were formerly employed as nurses or washerwomen, were over 50 years of age and were seamen's wives or widows (Stark, 1998, p. 68). Despite the male dominance in the maritime sector, around the second half of the 20th century the first officer positions occupied by women on merchant and naval vessels appeared. There were women working as radio officers - in the Norwegian fleet, and since the 1970s - in the Irish, German and Polish fleets. The Canadian Maude Steane, employed in the Norwegian fleet (1944), is mentioned here as a pioneer, as at that time women who graduated with their radio operator diplomas were banned from joining Canadian or any other Commonwealth ships (Greenlaw, 2002; Sharpe).

Contrary to previous centuries, since the last decades of the 20th century, women have encountered increasing quasi-emancipatory challenges, regarding the importance of employment of women in the maritime sector and encouraging them to take up work on-board. The slogans of equality between men and women are raised here, and the mythologisation of the sea (and work at sea) as a male-only domain is criticised. However, this rhetoric seems to be guided mainly by economic interests, as the interest in women involved in work at sea is linked to the potential of this social group in regards to being an underutilised human resource that is especially valuable in a situation where employment forecasts in the maritime economy on a global scale indicate an increasingly growing deficit of maritime personnel (UNCTAD, 2018; UNCTAD,

4 Certainly, the maritime sector also employed men in non-prestigious and low-paid jobs. Especially in the era of steam, low-skilled male workers were hired to perform work that required physical strength (e.g. coal trimmers).

2019; ILO, 2019; BIMCO/ISF, 2015). Indicators concerning the proportion of employment of women to men show that the maritime industry is almost wholly dominated by men, with women making up only a small fraction up to 7,5%) of the marine workforce (ICS, 2020)). Moreover, the employment of female seafarers is concentrated in the cruise and ferries sector – the IMO reports that 94% of female seafarers are working in the cruise industry (IMO 2019, Belcher et al. 2003, p.9).

These women primarily take on service roles, such as staff, catering, kitchen duties, cleaning, etc. (ITF, 2017). Please note that although the quantitative indicators are changing, in the qualitative dimension, a similar situation occurred during the nineteenth century, when, with the increase in the range of passenger transport and the emergence of demand for specific 'female' roles as well as cheap labour, women dominated the lowest positions on passenger ships (this same situation continues to this day). To summarise this part of the chapter, let us emphasise that when analysing the history of women in maritime professions, it can be seen that the sea has always offered women jobs but has not created the conditions for respecting and developing their professional identities. In this sense, they were denied their subjectivity.

2 Professional Identity Construction Among Female Seafarers as the Scope of the Current Analyses

Through analysis of the issues of discursive contexts in constructing the professional identities of seafaring women, we present this process in terms of lifelong learning that occurs during the development of professional experience. There is consensus, both across professions as well as within the academic environment of adult education, that formal education forms the basis of learning processes that continue throughout professional life (Day, 1999; Davis, 2003; Dall'Alba, 2004; Jarvis, 2004).

Development of professional identity within the workplace is strictly bonded to respecting an individual's subjectivity and agency. Many contemporary researchers emphasise this issue and critique 'classic' workplace learning theories, i.e., employment presenting the so-called 'training model', focused on the direct transfer of knowledge and skills from experienced practitioners to novices (Billet, 2008; Eteläpelto, 2006; Webster-Wright, 2009; Billet & Pavlova, 2005; Billett, Fenwick, Somerville, 2006). However, by exploring the topic of learning, the following issues are analysed: relations between individuals, identity construction issues, social aspects of the work environment, cognitive tasks and challenges in which learning processes are played out, and so forth.

Development of professional identity within the workplace involves learning taking place within a community that supports learning (Webster-Wright, 2009, p. 703). Together with engagement in authentic work experiences, a predominant role is played by problem-solving activities that individuals undergo during the process of social interactions. In this context, the key aspects of the process of constructing professional identity involve cognitive engagement combined with critical reflection; the community context of learning in the workplace related to the presence of social ties; genuine cooperation and cooperative learning; involvement of one's agency related not only to the aspects of creating solutions but also to the possibility of achieving one's own goals and the continuous process of negotiation and redefinition of one's personal and professional identity. All these aspects mean that acquiring a professional identity in the workplace does not involve forcing the employee into the rigid matrix of a predefined role but is related to the process of individuation within the role of which the form is negotiated. In this sense, constructing/developing professional identity is understood in terms of respecting one's subjectivity and autonomous development. As such, learning, that involves agency, is transformative for professional identity construction (Billet 2002, Billet 2004).

The concept of professionalism (in relation to 'professional identity'), which appears in the text, is not a central issue in our study, which means our empirical research focuses more on identity issues (i.e. formative role of discourse for the construction of seafaring women's identities) rather than on the specificity of the profession performed by female seafarers. Therefore, the term 'professional identity' refers to one of many possible dimensions of identity. In general terms, professional identity is understood here as professional self-concept based on one's attributes, beliefs, values, motives, and experiences (Slay & Smith, 2011, p. 85). In the case of our study, it is revealed at the intersection of two dimensions constructing identity, which include gender and seafaring (the domain and cultural environment of performing the professional role). Such an 'intersectional' approach remains consistent to current tendencies of investigating identities in context in order to explore how multiple categories of identity (such as gender, age, class, occupation, etc.) intersect and interact (Taylor 2015, p. 715).

Based on the assumption that an individual and their social world are co-constitutive, an extremely important role in this process of constructing a professional identity is played by the individual's structural embeddedness in the cultural space. In light of the post-structural perspective, the cultural space is the domain of influence of knowledge-power discourses. This interdependence has been explored from the perspective of a post-structural theoretical framework (predominately Foucauldian) and is still developed within critical discourse studies. In its fundamental, i.e. Foucauldian, terms, discourse constitutes both conceptual and linguistic expressions which have the power to define and impose different ways individuals define/perceive/understand social reality. Discourses carry meanings; they set the field of what and how things can be said/thought out, and, ultimately, put into practice – which means that they are constitutive for various forms of social practice. For Foucault, discourses also imply who is allowed to speak/act, when he or she may do so, and with what authority. They constitute subjectivities and social relations; they are 'practices that systematically form the objects of which they speak' (Foucault, 1972, p. 49). All in all, discourses constitute 'frameworks' thorough which power operates within the society in its subtle, unrevealed forms.

Discourses form cultural/linguistic contexts of identity construction – the latter was analysed by Foucault mostly in terms of "*subjectification*" (Foucault, 1977), "*governmentality*" (Foucault 1982) or "*technologies of the self*" (1988). While the first involves plain disciplinary techniques creating 'docile bodies', the last two operate through covertly persuasive forms of social pressure – which in fact makes individuals convinced of their own autonomy and govern themselves in accordance with the models culturally imposed on them (Foucault, 1982). Discursive formations involve norms, forms of knowledge (including knowledge about oneself), and practices that individuals are subjected to, and which influence their identity construction and representation. These deliver frameworks for constructing identities (Taylor, 2015), providing patterns of identification, generating aspirations, offering ways of thinking about oneself and reality. Finally, these discursively constructed identities become social realities (Slay, Smith, 2011).

3 Critical Discourse Analysis in the Current Investigation

Critical discourse analyses (CDA), in its contemporarily dominant form (Fairclough 1995, Wodak, 2015; Van Dijk, 2009; Lemke, 2003) involves a critical examination of how discourses are carried out by linguistic forms of expression of any kind. For this reason, the core of CDA is semiotic analysis. However, it must be kept in mind that 'texts play a constitutive role in social structuration' (Lemke, 2003, p. 130). Since discourses, as linguistically mediated models of reality (Foucault, 1972), refer to both linguistic practices (with their conceptual bases) and social practices that constitute one another, while in critical discourse studies, language is always perceived as a form of social practice (Fairclough, 1995). Hence, semiotic practices are always investigated in their relation to specific fields of social practices (Reisigl, Wodak, 2009, p. 87).

Discourses are complex semiotic structures which involve discursive scripts that form perspectives of social reality and its particular segments (Van Leeuwen, Wodak, p. 1999). Based on discursive scripts, people construct their beliefs concerning reality itself as well as its various (individual and collective) social actors, events, processes, etc. Thus, one may say that discourses create their 'ontologies' as reality representations. Moreover, discourses represent and reflect aspects of power asymmetries that pertain to structural inequities embedded in various domains of social practice. As such, power relations might be both legitimised or delegitimised in discourses. A discourse, as an object of investigation, is not a monolith, but 'a dynamic semiotic entity that is open to reinterpretation and continuation' (Wodak, 2015, p. 89). Consequently, it may be argued that discourses do not form homogeneous structures but are never completely heterogeneous either. They may overlap and intersect each other, including elements that belong to various discourses.

Using CDA as the methodological approach allows us to examine how the representations of female professional identities are represented, constituted, distributed and recontextualised in discursive scripts embedded in common knowledge or 'folk wisdom' of female seafarers.

Since CDA always involves problem-oriented research, research questions were formulated during the investigation. In literature devoted to this approach, various manners of formulating research questions are suggested. In this study, selected suggestions offered by R. Wodak (2015) were employed, and, consequently, the following research questions emerged in the course of the semiotic analyses:
- From which positions/whose perspectives are clusters of discursive scripts expressed?
- How is the domain of seafaring represented and recontextualised in the identified discourses?
- How are female subjects positioned within particular discourses?
- How are female subjects reflected within particular discourses: what characteristics, qualities, and features are attributed to them?
- How are the trajectories of female seafaring careers represented and construed within particular discourses?
- What patterns of conduct and strategies for action in their relation to professional identity construction are represented and construed within particular discourses?

4 Data Analysis

The data chosen for this analysis was obtained from a corpus of 65 fragments of various linguistic expression sourced from focus interviews conducted with groups of Polish seafaring female professionals and apprentices; individual in-depth interviews conducted with seafaring females; informal interviews conducted in maritime social settings; various promotional, reporting and information material published by organisations and institutions active in the maritime field. Some of the data used in this study (i.e. transcriptions of interviews) were previously used by us in other studies (Królikowska, Męczkowska-Christiansen, 2018; Męczkowska-Christiansen, Królikowska, 2019) and for the purposes of the current study, were re-analysed. Semiotic analyses were conducted on transcribed or printed texts. Additionally, selected photos and visualisations were used to present female seafarers present on internet portals dedicated to maritime issues. Herein, visually expressed content was subjected to semiotic analysis, according to assumptions of multimodal CDA (Djonov, Zhao, 2014; Machin, Mayr, 2012). Qualitative data used in the analyses were collected during the years 2017–2020.

The collected statements were treated as 'texts', and constructions of discursive categories were investigated (Sondergaard, 2002). Following the inductive research procedure, we identified broader 'genres' representing the structure of discourses. During the study, structural conditions of discourse were systematically referred to. Hence, the employed research procedure involved multiple cross-investigations of the relationships between acts of speech, genres, and the structural context of the identified discourses. Such a procedure refers to a three-dimensional discourse analysis proposed by N. Fairclough, consisting of micro-, meso-, and macro- levels of interpretation (Fairclough, 1995).

5 Results of the Study: Discursive Contexts of Constructing the Identity of Female Seafarers

As the result of the study, three types of discourses were identified a *patriarchal discourse of exclusion* (PDE), a *discourse of openness of the labour market* (DOLM), and a *discourse of maritime career instrumentalisation* (DMCI).
Below we present their descriptions, taking into account their structure, including:
- Positions from which discursive scripts are expressed;
- Semiotic representation of the seafaring domain within discursive structures;

- Semiotic representation of female subjects and the strategies of positioning them within discursive structures;
- Semiotic representations of female seafaring careers;
- Patterns of conduct and strategies for action in their relation to professional identity construction within discourses.

6 The Patriarchal Discourse of Exclusion

PDE is a traditionalist discourse, encompassing content embedded in the maritime patriarchal culture that assigns a legal role to a man at sea. This is a derivative of the stereotyped division into 'male' and 'female' professions, with the latter having a lower social rank. It is a discourse that excludes the presence of women from the seafaring domain – however, it is not about excluding their physical presence but includes a refusal to recognise their (fully-fledged) subjectivity in maritime professions. The patriarchal character of PDE assigns a higher value to masculinity than femininity and favours 'masculine traits' in performing professional roles within the seafaring domain.

6.1 *Positions from Which PDE is Expressed*

From the 'male' perspective, PDE is articulated in defence of the exclusivity of seafaring as the domain of men's work. The 'male perspective' or 'male positions' (in the gender-related sense) do not mean that the contents of the PDE only comes from what men say. They can be expressed by both men and women. For example, a female officer aspiring to the position of captain expressed that: "*I will never let any woman to get on board my ship!*"[5] In the patriarchal system, not only men but also women are in positions as protectors of traditional patriarchal social structures. From the perspective of postcolonial studies, as Said's *Orientalism* (1979) details, also native, colonised, dominated people make their efforts to support mainstream colonial discourses. The key to understanding such a 'postcolonial syndrome' is to give up the illusion that people always articulate their 'authentic voices' and speak from their 'native' positions. Instead, especially in CDA, it is necessary to ask the following: 'who says this and whose voice are they expressing?'.

5 The italicised fragments come directly from the statements of the female seafarers interviewed.

6.2 *Semiotic Representation of the Domain of Seafaring in* PDE

From a PDE perspective, access to the domain of seafaring is marked by legitimate inequalities for women and men and by the status of male and female subjects. PDE legitimises these inequalities, considering them legitimate, desirable, obvious, resulting from the nature of women and men, as well as from ancient traditions in the seafaring domain. The legitimacy of inequality concerns:

i. Wage inequalities: "*A male friend came, and he got a larger salary. Ashore, it does not make any difference at all*".
ii. Inequalities in recognition of achievement (women are expected to do more and affirmed less);
iii. Uneven access to formal positions on board;
iv. Uneven access to training;
v. Pre-entry discrimination of various kinds. For example: In Poland, when candidates for maritime apprenticeship are selected, women's applications are rejected immediately. Such practices indicate the existence of elements of horizontal occupational segregation in the recruitment process based on gender criterion (it is also worth noticing that completing a maritime apprenticeship is a prerequisite for graduation from maritime academies);
vi. Justification of stereotypes that are widespread in society. The results of Polish studies (Królikowska, Męczkowska-Christiansen, 2018, 2019) show that some women feel that they are not allowed to choose seafaring as a career because of the extended stay at sea, which is in contradiction with the traditionally perceived role of women, especially with the societal belief that children must be brought up by women; for that reason, women generally do not receive adequate social support to choose seafaring as their career and feel deprived of family support, which is essential for them to establish their own identity in a male-dominated sector.

Seafaring is perceived as a 'male territory'. In the area of PDE discourse, however, there is a noticeable shift of the centre of gravity from the lack of 'physical access' to the lack of recognition of the subjective (i.e. fully-fledged) position of women on board.[6] Male resistance to the presence of women on the ship is therefore rather resistant to equating her status (including her professional position) with that of a man.

6 This refers to seagoing vessels; on drilling platforms, which constitute a specific, but absolutely male-dominated work environment, this situation is less noticeable.

The positioning of female subjects within PDE is a derivative of gender inequalities which are inscribed within the PDE, where a woman is considered inferior to a man. Male dominance is definitely legitimised by the patriarchal dimension of the PDE semiotic field. Domination breeds violence, which comes in two variants: explicit violence or paternalism (understood in terms of symbolic violence). The facets of overt violence against women working in male-dominated crews of seagoing vessels have already been described by us (2018; 2019) and seem less interesting from the perspective of the adopted methodology. We can list here the cases related to the use of gossip as a tool of humiliation, sexual harassment, mobbing, strong unjustified criticism, etc. These types of violence allude to the disciplinary techniques of subjugation, as described by Foucault (1977). Moreover, the participants of the empirical analyses noted the severity of being constantly monitored. Their constant 'visibility' evoked the acute feeling of 'being observed', which seafaring females talked about in terms of violence against them: This is associated with psychological torment, for example: "*I am correcting a chart and he* (*the captain*) *looks over my shoulder and watches*". Again – the situation of permanent observation can be described in Foucauldian terms referring to Panopticon, providing subjects with continuous visibility, as an oppressive device (Ibid.).

Linguistic analyses, among which CDA falls, focus primarily on issues related to symbolic violence which is located in the signification of language itself. This form of violence is created and distributed within the language; it is constantly present. However, it is invisible in everyday acts of speech, sustaining relations of domination (Žižek, 2008). One of the modalities of symbolic violence is so-called 'soft violence' - this type of violence refers to acts that are 'gentle', paternalistic, and sometimes even 'kind' (from the point of view of the subject), however, taking away the feeling of agency, restraining the development of competences and invalidating the voice of the oppressed subjects. The following is an example of a description of a woman's experience of 'soft violence':

> Welding, grinding - I wanted to learn how and of course I heard: 'girl, you won't be able to do it; you better go to the bridge.' I replied: 'if I am to be with you, I must learn'. And then there were some unpleasant comments and then I could not stand it any longer, I said I was getting off (the ship) and I had enough.

The above situation is a description of some form of (discursive) practice. Why discursive? Because it perfectly corresponds to one of the types of representations of femininity present in PDE ('the fair sex'). More about this below.

6.3 *Representations of Female Seafarers Within* PDE

The construction of the representation of female seafarers takes on various forms within PDE. However, all of them have the potential to depreciate the potential of women as professionals or potential professionals. Below we present different variants of this representation.

i. The representation of woman as the *fair sex*,[7] which refers to an exaggeratedly romanticised, feminine portrait of a delicate woman who simply 'does not fit for this (hard) job'. Such a 'fair lady' is also considered mentally weak, she is not immune to critical remarks concerning the method of fulfilling professional tasks: "They were sometimes afraid to say something to me, so as not to offend me". In this sense, the lack of feedback can be a serious barrier to acquiring professional skills.

ii. The representation of a woman as a sexual object: a woman at hand. At the same time, she is perceived as an easy lay – a woman who seems easily persuaded to engage in sexual acts. As voiced by a female chief officer: "As we usually have five-month contracts, and do not always go shore in the port or do not want to catch something in such a port, you know, some kind of venereal disease, then such a lady on-board, who is still at hand, seems useful". This type of representation is sometimes accompanied by the legitimacy of sexual violence (in line with the principle: she is the one to blame, she brought it upon herself): She said: "*My God, how terrible, an officer comes to her and knocks at night, and there he torments her, but in the meantime, she publishes photos on Instagram, of her going ashore in such skimpy shorts, and she is a beautiful girl with a great figure*".

   A woman who successfully pursues a maritime career is also perceived in this context as one that pursues promotion 'by sleeping around'. In this case, the increase in professional position is considered a 'gift' or the fulfilment of obligations by the high-ranking men with whom she has slept:
   - *"If (she) gets promoted, it is because of who she slept with"*
   - *"For sure you slept around to have gotten this promotion ..."*
   - *"Oh yes, there were so many stories with whom I did sleep with on ships ..."*
   - *"I have also slept with so many board chairmen...."*

   (A fragment of a focus interview conducted among high ranking female officers)

7 *Fair sex discourse* itself, as presented in eighteenth century American and English culture, referred to women as the 'more virtuous gender'. The term derives from the Renaissance Era as referring to light skin tone, natural beauty, and moral purity as well as sexuality that must be constrained (Schloesser, 2002).

The representation of women as sexual objects is also accompanied by the perception of a young, unmarried woman on the ship being a gold digger - a woman who is looking for a husband on-board and will work until she finds a husband on board.

iii. Women are perceived in the context of their life-cycles and reproductive abilities, so their place on the ship is only temporary. This relates to social norms that impose the social roles of women as defined by biological sex: preferably in roles as mothers and wives. This means that women's maritime careers, might be a misunderstanding to start with and are short-lived and are/should be ended with motherhood. This translates, inter alia, on the recruitment process and access to training: "we will not invest in her, because she will soon leave the ship".

These stereotypes seem to discourage women themselves from taking up work at sea or cause environmental pressure (families, life partners) to abandon plans referring to maritime careers.

6.4 *Representations of Female Seafaring Careers Within PDE*

PDE includes beliefs about the temporary employment of women at sea. This is related to linking the image of women primarily with procreation and innate delicacy, therefore making them incapable of fulfilling demanding professional roles in an unfavourable maritime environment: This is how men commonly perceive women at sea: "*she will come for a while and soon become pregnant*". From the perspective of PDE, we can therefore talk about temporary employment but not about the career development of seafaring women.

6.5 *Patterns of Conduct and Strategies for Action in Relation to Professional Identity Construction Within PDE*

PDE is exclusive by nature. That is why we talk about building 'on board survival strategies' for women rather than building professional identity strategies. The former may include the strategy of 'playing dead', i.e. staying out of sight: withdrawing from the field of action, abandoning aspirations, and finally getting off the ship. It is also possible to adopt a mimicry strategy - to become similar in the way of fulfilling the professional roles of male models. Then appears (also represented in the course of empirical analyses) the representation of a 'manly woman'; a woman who has strong masculine traits, who is considered unnatural and alienated from her femininity - which is also rejected by the male community. Herein, women seem to deal with double binding effects of gender oppression, becoming victims of a situation that offers conflicting models of the woman and the professional. As a consequence, women feel obliged to deny the stereotype of feminity. However, if they do so, they will experience criticism and exclusion.

7 The Discourse of Maritime Career Instrumentalisation (DMCI)

DMCI concerns the perception of women's work at sea as a 'personal project' focused on the implementation of specific life tasks related primarily to caring about one's material standard. In a nutshell, for women, the sea is there to make enough to 'settle down' comfortably, and from the very beginning of their professional career they think about leaving the sea - of course after fulfilling certain life tasks: "*To tell you the truth, in fact, intelligent people leave the sea*".

DMCI is mostly expressed from positions of 'successful women' - i.e. those women who actively climbed all or almost all levels of their on-board professional career (including holding the position of the captain of large merchant ships). These women share the fact that working at sea was for them the starting point for (sometimes spectacular) land-based maritime careers. They are women who are aware of their high professional position and enormous value as an employee. It seems that, in contrast to PDE, we are dealing with a departure from representing the 'male point of view' and 'male interest' in maintaining male domination within the seafaring industry. It is worth adding that the social and professional position of women, from which they articulate the discursive patterns of DMCI, is privileged - it gives them the opportunity to choose how to pursue or even interrupt their professional careers and to express resistance to existing norms and conventions. They also express a critical awareness of the presence and modalities of the patriarchal discourse of exclusion (PDE) dominant in the maritime industry.

7.1 *Semiotic Representation of the Domain of Seafaring in DMCI*

Seafaring is perceived as a profession that gives financial gratification, allows one to become 'set up comfortably', but, however, is temporary in nature: "*to start with to get big money that is difficult to earn elsewhere*". It is also a profession associated with high personal costs (separation from family, exposure to stress, work in an unfavourable misogynistic environment requiring a high degree of assertiveness from a woman and a very high level of competence, exceeding the competences of men holding comparable positions): "*I believe that it is men that aren't prepared for having women work on the ship, not that the women aren't prepared to work on a ship; You pay a high price for selling yourself to the sea.*"

The temporary aspect of women working at sea is due to the aspirations of women regarding family life and high aspirations to take on future land-based professional positions in the maritime industry: "*You must have a plan B. My plan is to go to sea for a few years and reach an officer position and then go ashore. To have a family life.*"

The seafaring domain is attractive to women, although they are aware of the gender inequalities occurring in the field (payroll, personnel, and unequal requirements for women versus men). Thus, they consciously enter a male-dominated environment, trying to 'win much for themselves' in a field of unequal competition.

7.2 *The Positioning of Female Subjects Within DMCI*

Despite the fact that in the field of seafaring, men occupy a privileged position, women are perceived as more responsible, perhaps more capable, with full volitional and intellectual potential, as well as professional competence resources to occupy high positions on board. In this sense, we can talk about their positioning within DMCI as empowered subjects.

7.3 *Representations of Female Seafarers Within DMCI*

Women are perceived here as pursuing their own personal interests with a priority being high earnings. Career development, which includes all (or almost all) steps in the occupational hierarchy, is seen as subordinate to the main goal. Additionally, career development is combined here with expanding personal autonomy and gaining power in the male world. In this sense, it has an emancipatory dimension.

It happens that the 'female subject' is contrasted in this aspect with the 'male subject': women work at sea for money, and men (who do not think about ending their career at sea), work at sea for convenience: "*I think that in fact, men are cowards because it's comfortable to work at sea. It is really comfortable to work at sea and earn good money because they do not understand what the price in life of this is. Really intelligent people leave the sea.*"

Women are perceived as competent and professional, this image is sometimes juxtaposed with the image of men being less predisposed to this type of job:

> We are very suitable for the job, more so than men, only there (on a ship) you have to put your foot down; there is no other way; When we do something, we do it. Here it seems to me that we have a different mentality; For them (men), responsibility ends very quickly; We are more diligent. We think about what we do and not just, 'whatever' then it has done.

Roles and areas of responsibility borne by women (including family life) are the results of a multitude of good organisational skills, an innate sense of responsibility and persistence: "*When I am at sea, I am responsible for the ship and its cargo, but I am also responsible for my family.*"

Women who articulate their voices from positions of DMCI perceive themselves as natural-born leaders:

> I must have always been a natural social activist, I held positions in social functions since primary school, I was the chairwoman of students' school council. In high school, the same. (...). When I graduated from school, I already had total ease in managing my (male) colleagues (...). I simply entered the ship with the benefit of my own inventory. As a public figure, I was involved in cultural life on the ship (...); I had everything under control, which also established my position.

Such women are desirable employees. They present themselves as an 'object of professional desire': "*We ended up with a guy who took care of recruitment, and that is how these two captains met, mine and another one. 'You know, Madam, it amazes me. How is it possible for two flagship captains to argue about you?' So I replied, I guess that is good.*"

Women, as objects of 'professional desire', should be deprived of the obvious feminine attributes: "*I had no problems in the male environment, maybe because I am not that pretty, I do not have long legs, and I did not arouse men's emotions right away.*" They should considerably constrain their femininity: "*no cleavage, no short skirt; better to not be pretty.*" At the same time, they should not assume the external attributes of masculinity: "*this measure is important, however, if you go the other way, it will also be wrong; a woman (on board) cannot be overly masculine.*" The task of a woman on board a ship is to also reduce the emotional attributes traditionally attributed to femininity: "*They (seamen) knew that I would tell them off if necessary, but they would also come to cry on my shoulder when needed.*" "*Have you ever cried?*") "*Not in front of someone. By myself, yes, of course; A woman on a ship cannot be a sensitive person who will cry on my shoulder and seek comfort.*"

The desired professionals consciously give up the traditional ways of fulfilling typical domestic roles traditionally assigned to women - it is not about negating them, but it is about choice, nor is it about abandoning traditional roles but rather negotiating and transforming how they are fulfilled: "*What does the sea do to a woman? Well, you work at sea for a decade or so, like me, so you stop being so multifunctional when it comes to household things. (...) Because you have a steward who cleans your cabin, a cook who cooks for you, a steward who serves meals and takes away the dishes.*"

7.4 *Representations of Female Seafaring Careers Within DMCI*

The maritime careers of women are perceived by them as compelling personal sacrifices, but - as mentioned before - they have an instrumental purpose: "*I have this fantastic piece of advice that I think is worth following: if someone wants to sell themselves to work at sea, get the right price. If you have to spend time at sea, it must be for good money.*"

The situation of the women on the ship is initially disfavoured. Then, thanks to the intense efforts and at the same time, the strategy of 'taking advantage of the opportunities' adopted by women, they gain an increasingly higher professional position. By the way, they try to carefully choose the employer and the ship they will embark on, taking into account the social climate on board, the characteristics of the captain, the length of voyages, etc. For this reason, they are able to stop employment and, at some risk, wait for better employment circumstances. They seem entirely conscious of the disfavoured position of females at the beginning of their seafaring careers: "*Women go to see with a negative load. You have to hit zero to be able to move forward.*" For this reason, the stress period of building a professional position is seen here as a period of proving by a woman of her value as an employee in a male-dominated environment, often presenting misogynistic attitudes. This is a key period for women's maritime careers. Then comes the 'harvest' period - involving the use of a position that equates a woman-officer on a ship with the status of men in similar positions:

> It took me a few years and when I was the chief, I did not stress anymore, because when I got to this place, I had already proven to everyone that I know what I am doing. Then I was able to relax and work normally, not as before – by needing to prove something to someone; When you get to become an officer, it will be easier.

Representation of a professional trajectory in DMCI could be described as a 'broken trajectory', because at some point, women should make the decision to leave the sea in order to effectively, and with greater gratification (personal and professional), realised in other domains (top managerial positions ashore and also in family roles). This is combined with expanding the dimension of professionalism:

> I think a person can change what they do and still be a professional. You cannot pin yourself to one thing. You have to be a little more flexible in life. I am not saying that I am going to do this (work on a ship) for the rest of my working life; I cannot imagine having my one-year-old toddler and leaving him for a three-month contract. It is bad enough when the father is not around, but at the beginning of this young man's life, the presence of the mother is a must.

During one of the focus interviews, the decision to leave the sea was described by the women as 'plan B' - a plan that women should have in store from the very beginning of their seafaring careers, just as they should always be ready to take advantage of opportunities unexpectedly arising for professional development and being ready to change their professional position: "*Yes, exactly, you have to be ready for a change.*"

DMCI does not ignore the issue of life-cycles and motherhood. It embraces the belief that decisions regarding parental and professional roles should be carefully considered, in their mutual contexts, in consultation with partners. This can translate into postponing the decision to become a mother: "*I just turned 40 and half a year earlier, before I was 40, I gave birth to my first child.*" Despite the attention paid to the realisation of family careers, women consciously give up fulfilling the domestic roles traditionally assigned to women in a patriarchal culture (i.e. 'running a hotel and restaurant').

7.5 *Patterns of Conduct and Strategies for Action in Their Relation to Professional Identity Construction Within DMCI*

In the area of ship life, the importance of women's resistance to disregarding women's positions and competences is emphasised. In this respect, women must react (not ignore) so as not to be pushed into a position inferior and subject to men: "*Girl! At the very beginning* (*they called me*) *'girl' ... Sometimes you also have to put your foot down.*" With the increase in the formal position of a woman on board a ship (i.e. with her professional promotion), resistance to the discriminatory positioning of a woman on a ship takes a disciplinary form, using the overt and formal domination of women over men - in this sense the dominance relationship changes:

> An Indonesian boatswain had a problem with having a female boss. (...) He ignored everything I said. He got my warning saying that the next (warning) would be from the company and he would be sent home. He got scared. I took away all of his overtime because that is the right of the boss, any boss. When he got zero, just zero, he came to the conclusion that maybe it is not profitable to rebel.

From the perspective of DMCI, the key to raising the social position of a woman on a ship (which is a condition for her further professionalisation and professional promotion) is building authority based on substantive competence. If a woman wants to be an officer, she has to be more competent than her male counterparts and must constantly prove her competence. More so - because in a male-dominated environment, women are always being 'observed':

"You have to be a professional, you have to be good in your profession and do all these things well, it is obligatory, nobody can accuse you of not doing your job; the guys can get away with such things, but if you do it they will point it out and nag you about it; Knowledge, this is it, if you have knowledge, you can say something confidently, with conviction. So 'knowledge is power'" - the literal meaning of this phrase from Bacon gets a literal connotation within DMCI.

Long-term strategies of action and building a professional identity in the DMCI area are based on thoughtful choices, such as:

- Choosing a ship carefully, bearing in mind: earnings, environment (prejudices and exposure to sexual harassment): "I had an offer to go on (certain company) ships, and because there were girls there before, I knew there was always something going on there, although I could earn twice as much, I didn't go there";
- Careful consideration of the seafaring career path, its reconciliation with family life and choosing when to end it;
- Planning for the future related to the land-based sector of the seafaring industry, where it is possible to use the accumulated competence resources.

8 The Discourse of Openness of the Labour Market (DOLM)

DOLM is weak in the statements of the respondents; it is strongly present in numerous documents and online forums concerning the maritime industry, e.g. in: official positions and interpretations of personnel policy, it is marked in the press statements of 'successful women' presented by maritime organisations as role models, its content is expressed in the area of official EU documents, supranational organisations (ILO, ITF), including maritime organisations (IMO, WMU), maritime women's organisations (WOMESA, WISTA, WIMA, Red-MAMLa), and transnational organisations of an educational nature (UNITAR). This discourse mainly regards postulates - encouraging governments, shipowners' organisations and other entities to take steps to increase female employment at sea and reduce the gender gap, as well as encourage women themselves to pursue careers within the sector of the maritime industry.

8.1 *Semiotic Representation of the Domain of Seafaring in DOLM*

Seafaring is depicted as an attractive profession for women, offering financial gratification and allowing them to be economically independent; often - as a justification - in this context, the argument concerning feminisation of poverty on a global scale is raised. In this sense, the (assumed) emancipatory value of increasing female employment in the maritime economy is argued. It is claimed that the openness of seafaring careers for women is high. Seafaring is usually presented as a 'dream job', especially by role-models in this discourse: *"It makes me proud to work in a company that gives targeted support to young women in their careers and enables me to pursue my dream job, looking forward to my new role as captain aboard AIDAsol, and aware of the great responsibility"* (safety4sea related to IMO).

Despite that DOLM draws attention to the fact that there are still 'barriers' in this domain related to the employment of women (the general thesis on seafaring as a male-dominated sector is cited), the current progress is enthusiastically emphasised concerning the lifting of the above-mentioned barriers (IMO 2020) or a thesis about their absence is formulated: *"I have never had any specific challenges because I am a woman; thus, I am embracing it and working to turn it from a negative image into a positive one"* (a female leader in the maritime sector in a promotional video; IMO).

In the DOLM area, the importance of women leaders in the maritime sector is emphasised, including officer positions occupied on board. In this sense, it can be said that in the DOLM seducing strategy, aiming at attracting female workforce, is employed: *"Despite the persistence of gender inequality, female champions, role models and success stories exist in every sector of the maritime and ocean communities"* (WMU 2019).

The multicultural addressees of messages about the openness and attractiveness of the seafaring industry are being convinced that this work domain enables a woman to reconcile personal and professional roles, provided that she 'finds a suitable husband': *"Choose your husband! I would never choose a husband who would not let me have a career and would not do half the work at home"* (WMU role model); *"One does not have to sacrifice a family life in order to move forward with a career in shipping. I brought up two children largely on my own while climbing up the career ladder"* (another WMU role model).

8.2 *Representations of Female Seafarers Within DOLM*

In DOLM, women are represented as a human resource, understood in economic terms (and in this sense, they become objectified): *"Female seafarers are an under-utilized, underdeveloped but valuable resource that could provide part of the solution to the increasing problem of finding sufficient, adequately trained personnel to manage and operate the world's growing and sophisticated merchant fleet."* (Secretary-General of the IMO, 2008). *"Convincing women from a young age to seek a long-term career in the maritime sector will go a long way to solving many challenges in the industry, including the shortage of seafarers."* (WMU, 2019, p. 15)

The principle of the professional presence of women in the maritime sector should be their visibility. As part of the discourse, practices are implemented to increase the visibility of women's representation in the maritime sector: "*IMO has invited women of the maritime sector to share photos of themselves at work, using the hashtag #MaritimeWomenPhotoShare.*" (https://www.imo.org/en/MediaCentre/PressBriefings/pages/43-promoting-diversity.aspx). The collected photos provide an interesting collection of portraits of seafaring females, that 'embody' cultural attributes of visual representations of professionalism. The women's postures are proud and upright here, presenting the attributes of a 'male' position of leadership. At the same time, warm smiles (as female attributes) are reflected on their faces. The expression of the body of the depicted women exudes self-confidence, self-esteem, professionalism and satisfaction. The principle of women's visibility implemented in the public sphere also applies to individual shipowners who employ such strategies in order to be 'politically correct' and build a positive image in line with the expectations of maritime organisations: "*The company wanted me as a captain, because they would have their first female captain on one of their gas tankers to prove themselves and show off.*"(An interview)

Representations of female seafaring careers within DOLM are not as clearly outlined as in the other types of discourse. The only thing emphasised is its openness to women from different cultures. DOLM assumes that the conditions for pursuing a professional career by women and men are equal, and effort, as well as competence, are presented as guarantees of its effectiveness. In a sense, we are dealing here with reference to the (neo-) liberal myth of equal opportunities for all.

8.3 *Patterns of Conduct and Strategies for Action in Relation to Professional Identity Construction Within DOLM*

DOLM both postulates and illustrates the (positive) experiences of women in the shipping industry. The formulated postulates regarding the methods of action, behaviour or building the aspirations of women at sea include:

- The postulate of ignoring maltreatment of women in a male-dominated work environment, which resembles the topos of "victim blaming" widespread within mysoginic discourses: "You cannot allow yourself to be unsettled by every outlandish remark made. It is better to ignore them and move on" (WMU 2019: 15);
- The postulate of 'hard physical work: Work hard; (WMU 2019: 17);
- The postulate of integration of women's communities related to the maritime industry and implementation of the idea of mentoring among novices;

– The postulate of continuous improvement of professional qualifications;
– The latter is also seen as a path to professionalisation and professional identity by seafaring women.

9 Discussion and Concluding Remarks

The presented types of discourse as contexts for constructing the professional identity of seafaring women certainly do not provide a full picture of the conditions in which women performing or aspiring to maritime professions become professionals. We also notice the absence of a certain - seemingly - 'necessary discourse' illustrating the fluidity and continuity of the professionalisation by women which would be possible under the conditions of their full commitment as well as combining the challenges of acquiring professional identity with the challenges of personal self-realisation. At the same time, the discourse would represent a supporting role of the work environment as providing cognitive and ethical challenges and involving a cooperative climate of workplace learning, in which gender-related issues do not matter. This - idealistic - type of discourse comes to mind when we compare the results of the conducted critical discourse analyses with the desired visions of the workplace learning environment present in the field of adult learning theories. However, the image of the research field constructed from the perspective of qualitative research is never complete – perhaps, we have not found articulations that would give hope for the convergence of theory and practice. And yet, from the perspective of the epistemological layer accompanying the critical analyses of discourse, it is worth noting that this kind of convergence would seem to us – the researchers - a trap for the imprisonment of the subject, along with the potential of their agency, in a perfectly polished reality. The autonomy of the subject, her agency and critical reflection is better seen from the perspective of post-structural positions (Foucault, Deleuze, Laclau, etc.) where, instead of discourse hegemony, inter-discoursive contradictions and tensions appear; where subjects' autonomy develops in areas of irregularities, discontinuities and gaps; where, instead of the universalism of one discourse, there appear competing multiplicities. It seems tempting to apply the above remarks to the problem of young women entering professional roles in the maritime field. Their familiarisation with the diversity of women's experiences and, at the same time, with the diversity of discursive propositions regarding the construction of the identity of women at sea could provide 'fuel for thought' for the emerging reflection on one's own position in the discourse as well as for resistance against forced conventions and self-awareness in the field of shaping professional identity.

References

Aggrey, H. A. (2000). *Women in the Maritime Industry: A review of female participation, and their role in Maritime Education and Training* (MET) *in the 21st Century*. World Maritime University Dissertations 383. Retrieved from: http://commons.wmu.se/all_dissertations/383.

Belcher, P., Sampson H., Thomas M., Veiga J., & Zhao M. (2003). *Women Seafarers: global employment policies and practices*. Geneva: International Labor Office.

Berggreen, B. (1979). Skibet som hjem. *NordNytt* 5, pp. 40–49.

Berggreen, B. (1985). *Sjökvinner, om a uppdage et forskningsfelt' Skärgård* 2, 4–12.

Billett, S., Somerville M. (2004). Transformations at work: Identity and learning. *Studies in Continuing Education* 26(2), 309–326.

Billett, S. (2008). Subjectivity, Learning and Work: Sources and Legacies. *Vocations and Learning* 1, 149–171.

Billett, S., Fenwick, T., Somerville (eds.). (2006). *Work, subjectivity and learning*. Dordrecht, The Netherlands: Springer.

Billett, S., Pavolva, M. (2005). Learning through working life: self and individuals' agentic action. *International Journal of Lifelong Education*, 24(3), 195–211.

BIMCO/ISF. (2015). *Manpower Report. The global supply and demand for seafarers in 2015*, Retrieved from: http://www.ics-shipping.org/docs/default-source/resources/safety-security-and-operations/manpower-report-2015-executive-summary.pdf?sfvrsn=16.

Brit, B. (1979). Skibet som hjem' *NordNytt* 5, 40–49.

Burton, V. (1999). Whoring, Drinking Sailors, Reflections on Masculinity from the Labour History of Nineteenth-century British Shipping'. In M. Walsh (ed.). *Working Out Gender, Perspectives from Labour History*. (pp. 84–101). Ashgate: Aldershot

Butler, J. (1990). *Gender Trouble*. New York: Routledge.

Chia-Ling W., Shiou-Yu Ch., Kung-Don Y., Yi-Wei H. (2017). Career development for women in maritime industry: organisation and socialisation perspectives. *Maritime Policy & Management*, 44(7), 882–898.

Cordingly, D. (2007). *Seafaring Women: Adventures of Pirate Queens, Female Stowaways, and Sailors' Wives*. New York: Random House.

Creighton, M.S., Norling, L. (eds.). (1996). *Iron Men, Wooden Women: Gender and Seafaring in the Atlantic World, 1700–1920*. Baltimore: Johns Hopkins.

Dall'Alba, G. (2004). Understanding professional practice: Investigations before and after an educational programme. *Studies in Higher Education*, 29(6), 679–692.

Davies, B. (2003). Death to critique and dissent? The politics and practices of new managerialism and of "evidence-based practice". *Gender and Education*, 15, 91–103.

Day, C. (1993). Reflection: A necessary but not sufficient condition for professional development. *British Educational Research Journal*, 19(1), 83–92.

Davies, B., Harre, R. (1990). Positioning: The discursive production of selves. *Journal for the Theory of Social Behaviour*, 20(1), 43–63.

Djonov, E., & Zhao, S. (2014). From multimodal to critical multimodal studies through popular discourse. In E. Djonov, & S. Zhao (Eds.). *Critical Multimodal Studies of Popular Discourse* (pp. 1–14). London: Routledge

Eteläpelto A., Saarinen J. (2007). Developing Subjective Identities Through Collective Participation. In: Billett S., Fenwick T., Somerville M. (eds). *Work, Subjectivity and Learning. Technical and Vocational Education and Training: Issues, Concerns and Prospects, vol 6.* (pp. 157–197). Dordrecht: Springer

Fairclough, N. (2001). *Language and Power*. Malaysia: Longman.

Fairclough, N. (1995). *Critical Discourse Analysis: The Critical Study of Language*. Malaysia: Longman.

Foucault, M., Sheridan, A., Foucault, M. (1972). *The archaeology of knowledge*. New York: Pantheon Books.

Foucault, M. (1977). *Discipline and Punish: the Birth of the Prison*. New York : Pantheon Books.

Foucault, M., Martin, L. H., Gutman, H., Hutton, P. H. (1988). T*echnologies of the self: A seminar with Michel Foucault*. Amherst: University of Massachusetts Press.

Foucault, M. (1982). *The Subject and Power*. Chicago: University of Chicago Press.

Greenhill, B., Aiffard, A. (1971). *Women under Sail. Letters and journal selling or working in sailing vessels between 1829–1949*. Newton Abbot: David & Charles.

Greenlaw, J. (2002). *The History of the Radio Officer in the British Merchant Navy and on Deep-Sea Trawlers*. UK: Dinefwr Publishers Ltd

Guo, J. L., Liang, G. S. (2012). Sailing into rough seas: Taiwan's women seafarers' career development struggle. *Women's Studies International Forum*, 35(4), 194–202.

Henning, H. (1981). *Sömanden og Kvinden. Ett kapitel af sömandslivet i sejlskibstide. Söhistoriske skrifter XII*. Danmark: Høst og Søn. Retrieved from https://tidsskrift.dk/historiejyskesamling/.

International Chamber of Shipping (2020). *Diversity Tracker*. Marisec Publications. London.

ILO, International Labour Organization (2019). *Recruitment and retention of seafarers and the promotion of opportunities for women seafarers*. Report for discussion at the Sectoral Meeting on the Recruitment and Retention of Seafarers and the Promotion of Opportunities for Women Seafarers (Geneva, 25 February–1 March 2019). Geneva: International Labor Office.

IMO, International Maritime Organization. (2012). Integration of women in the Maritime sector. Report on 2011.

IMO, International Maritime Organization (2018). *Women in Maritime*. Retrieved from: http://www.imo.org/en/MediaCentre/HotTopics/women/Pages/default.aspx.

IMO, International Maritime Organization (2019). *Women in Maritime - IMO's gender programme*. Retrieved from: http://www.imo.org/en/OurWork/TechnicalCooperation/Pages/WomenInMaritime.aspx.

IMO, International Maritime Organization (2020). *Resolution A.1147(31) Preserving The Legacy of The World Maritime Theme for 2019 and Achieving a Barrier-Free Working Environment for Women In the Maritime Sector*. Retrieved from: http://www.imo.org/en.

ITF (2017). *Women Seafarers*, http://www.itfseafarers.org/ITI-women-seafarers.cfm.

Jarvis, P. (2004). *Adult education and lifelong learning: Theory and practice*. London: Routledge Falmer.

Kitada, M., Williams, E., & Froholdt, L. (Eds.). (2015). *Maritime Women: Global Leadership*. Berlin Heidelberg: Springer. https://doi.org/10.1007/978-3-662-45385-8

Klausmann, U., Meinzerin M, Kuhn G.; Austin T., Levis N. (1997). *Women Pirates and the Politics of the Jolly Roger*. Montréal, London and New York: Black Rose.

Królikowska, I., Męczkowska-Christiansen, A. (2018). Edukacyjne doświadczenia kobiet-marynarzy w kontekście praktyk morskich. *Colloquium* 4, 55–72.

Lemke, J. L. (2003). Texts and Discourses in the Technologies of Social Organization. In G. Weiss & R. Wodak (Eds.), *Critical Discourse Analysis* (pp. 130–149). Palgrave Macmillan UK. https://doi.org/10.1057/9780230288423_7

Machin D., Mayr A. (2012). *How to do Critical Discourse Analysis: A Multimodal Introduction*. Los Angeles-London-New Delhi-Singapore-Washington DC: Sage.

Mäenpää, S. (2004). Comfort and guidance for female passengers: The origins of women's employment on British Passenger Liners 1850–1914. *Journal for Maritime Research* 6(1), 145–164.

Męczkowska-Christiansen A., Królikowska I. (2019). Perspectives on Women at Sea in the Light of Female Seafarers' Experience. Challenges for Maritime Education. *Colloqium* 4, 113–128.

Norling, L. (2000). *Captain Ahab had a wife. New England women and whalefishery, 1720–1870*. Chapel Hill: University of North Carolina Press.

Pettersson L, Persson A, Berggren A., W. (2008). Changing Gender Relations: Women Officers' Experiences in the Swedish Armed Forces. *Economic and Industrial Democracy*, 29(2), 192–216.

Reisigl, M., Wodak, R. (2009). The discourse-historical approach. In R. Wodak, M. Meyer (eds.), *Methods of critical discourse analysis*. London: Sage.

Said, E. (1979). *Orientalism*. New York: Vintage Books.

Schloesser, P. E. (2002). *The Fair Sex: White Women and Racial Patriarchy in the Early American Republic*. New York: NYU Press.

Sharpe, C. (n.d.) *Merchant Marine Woman*. Retrieved from: https://navalandmilitarymuseum.org/archives/articles/unsung-women/merchant-marine-women.

Slay, H.S., Smith D.A. (2011). Professional identity construction: Using narrative to understand the negotiation of professional and stigmatized cultural identities. *Human Relations* 64(1), 85–107.

Slope, N. (2011). *Women in Nelson's Navy*. Retrieved from: http://www.bbc.co.uk/history/british/empire_seapower.

Sondergaard, D.M. (2002). Poststructural approaches to empirical analysis. *International Journal of Qualitative Studies in Education*, 15(2), 187–204.

Splash247.com, https://splash247.com/ics-sets-targets-to-get-more-women-working-at-sea.

Stanley, J. (ed), (1995). *Bold in Her Breeches: Women Pirates across the Ages*. San Francisco: Harper.

Stark S. J. (1996) *Female Tars: Women Aboard Ship in the Age of Sail*. Annapolis MD: Naval Institute Press. (London 1998).

Stamarski C.S., Son Hing L. S (2016). Gender inequalities in the workplace: the effects of organizational structures, processes, practices, and decision makers' sexism. In: F. Autin, F. Butera (eds.), *Institutional Determinants of Social Inequality*. Lausanne: Frontiers Media SA.

Taylor, S. (2015). Identity Construction. In: K. Tracy, C. Ilie, T. Sandel (eds.), *The International encyclopedia of language and social interaction*. Vol. 2, (pp. 715–768). West Sussex: Wiley-Blackwell, Wiley.

Turley. H. (1999). *Rum, Sodomy, and the Lash: Piracy, Sexuality, and Masculine Identity*. New York and London: New York University Press.

UNCTAD (United Nation Conference on Trade and Development) (2018), *Review of Maritime Transport 2018*, UN, New York, https://doi.org/10.18356/cd4440fc-en.

UNCTAD (United Nation Conference on Trade and Development) (2019), *Review of Maritime Transport 2019*, UN, New York, https://doi.org/10.18356/17932789-en.

Van Dijk, T. A. (2009). Critical discourse studies: A sociocognitive approach. *Methods of Critical Discourse Analysis* 2(1), 62–86.

Van Leeuwen T., Wodak R. (1999). Legitimizing Immigration Control: A Discourse-Historical Analysis. *Discourse Studies*, 1(1), 83–118.

Walker, T. (2015). *Why we need more women in maritime industries*. World Economic Forum, 04, Retrieved from: https://www.weforum.org/agenda/2015/09/why-we-need-more-women-in-maritime-industries.

Webster-Wright, A. (2009). Reframing professional development through understanding authentic professional learning. *Review of Educational Research*, 79(2), 702–739.

World Maritime University (2019). *Third WMU International Women's Conference: 'Empowering Women in the Maritime Community'*. Retrieved from: https://commons.wmu.se/lib_reports/62.

WEF, World Economic Forum. (2015) *The Global Gender Gap Report 2015*. Geneva: World Economic Forum.

Wodak, R. (2015). Critical Discourse Analysis. Discourse-Historical Approach. In: K. Tracy, T. Sandel, C. Ilie (eds.), *The International Encyclopedia of Language and Social Interaction*. West Sussex: Wiley-Blackwell, Wiley.

Wodak, R., Krzyzanowski, M. (2008). *Qualitative Discourse Analysis in the Social Sciences*. Basingstoke: Palgrave Macmillan.

Žižek, S. (2008). *Violence: six sideways reflections*. New York: Picador

CHAPTER 5

Strategies and Struggle of Women Fishers for the Rescue and Conservation of a Coastal Lagoon System: "Mujeres Pescadoras del Manglar"

Nuria Jimenez Garcia

1 Introduction

This chapter is based on my postdoctoral research (2018–20) that was carried out at the Rural Development Postgraduate Program of the Autonomous Metropolitan University, Xochimilco Unit, Mexico City. The purpose of this research was to analyse the transformations taking place in communities of the Costa Chica of Oaxaca, which are predominantly comprised of "Afro-descendants". The objective of this research was to identify changes in familial-, and household-based formations within these communities and to explore the strategies adopted by women, particularly single women, who head household units for mutual aid (through the construction of support networks) and cooperation (Jiménez, 2015: p. 190). Many of the women I worked with have been involved in fishing since their childhood, both in pre-harvest and post-harvest activities, as well as direct participation in fishing extraction.

Some fisherwomen from Chacahua and Zapotalito told me that they had always fished but that their work had never been considered or valued.

> Comrade Minerva would go look for kids or teenagers, and she would go fishing with them; she would grab the motor. Yes! Aide, too, would go from the crab to Chacahua, alone, her sister [...] I mean, they had all worked there in the Laguna, and they know how to do things: they know to row; they know how to fish; they know what kind of net it is [...] And well, me too! But I started to fish with my son, with my children [...] In the beginning, well, it was all like that, no[...] (Interview with Cristina Arellanes, president of Mujeres pescadoras del Manglar, author's translation.).

These women often have to alternate between various economic activities and to diversify their areas of work since, in recent years, the situation of coastal spaces has shifted on multiple levels (social, economic, and family). These transformations have been the result of various factors, including tourist

 | DOI:10.1163/9789004518841_007

development, the dispossession of many of the natural resources by the state and both national and international companies, and the contamination of lagoon waters. There have also been changes and consequences that have occurred through natural processes within coastal lagoon systems and mangroves (hurricanes, earthquakes, droughts. As a result, today, it is very difficult for fishers to rely solely on fishing activities to meet their subsidence needs and those of their families. Given these facts and within this context, the *Mujeres pescadoras del Mangla*r cooperative was born. The cooperative was not formed with the explicit objective of environmental struggle and conservation but, rather, out of an economic need to formalise its productive fishing activity. Nevertheless, it has also adopted and developed practices with a sustainable approach of protection and defence of the environmental resources of its community.

Mujeres pescadoras del Manglar was founded in 2016, in the Zapotal or Zapotalito, Tututepec Melchor Ocampos community, located in the Lagunas de Chacahua National Park. It is made up of women who are engaged in fishing, conservation, and the sale of fish. These women are currently carrying out a community monitoring, conservation and management project for the *tichinda* mollusk (Mytella charruana), or mangrove mussel, which lives in the La Pastoría-Chacahua[1] lagoon system, in addition to developing different care environmental protection and maintenance activities for the Pastoría Lagoon, such as the opening of the El Palmarito canal to restore the flow of water from this canal to the lagoon and its drainage.[2] In the last year, the Cooperative has proposed several ecotourism projects to publicise its conservation practices for the *tichinda*, the lagoon ecosystem and is offering motorised boat rides to watch the luminescence. But let us return to the previous context, which led to the decision to form this cooperative.

In this community on the small coast of Oaxaca, women have always been involved in the practice of fishing. If not in extraction, they worked in preparation and sales activities. Some of the members of the *Mujeres pescadoras del Manglar*, who used to catch a lot to fish before,[3] could make from one thousand to two thousand pesos a day. Thanks to the fishing money, many arrangements were made in the community, and many families improving their economic situation.

1 Lagunas de Chacahua National Park

2 The muzzle that allows the entry of seawater into the lagoon has been closed for ten years

3 On September 7, 2017 there was an earthquake that caused the massive death of fish

> Yes, I liked it. I learned to fish. Before, there was a lot of fish. Yes, there was a lot of fish and a lot of shrimp, we would go out early. We would head out by 12, and then we would return at 1. A few hours [later] we would return, because there was a lot of fish, until 5 or 6 in the afternoon. Someone would throw the trammel and so many fish. Someone goes out, and there is already someone to buy it. Now, nobody goes out. There is a woman there whom I give it to. Before, there was also a woman there.
>
> There are many women who run the show, and I speak with them. Many are fishermen's wives, but they no longer fish; they go with them [their husbands] to sell. The one I am selling to sells in Jamiltepec; she has a store or wholesale delivery: she sells it to them, and they sell it [to customers]. Before, it was bass, snapper, mullet, common snook, depending on the size of the net. If you throw out a small net, you get the best quality. There has always been shrimp; before, when the river mouth was open, there was a lot of shrimp. I used to go out with my husband at night. You have to go deep and then pull and pull it out. When the shrimp are coming out – that's when you grab them. (Interview with Olmides López, cooperative member of *Mujeres pescadoras del Manglar*, author's translation.)

The Pastoría Lagoon stands out for having economic importance since it employs artisanal practices in the fishing for crustaceans (shrimp and crab), fish (smooth, snapper, red snapper, sea bass, ojarras) and the bivalve mollusc, known locally as tichinda. The balance of the lagoon was maintained thanks to the balance between fresh and saltwater. The sea and lagoon used to come into contact through a natural channel called a river mouth, located in the community of Cerro Hermoso, neighbouring Zapotalito. This channel opened and closed cyclically: in the rainy season, it opened; in the dry season, it closed. The federal government decided to intervene in this natural process to keep the canal open all year round.[4] Despite the objections of fishers that this would not work, a first attempt was made in the 1970s, followed by several more since then. These interventions resulted in an accumulation of sand around the river mouth, which caused the canal to remain closed and greatly reduced fishing, depriving the people of Zapotal of their main subsistence resource. The situation has been exacerbated by government budget cuts to finish the works, the rise in fuel prices, and increased corruption. As if this was not enough,

4 In 1999 the federal government built a rock jetty for the opening of the mouth, and it was proposed to do dredging works

the earthquake of September 7, 2017, caused massive destruction of fish in the lagoon.

In response to these challenges, Oaxaca's first and only fisherwomen cooperative was formed in the community of Zapotalito in 2016. The majority of the population is afro-indigenous and first arrived in the region in the 1970s and 1980s from other areas of Oaxaca and Guerrero, seeking to survive through subsidence fishing. One of the main objectives of the collective was that the government would open the channel's mouth to enable continued fishing activities as they had taken place before.

2 Analytical Perspective/Theoretical Framework

This work aims to contribute, on the one hand, to the field of anthropology of fishing or maritime anthropology. On the other hand, it also contributes to gender studies on women, fishing and natural resources. It starts with political ecology from a gender perspective to analyse the relationship between society and nature in the studied community.

Political ecology also helps us understand the responses of women and forms of resistance that they have generated in the face of the effects of climate change on coastal and socioeconomics derived from tourism projects, among others. According to Stott and Sullivan (2000), political ecology deals with tracing the genealogy of "the environmental", identifying the power relations that shape the narratives related to social and economic development. Similarly, for Bedoya and Martínez (2000), political ecology is a discipline focused on the analysis of the political, economic and social causes for the destruction of ecosystems. For Piers Blaikie (1996), political ecology is a hybrid derived from the natural sciences and the social sciences, which analyses the mutual production and reproduction of society and the environment. What characterises political ecology as a theoretical orientation is precisely the ability to understand, on a scientific basis, the causes and consequences of environmental degradation, including the role of the state in the access to critical resources, power relations, and the use, access, and control of natural resources by transnational individuals, organisations, and companies (Fraga, 1999).

The present study is an attempt to achieve an approach to a topic that offers a huge vein of research since fishing as an economic activity is one of the pillars that has supported the various human groups. Besides, it leads us to address various related discussions with the economic and social reproduction of minority groups excluded from the messianic horizon presented by modernisation and neoliberal policies.

The world is experiencing an environmental crisis caused by a capitalist logic that supports an uncontrollable growth in the consumption of resources, energy, and advance on territories, cultures and ecosystems. Amid this crisis, we find ourselves in a critical situation of small-scale and artisanal fishing. Women have been the most affected by this crisis mainly because they have a greater stake in the processes of social reproduction. In this situation, the women of these cooperatives develop different processes of subjectification and environmental struggles for the access and use of natural resources. Therefore, in this work, I analyse the struggles of women in defence of resources and life. We will conduct this analysis from a feminist-economy perspective, which defines economy and work as the set of processes that allows one to generate the necessary resources to live. Moreover, feminist economy shifts the analytical axis to centre the sustainability of life, understanding that market processes must be questioned in the light of their contribution to such sustainability (Perez Orozco, 2011). Continuing with the framework of feminist economy, we seek to understand the role that relations of inequality between women and men play in the economy since no economic policy or process is considered to be neutral in terms of gender (Agarwal, 1995; Arizpe, 1993). Therefore, in summary, this perspective proposes an economy that generates conditions for a life worth living in terms of equity and universality. It targets the multidimensional and accumulated crisis that makes the unsustainability of the economic system visible in ecological, social and reproductive terms. Thus, we start from the proposal to consider these women's activities and practices of environmental protection and conservation as socio-environmental struggles forming part of a process of resistance and appropriation of social wealth that puts the production of the common for the reproduction of human and non-human life (Navarro Trujillo et al., 2009; Salazar et al., 2012). The gender approach (central axis in this research) in studies on environment and development suggests analysing the rights and obligations that women have towards resources, as well as the institutions and property relations that rule the access to them in specific socio-environmental contexts.

3 Crisis and Transformations in Fishing Activity. Artisanal Fishing as an Alternative

Today, fishing has a preeminent place as a pillar of food security in contemporary society. It is also an activity offering employment to millions of people and represents the economic base of many developing nations and societies. In fact, it has been estimated that, in 2003, the world production of fish through marine capture and aquaculture was approximately 133 million tons, of which around 101 million were allocated for human consumption (FAO, 2004). Fish provides at least 20% of the animal proteins consumed by the world population. Thus, it provides food to more than 2.6 billion people (FAO, 2004).

Fishing also stands out as an important source of employment. It is estimated that, currently, about 38 million people earn an income from direct employment in fishing and aquaculture (FAO, 2004), and that fishing indirectly generates various economic activities that sustain around 200 million people worldwide (FAO, 2002).

Unfortunately, despite all of these benefits, fishing is in a rather critical situation worldwide. This is partly due to the increase in industrial fishing, which has grown uncontrollably, both in terms of capital investment and in human resources. In other words, a condition of overcapitalisation persists (too many boats in relation to the volume of exploitable resources) which is exacerbated by the use of technology, as well as production practices that have little respect for the environment. Another important part is the negative effects of marine pollution from land-based sources, as well as the appropriation of productive spaces. The expansion of cities, industrial areas, agricultural crops, thermoelectric plants, refineries, port traffic, tourism, among other elements, are sources that, to some extent, produce toxic substances that end up in the seas and affect the reproductive cycles of the species. Even more, those industrial activities often compete for the same space, displacing other productive sectors (Marín, 2007).

In the case of Mexico, despite official attempts by the state to regulate fishing activity and achieve a balanced administration, the national fishery faces serious difficulties. The fishing struggle increases every day. The contamination of rivers, lakes and marine waters is an unstoppable process, and the magnitude of the challenges state institutions must solve exceeds their operational capacity. Finally, practices in fishing areas are generally regulated within a climate of arbitrariness and impunity that encourages the exculpation of offenders and their accomplices.

This situation affects the living conditions of Mexican fishers, who observe how their environment and their lives undergo a general process of deterioration. They find themselves in an increasingly devastated environment and under a tenacious and growing competition for fishery resources. They are immersed in an environment where illegality prevails, amid enormous disadvantages to operating efficiently in markets, and are subject to disparagement within the supreme policies of the national economy (Marín, 2007). Currently, fishermen and fisherwomen in Mexico, as in most parts of the world, survive under marginal circumstances. They typically live in towns that lack basic services; subsist on a very low income; suffer from the indolence of political circles, and experience a degraded social status. Contemporary industrial, agricultural and tourist-commercial development anchored in the ownership of territories located on the coasts ends up having disastrous consequences on the exercise of artisanal fishing. The primary reason is the imbalance they generate in the use and control of the territory in the coastal river mouth and also in the seashore and the open sea.

New proposals have recently been discussed, and alternative notions for the proper management of fisheries have been implemented. In particular, ideas about sustainable development have had a great influence, as well as the revaluation of small-scale fishing systems, community participation models and the recognition of the cultural dimension, in order to understand forms of local administration. These influences are directly related to the potential of artisanal fishing. This, of course, does not escape the problems of overfishing but allows us to think about possible forms of control. Faced with the calamities associated with industrial fishing, which has always shown signs of a predatory logic, artisanal fishing emerges as an alternative with certain benefits and advantages. It is closely related to the sociocultural reproduction of small localities that, under certain conditions, can preserve the environment and uphold sustainable economic systems. The response of artisanal fishermen and fisherwomen to the scarcity of resources and the price of their catches - which they do not control - consists, now, in seeking less aggressive forms of managing their resource which, therefore, would be more beneficial for the subsistence of their trade (Alcalá, 2011)

4 Access to Environmental and Productive Resources from a Gender Perspective

Traditional knowledge related to strategies of social reproduction has been maintained and reproduced for generations. There is a gender divide in terms of knowledge and practices of environmental resource management in rural communities (both those dedicated to agriculture and fishing). The distribution of work and its recognition are influenced by gender and generational relations like the access to means of production, the number of members, the use of time and the distribution of workloads. In all these relations, women have a subordinate position, are not considered subjects with the right to access land or with fishing rights. Their contributions are not highly valued, and they also face a greater workload.

In rural communities, men and women develop reproduction strategies in which gender differences in the distribution of work, in the access and management of resources, and in decision-making are manifestations of inequity in social relations between genders (Parra-Sosa et al., 2007). Considering gender as a category of analysis in the study of society-environment relations is a recent approach, thereby overcoming the unitary vision of interests, knowledge and distribution of resources in domestic groups (Leach et al., 1995), which contributes to improving the approach to understanding rural realities.

Bina Agarwal points out that power relations between men and women are not easy to analyse in all their complexity. They include both material and ideological aspects, which are manifested not only in the division of labour and resources but also in ideas and representations, for example, the understanding that men and women may possess different abilities, attitudes, desires, behavioural patterns and personalities. This author considers that the woman-nature relationship is built through a series of mediations derived from the strategies used by women to fulfil their responsibilities in their families and communities, which imply differentiated gender relations between men and women in the processes of social production and reproduction (Agarwal, 1997).

Understanding the social and cultural processes that enable or deny differential access by gender to natural resources is highly relevant (Velázquez, 1996). It is necessary to recognise the existence of different ways of accessing natural resources for men and women, associated with cultural rights, constructions, assignments and differential learning by gender, as shown by various studies (Vázquez et al., 2004; Soares, 2007). There is also diversity in interests, perceptions, and control over resources. Access to natural resources by women continues to be reduced or conditioned by their gender.

5 Visibility and Importance of Women's Work in Fishing Activities and in the Conservation of Natural Resources

In the case of fishing, there is a marked sexual division of labour worldwide where women traditionally participate in the tasks that take place ashore and require specialised skills and time, such as making and repairing nets, pre-processing of marine resources after the harvest and their commercialisation. However, women are seldom present in the direct capture of fishery resources. This differential access to resources has been and is one of the main causes of inequality between men and women as users of fishery resources. The right that is granted, how it is granted and who the recipients are in particular areas has generated a critical situation between users and the state and between men and women involved in fishing activities.

Currently, in Mexico, women represent approximately between 38 and 40% of the labour force and 10% of workers in the fishing sector. However, among the women who work in the fishing sector, 70% lack a fixed income and they are rarely recognised as legitimate businesswomen, experts and licensees. Cooperatives and businesswomen agree that official permits and supports are obstructed for gender reasons.[5]

Women participate at all levels of marine and inland fisheries production, as well as in aquaculture. In the 17 coastal states of Mexico, 14,311 women work in the fishing sector, compared to 158,227 men. Out of those women, 70% do not receive a fixed income, according to an analysis of dataMares[6] and Community and Biodiversity (Cobi), based on the figures of the last economic census of the National Institute of Statistics and Geography (Inegi). This number is so low because, in Mexico, there are limited efforts to collect data about women's participation in the processes before and after extraction. When this work is recognised, it is primarily discussed in terms of low-skilled labour, overlooking women's roles in decision-making, expertise, and managerial labour. This is reflected in the lines of action and government programs of the 21st century, in which the participation of women in the rural fishing sector is recognised only as workers in the processes before and after the capture, but not in the capture activities. When observing the role women play in social and environmental dynamics, several authors (Kleiber, 2014; Uc-Espadas et al., 2017; Velazquez et al., 1996) point out the tendency of women to make decisions that favour conservation while men show a more extractive-productive and immediate-benefit approach. Failure to consider women in fisheries statistics and decision-making implies an important bias towards aspects solely related to the extraction of the fishery resource, underestimating the socioeconomic impact of fisheries. It ignores the jobs and the value generated along the production chain, not to mention social justice aspects by leaving out one in two workers who contribute to the fishery (Lopez-Ercilla et al., 2019).

In Mexico, women play an important role in coastal fishing, which represents one of the main productive activities from which coastal families subsist. Some women fish with their parents, children, husbands, and even alone. In this way, the profits and the total catch remain in their homes. Faced with the need to

5 Enrique Alvarado, Alejandro Melgoza y Andrés M. Estrada, "Viento a favor, mujeres con éxito en la pesca", 17/10/2018, El Universal. URL: https://www.eluniversal.com.mx/nacion/sociedad/viento-favor-mujeres-con-exito-en-la-pesca

6 http://datamares.ucsd.edu/. Facilitate access to scientific knowledge and data to promote transparency, education, and a deeper understanding of Mexico's ecosystems and their biodiversity to bridge the gap between science and the design process of conservation and resource management programs.

diversify their economic activities, women have begun to organise themselves in fishing cooperatives in order to raise their profile at the government level and within fishing communities, such as in the states of Veracruz, Baja California, Sinaloa, Oaxaca, Chiapas, etc. The formation of women's cooperatives has, on many occasions, resulted in confrontations with the men within the families and the communities where they live – husbands, fathers, and neighbours. The resistance of men to women's cooperatives could be in response to what they perceive as a transgression of tradition, of the established order, and an invasion of a productive space historically and socially considered masculine. To this rejection, we must add the physical work of fishing and the situation of vulnerability they experience as women. In general, these problems are particularly acute when access to natural resources depends on technological means and community permission. In many cases, those factors lead to establishing a working or productive subordination dependent on cooperatives or people (men) with whom they have conflicts that segregate them (Munguía et al., 2013).

6 Zapotalito: Between the Lagoon, the Mangrove Swamp, and the Sea

Zapotalito is located within the Chacahua Lagoons National Park. The National Park is on the Costa Chica, a name for the territory that extends from Acapulco in the State of Guerrero to Puerto Ángel in the State of Oaxaca. The park's area of influence forms a micro-region within the municipality of Tututepec, with particular development dynamics. These dynamics directly influence the park in demographic (population concentration and accelerated population), productive (orientation of the pattern of commercial crops, extensive livestock, and fishing), agrarian (focus of conflicts between communal, ejidal and private property), ethnic (construction of identities between indigenous, afromestizos, and mestizos), and socioeconomic terms (strong polarisation between rural and urban areas) (Alfaro and Escalona, 2000, p. 92). The park comprises two lagoons: the Chacahua lagoon and the La Pastoría lagoon. Both communicate with each other through a narrow channel, El Corral, and with the ocean through the Chacahua river mouth and the La Pastoría river mouth. There are six fishing locations in the park: Chacahua La Grúa, Chacahua Bahía, El Azufre, Cerro Hermoso and El Zapotalito. The *Mujeres pescadoras del Manglar* is located in the latter.

The national park was declared a protected area in 1937 and is the first Mexican national park of tropical ecosystems. The park's six locations belong to the Municipality of Villa Melchor Ocampo de Tututepec, Juquila District,

FIGURE 5.1 Fisherwoman after fishing
SOURCE: NURIA JIMÉNEZ GARCÍA

in the Costa Chica region of Oaxaca. It borders to the South on the Pacific Ocean, to the West on the Green River, and to the North and East on the foothills of the Sierra Madre del Sur (Huerta-García and Propin-Frejomil, 2000, p. 6). El Zapotalito is located in La Pastoría Lagoon. This community is the closest to Federal Highway No. 200 and the disembarking area when accessing the Protected Natural Area by water. Zapotalito also houses most of the authorised tourist services cooperatives (INEGI, 2010; CONANP, 2014).

The main activities of El Zapotalito, along with the other towns in the park, are fishing and seasonal tourism. In addition, agriculture and cattle ranching are practised. The product is fished in the lagoon (see Figure 5.1), in the ocean or the river (Río Verde, mainly the inhabitants of Chacahua La Grúa fish there). Despite its wealth and natural beauty, this territory continues to be highly marginalised for various reasons rooted in problems of political, social and environmental origin, as pointed out at the beginning of the text. Reviewing the history of the park, I am going to explain the problems that affect the lives of the residents of the park and, in particular, of El Zapotalito.

Between the twenties and thirties of the last century, the area in which the park is located today began to populate with the arrival of people from Tututepec. However, it was not until the mid-sixties, when the federal highway was built in 1965, that immigration peaked to this area. As Alfaro and Escalona (2002) present, one of the most serious and complex problems in the park is its rapid population growth during the last three decades. The authors continue to delve into the antecedents of the colonisation process that affected the area, from the 1920s to the early 1960s, as well as agricultural development policies that fostered the demand for the best land and the supply of work around a purely commercial production. Starting in the 1980s, the proximity of the park to the most important tourist and commercial development poles of the coast indirectly influenced its settlement (Alfaro and Escalona, 2002, p. 87). In fact, thanks to the highway, people came from other locations in the state of Oaxaca, as well as from other states such as Guerrero, Veracruz, Chiapas, Morelos, Puebla, and Michoacán (Rosas Narvaez, 2017, p. 21).

The population of Zapotalito is mainly of afro-descendant and indigenous origin. The afro-descendant population came from other coastal municipalities of the Costa Chica, unlike the indigenous population that came from the most mountainous part of it (Escalona, Alvarado and Saldívar, 2018, p. 1). In this same period, the Chacalapa river[7] did not provide enough water to open the two river mouths of Cerro Hermoso and Chacahua. Only the latter opened while the former continued to gain altitude until its opening became more difficult (Rosas Narvaez, 2017, p. 21). As this author points out, in the 1970s and 1980s, due to the abundance of fish, the strong immigration to the region, and the deregulation of fishing, the lagoons became heavily exploited, as fishing became a consolidated commercial activity. In the same time period, cotton, peanuts, papaya,[8] coconut, and lemon agriculture flourished, products that are still produced and processed into derivatives such as lemon, coconut, and other oils. In 1985, the river mouth of Cerro Hermoso was closed, and water was diverted for the irrigation of crops. In fact, from 1980 to 1994, there was an impressive increase in hectares dedicated to permanent crops, from 125 to 420, and of temporary crops, from 370 to 610 hectares (Rosas Narvaez, 2017, p. 23). In 1990, a containment curtain was built on the Verde River, which, alongside deforestation, caused less freshwater to reach the lagoon, further disrupting the delicate balance of the lagoon ecosystem. In 1999, the federal government

7 The relationship between the lagoons and freshwater is, basically, through rain and surface runoff through the San Francisco and Chacalapa Rivers, which in the dry season remain dry, because they are affected by the local climatic conditions and the reduced size of its catchment areas (Municipal Development Plan, Tututepec, 2014–2016)

8 Papaya is produced for national and international export (Jiménez García, 2016, p. 146, 2015, p. 184).

built rock breakwaters to open the river mouth. It also intended to do dredging works, but for different reasons, the following year, in 2000, to close the river mouth. The first breakwater, a kind of wall made of rocks whose function is to help redirect currents to increase water flow and improve the drainage of sediments, was built in 1972.

After opening and closing again in 2014, the federal government began works to dredge the sand and reopen the bar. However, it went on to build two new breakwaters that would strengthen the existing one and help to have more fish, thus benefiting the local fishing. However, due to a lack of political will, mismanagement, and corruption, the works did not continue as planned and, to date, have been arbitrarily stopped. In informal talks and in interviews on the subject, many local people (interlocutors) in my study stated that the problem was the construction of the breakwaters themselves because they (the engineers and the government personnel) did not take into account the local knowledge of the fishers about the Marian currents and waves. The local people relayed that the government personnel ignored them, which led to the closure of the river mouth. This, in addition to the problems caused in the Lagoon, has also caused the Cerro Hermoso community to cease to attract tourists. They told me that, years ago, people hardly ever visited Chacahua (a popular tourist site); most people preferred to go to spend the day at the beach in Cerro Hermoso, due to its proximity, ease of access and because it was very beautiful. But since the river mouth closed, hardly anyone goes there. This has been detrimental to both Cerro Hermoso, as well as nearby communities that also benefited from the arrival of tourists.

On my last visit, in December 2019, I was able to be present at a meeting[9] that took place in the Municipality, which was widely attended by members of the different fishermen's cooperatives and women from the fisherwomen's cooperative. The purpose of the meeting was to explain to the inhabitants of Zapotalito how the dredging works of the river mouth were going. Apparently, a new company had accepted the project and was beginning with the opening works of the river mouth. What could be clearly understood from the explanations of the engineer in charge was that the works would produce the opening of the river mouth, but that this opening constituted a small recess, that is, it could last a few hours, a day or a few days, but it would then close again.

In short, the main problems that affect the lives of the people of El Zapotalito are the closure of the river mouth that does not allow an exchange of water in the lagoon, meaning that there is fewer fish in the lagoon, a lack of freshwater

9 This meeting took place on 12/11/2019 on the basketball court, in front of the Zapotalito Municipal office

due to diversion for crop irrigation, contamination due to the use of agrochemicals[10] in plantations of marginalised peasants, and waste from larger haciendas, such as the lemon one, which are particularly harmful to flora and fauna of the lagoon (Sartini, 2019, p. 27). Agrochemical residues from fertilisers and herbicides used in agricultural crops are carried by channels, permanent or intermittent currents towards coastal water bodies. These agrochemicals come mainly from the municipality lowlands, where the intensive activities of agriculture and livestock are concentrated. Nitrogen fertilisers are common, followed by phosphorous, potassium, lastly micronutrients and foliar crops in horticultural crops. Virtually all insecticides cause injury on chronic exposures in fish. Likewise, fertilisers favour the growth of microorganisms that consume the available oxygen (Ecosta Yutu Cuii, 2000).

Compounding these problems is the mismanagement of resources and lack of care by the population towards the territory where they live. Marginality and lack of employment in surrounding regions continue to drive immigration to El Zapotalito, which contributes to ongoing population growth and limited resources. This situation is the result of excessive population growth that has led to the depletion of resources. In fact, since the park's foundation (1937), the first management project was implemented in 2014. To make matters worse, the Management Plans and the organisation of fishing and fishing gear end up damaging the lagoon and its inhabitants.

Fishing permits and state aid are granted only to cooperative members, so throughout the park, and especially in El Zapotalito, many cooperatives have been formed (there are a total of ten) to obtain permits without having a true spirit of collaboration. In fact, the members of the cooperatives each fish to earn their daily livelihood. There is no true cooperative structure (Sartini, 2019, p. 28). My study participants told me that there is a lot of division between the cooperatives and that everyone joins the cooperative that interests them the most, either because their relatives are there or because of political or religious harmony, among others. However, they claim that cooperatives do not seek the common good and that they are not intended to sell fish and distribute it; people go out to sea whenever they want and fish and sell whatever they can (Ruperto Arellanes and Hermes Arellanes, fishermen).

The lack of collaboration and organisation in the cooperatives has led to further overexploitation of the fishery resources from the lagoons. Many go

10 Currently, the lagoon system receives water throughout the year through drains from the agricultural system. These return waters have the inconvenience of being a vehicle to transport, to the lagoons, residues of the agrochemicals used by farmers throughout the irrigation area (Municipal Development Plan, Tututepec, 2014–2016)

fishing without permits or with prohibited fishing gear, using smaller-meshed nets with which young fish are caught, which prevents the growth of the marine species and its reproduction in the long term, hitting the bottom of the boats (which is also prohibited) to disturb the fish and make them easier to fish, etc. This is possible due to the low vigilance by the park authority (Mijangos Rosario, 2017, p. 54). Also, some fishers use a mixture of gasoline and oil for the motors of the boats that, while it is cheaper, mostly pollutes the water in the lagoon (Sartini, 2019, p. 28). This has caused confrontations with fishers from other lagoons such as those in the Chacahua Lagoon, which prohibit Zapotalito fishers from fishing in its waters. Chacahua residents say that they do not respect fishing regulations or the environment, so, sometimes "they hijack the work tools, such as boats, trammel nets, other nets, etc., from the fishermen of Zapotalito and I ask them for money or to leave to return their work tools" (Hermes Arellanes, fisherman). This was confirmed to me by a fisherman from Chacahua claiming that "those of Zapotal" do not know how to take care of the fish and the lagoon (e.g., they use smaller-meshed nets than they should, that they do not use rods, that they hit the bottom of the boats, etc.).

The illegal logging of mangroves is another of the great problems that the Park suffers, and that affects its inhabitants. It affects the ecosystem in several ways: the amount of *tichinda* decreases, which is serious since these molluscs act as an "aquatic filter." They serve as a kind of "kidney", or filtration system, for the lagoon, so when they are destroyed, the lagoon is even more dirty and polluted. Mangroves also serve to provide protection against hurricanes; their roots are a good place for the growth of various species of fish, and various species of birds reproduce on their branches. Deforestation throughout the basin is causing tangible effects in the permanent rivers that supply the wetland complex in the lower part of the basin. These natural sources of hydrological contribution have gradually decreased their water loads, exacerbating the problems of dragging of agrochemicals, salinity and eutrophication. (Rodríguez- Castañeda, 1998). Naturally, the supply of freshwater to the lower zone is supplied by the rivers that flow throughout the Sierra Sur, which coincides with the hydrological zone 21.[11] These natural

11 In the lower part of the Green River Basin, one of the most important in the State of Oaxaca, within Region 21, are the Chachua and Pastoría lagoons, which are two permanent bodies of water. The Chacahua lagoon has an area of 612 hectares and the Pastoría lagoon of 2,228, the two lagoons communicate through an approximately 3.0 km long canal called El Corral. The system is part of the Lagunas de Chacahua National Park, which constitutes 14, 187 hectares of Low and Medium Tropical Forest, Coastal Dunes, Mangroves and Coastal Lagoons, in the area the abundance of species of commercial interest such as mussels, shrimp and various species of fish stands out, it is a natural

sources of freshwater have their water loads gradually decreased, attributable to deforestation in the upper part of the basin. In addition, a containment curtain is built on the Green River, which alters the drains adding to the water contributions. This problem directly affects the lagoon area, the mangrove, and all the fauna associated with it, in particular the shrimp production in the area.

In the upper part of the Green River, tropical vegetation is slashed to give space to cultivated fields. Due to the lack of forest, this has resulted in land erosion and soil entering the lagoon. This process has, in turn, led to closing the channel that connects the La Pastorìa Lagoon and the Palmarito Lagoon. The *Mujeres pescadoras del Manglar* are carrying out a project to free the channel and to fish in this other lagoon as well (I will talk about this later).

The lagoon does not currently guarantee the same fishery production as in previous decades. This means fewer jobs and a lower and more fluctuating profit, which translates into greater vulnerability for the inhabitants of the park, in addition to the already high marginality of their localities lacking basic services (water, electricity, drainage and telephone services) and doctors (health centres are not found in all localities and doctors usually are medical internists), (Sartini, 2019, p. 30).

The federal government has not taken concrete measures to change this situation and, in the words of Escalona, Alvarado and Sadívar:

> The state is guilty of environmental racism to the extent that it has prioritised other interests over the right to a healthy environment of the Afro-Mexican population that depends on the lagoon. It has also engaged in institutional racism by belittling local knowledge and ignoring the recommendations made by communities on the use and management of local natural resources and excluding them from administration and decision-making (2018, p. 1).

7 Cooperative "Mujeres Pescadoras del Manglar"

In 2017, the Fisheries Law was amended so that women were formally and legally incorporated into fishing production activities. However, legal changes always take time to be applied in practice. According to the law, obtaining a fishing permit requires membership within a fishing cooperative. For this

---

breeding ground for lizards. Turtles are spawned on the Costa Marina, as well as the presence of numerous birds, mainly herons and ducks.

reason, in the town of El Zapotalito, there are nine fishermen's cooperatives and one fisherwomen's cooperative: *Mujeres Pescadoras del Manglar*. To be a member of a cooperative, one undergoes an "observation period" as a candidate for one or two years. Once the permit is obtained, the fisher is also

FIGURE 5.2 Fisherwomen fishing
SOURCE: NURIA JIMENÉZ GARCÍA

entitled to state support to renew have their fishing equipment replaced if it is destroyed in the event of a natural disaster. Here, being a member of a cooperative (as we previously discussed) does not necessarily mean working in a group and paying a fixed fee. Being part of a cooperative only means having a fishing permit with which one can fish as many fish as possible in one day. Two people are needed to fish by boat or panga, although many go out fishing alone, so the members of the cooperatives usually fish with their wives, sons and daughters so as not to have to divide the daily profit with another partner (Sartini, 2019, p. 35). Several of the members of *Mujeres pescadoras del Manglar* have always fished with their husbands. However, prior to membership in the women's cooperative, they were never granted recognition as cooperative members. They did not have a permit and, therefore, no access to resources. It was seen as "normal" for women to help their husbands so that their husbands did not have to hire anyone else and to ensure that for the benefits would to remain within the family (see Figure 5.2). Since the *Mujeres pescadoras del Manglar* cooperative was created, they have had their fishing permits.

This changed in 2014, at which time La Ventana A.C., an organisation that specialised in projects and studies in marginal wetlands, mangroves and marginalised women, arrived in El Zapotalito. It was at this time that the project of the Mujeres Pescadoras del Manglar cooperative originated and began to take shape. La Ventana A.C. had started been working with Afro women from the Oaxacan Costa Chica since 2010 and was the organisation responsible for founding the Costa Chica Women's Network, which brought together the women who benefited from the association. In 2014, Yolanda Camacho,[12] an activist for the recognition and rights of Afro-descendant women, invited members of La Ventana A.C to El Zapotal:

> So what I can tell you is that we started as a group. First, we, we started as a group, first, they were formed, an organisation called the Window came. We fish, we are fisherwomen, but there was a woman [Yolanda] who began bringing us together to meet. Yolanda told La Ventana that there were women who were doing the fishing.
>
> So the La Ventana came for the first time. So I didn't go, well, I didn't know, right? And then, one night, a friend says to me, "Hey! Can you believe it, this organisation has shown up and says that they want to help us, as fisherwomen. And you say, Wow! They hardly help you well, ahh yeah!

12 President of the Costa de Oaxaca Na'a Tunda Collective (Black Woman)

> When is the meeting going to be? Well, such a day, let's go! And we went to do it and we went! When I arrived there were few people, little by little they arrived and then they arrived; there I met Inti and Karina. And we started, they began to talk about ... what would they like, how much did you earn, how much did you get from fish, I mean to ask questions, right?
>
> And [...] there was, following the meeting, from there they had us do a survey. After the survey, they continued, we continued organising as a group – we were 26 women. But, [because of] riots with Chacahua, only four of five women from Chacahua would come [...] to attend the meetings. And there were meetings in different places. First, it was at Yolanda's house, then at [the home of] a colleague named Minerva, then at the Agency, like this in different places. And they said no! What is that you all would like to do? Ahh, a store to sell fish! Because there aren't really any stores to sell fish around here. (Interview with Cristina Arellanes, president of Mujeres pescadoras del Manglar, author's translation.)

The La Ventana A.C. team began by gathering the fisherwomen from the Chacahua-Pastorìa lagoon system in an assembly in El Zapotalito. Their first objective in bringing these women together was to learn more about their situation (and the challenges that they face) within their communities. Through questionnaires, they inquired about women's labour activities, family composition (e.g., what type of family they had, whether they were single mothers), marital status, education background, and fishing experience. The La Ventana A.C. then organised a participatory workshop with the aim of bringing together the thirty women and preparing proposals for long-term projects to address women's primary concerns.

Once the problems related to gender violence, low self-esteem, lack of recognition of their importance at the community level and in the fishing activity were identified, they began to work on some issues, such as self-esteem, in order to obtain an effective workgroup. An extremely enriching experience for these women was the experience exchange workshop in Veracruz, which was carried out between the group of women from the Chacahua-La Pastoría lagoon system and the fisherwomen from two cooperatives in the state of Veracruz, one in Alvarado and the other in the Costa de San Juan[13] township.

13 Twenty women from the port of Alvarado, in the Mexican state of Veracruz, were the pioneers of this form of organisation and work that has been spreading along the coasts of Mexico: the women fishermen cooperatives. Experimenting Women was the idea of the sisters Azucena and Araceli Palacios. They say that the idea arose six years ago in the face

Both experiences (two cooperatives in Veracruz) have existed for more than ten years since the fisherwomen organised into cooperatives. Currently, they are engaged in fishing, cultivation of hatcheries for cherry snapper and soft crab, selling the product in a market fishmonger (Alvarado) and production of manufactured lily pads.

> The thing is that a women's cooperative had never been established here. Many women came, really quite a lot, but they wanted to be given money right away. But not us; we went to Alvarado Veracruz to see the fisherwomen. There were also fisherwomen in Chacahua. There, we had just started meeting with Inti and Karina. Many of us went to see what could be done, but many wanted to receive the money right away. But we stayed – there were 20 of us – and we started working in a restaurant; we worked in teams. The psychologist came because, at first, we had a lot of conflict. There were issues between some and among others, so the psychologist called them in and they discussed many things. They told each other what they felt, what they had worked out, and so on. (Interview Olmides López, member of Mujeres pescadoras del Manglar, author's translation.)

This meeting and exchange of experience greatly helped them to think of themselves as capable and to see the experiences of other women who had "been able" despite the difficulties (collectively organise). Thus, they decided to establish themselves as a fisherwomen's cooperative, the first cooperative of Afro-indigenous fisherwomen in the whole country. In the constitutive statute of *Mujeres pescadoras del Manglar* there are two fundamental points that differentiate them from the rest of the fishing cooperatives in El Zapotal and show that it is not a cooperative that was constituted for the mere monetary interest and access to permits. 1) The fact that men cannot be admitted to the cooperative (to create a freer and less violent environment for women) and 2) that environmental education is promoted. Environmental education includes actions that are taken to maintain natural biodiversity, women's rights, gender equality, and community development, in addition

of the decline of fishing and the failure of their husbands' cooperatives. With the help of biologists from the Universidad Veracruzana, the women organised themselves, created rustic clam and fish cultures in semi-freedom, investigated sustainable fishing systems, and also launched into the lagoons and the sea in search of livelihood for each day. After Mujeres Experimentando, with 11 members, she was born in La Mujer Costeña, with eight. Later Laguna la Flota saw the light, the only female cooperative that admits men.

to carrying out productive activities generating an income for associates (Statute of *Mujeres pescadoras del Manglar*, 2016). In these two points, there is a clear commitment to the community; women's work is simultaneously understood as care for the common good, the environment as well as human and social development of the population.

After becoming a cooperative, the members began working on opening a fish shop, for which they rented an establishment near the main road and equipped it to sell the fish they caught. But due to some problems, such as rivalries and little common work experience[14] (they had rarely worked in groups on projects), the shortage of fish in the lagoon and the sales did not cover their expenses. Hence, they decided to close the fish shop and open a restaurant La Flor del Manglar.[15]

> That's where the fish died and, well ... We want to have a fish market, but, well, we don't have it! How are we going to have a fish market if there is no fish, right? And they said, well, what do they want? What do you want to do? No! Well, we are going to start this ... a ... a restaurant, or not a restaurant but a dining room, where you sell things like tortillas, enchiladas, things from the region then ... and yes! And so it was. At first, we were doing very well! But later they said ahh we are going to build it up; we are going to have a social purpose because with that you can start projects, you can do things, right? And so it was done! The cooperative was named "Fisherwomen of the mangrove", and many mothers may no longer fish as the one that you saw, Doña Victoria. She no longer fishes, but she did sell fish. (Interview with Cristina Arellanes, president of Mujeres pescadoras del Manglar, author's translation.)

14 Doña Brígida is the mother of Cristina Arellanes, president of the cooperative, and she also belongs to the cooperative although she does not go out fishing because she is scared, she goes out every day to sell fish, she sells throughout the Costa Chica area of Oaxaca, House for house. One of the days I went out to sell fish with her, we were invited to the fiesta-posadas of a nearby town, where the whole town and particularly the women had organised days preparing the party. Doña Brígida told me that she was envious of how in these towns women organised themselves for any community event, unlike in Zapotalito, where each one was more in their interest and where it is very difficult to organise community events or activities where women go to house to house preparing food, and what is necessary to organise the party and invite people from nearby towns. She thought that one of the explanations for this could be that the people who live in Zapotalito come from different areas and communities and that the town is very new and in a certain way disintegrated, another option was that since it is a tourist crossing point, traditions have been lost.

15 The Mangrove Flower

The experience of this second project was really difficult, exhausting; but on the other hand, it was enriching and fostered personal growth. They started by renting a cabin on the banks of the lagoon that they furnished and decorated. All the members of the cooperative began participating in this project, which was organised in shifts of three people, each shift working once a week. At the same time that they organised to attend and run the restaurant, they attended customer service workshops, hygiene standards, etc. It also provided a space of empowerment, where women were able to reflect on and address their problems, including the negative effect of familial conflict on the continuous operation of the cooperative. The internal conflicts fuelled by gossip and the rejection of women's spouses towards the activities carried out by the cooperative eventually led to the abandonment of a large part of the cooperative members, leaving only five people out of the original members. The remaining members relay how difficult it was for them to continue. There were some women who did not contribute all the money they earned to the cooperative; there were those who stole materials from the restaurant; some women did not respect the hygiene rules that they had learned in the workshops. Many of the women's husbands were angry because they said that their wives hardly made any money and were away from home all day when it was their turn at the restaurant; this led to conflicts among some couples. In order to try to solve the problems of the group, a psychologist was hired. She orchestrated group and individual activities, which greatly helped the group and the members who remained in the cooperative to face existing problems.

The low sales in the restaurant reduced economic activity, so the members decided to open the restaurant only when necessary or when there were important events. The financial support to cover the expenses of the constitution as a cooperative, the fishmonger and the canteen, was derived from the INMUJERES government fund (years 2015 and 2016) and from the organisation Semillas (from 2017 to 2020). With the support of Semillas, they have managed to buy a boat to give tours to tourists, academics and technicians who work on reducing the contamination of the lagoon and its fauna. They also organise workshops where they invite all people in the community to participate. In these workshops, ideas for productive projects of community interest have emerged, such as the construction of pedal boats to give eco-tourism tours around the Lagoon.

In 2017, there was a strong earthquake in the state of Oaxaca, in which many fish in the lagoon perished. The earthquake exacerbated their problems, and so they decided to clean the channels of the lagoon for better water circulation. Two main projects are currently underway. The first project aims to clean the Palmariro channel so that it is once again connected to the La Pastoría

Lagoon and will allow them to resume fishing activities in that location. This was supported by the training of a biologist from Tabasco (a state in Mexico) who taught them about cleaning the canal. They called upon the other fishermen's cooperatives to help them with the task of cleaning the channel, and some cooperatives gave them boats to transfer the workers to the Palmarito channel. In fact, they hired workers who daily to clean the canal daily, employing women in need and thus generating income in the community.

> We do work. The Canal del Palmarito dried up. Shrimp used to come in through there. Now it is open, but the water has gone down again. But we continue to monitor the canal because there is another little lagoon there. Semillas supported us because we started a project, and we brought in many women to work. If the project came from there, we were paying women to work. For example, there is a meeting every month for men's cooperatives, and we went, and from there they went to support us, to work. That channel was lost; they had a place for the animals to pass through. Now the big boats were coming in, now that it was opened. We told the cooperatives to help us. We gave them food and so because it was also convenient for them, they also went fishing there. Afterwards, they did not go, but we have been maintaining it. We also have been monitoring the tichinda. What we most need to know is the analysis. (Interview with Olmides López, member of Mujeres pescadoras del Manglar, author's translation.)

The *Mujeres pescadoras del Manglar* cooperative has also involved in a sustainable management project for *tichinda* since August 2019. This is carried out in conjunction with three biologists from the Universidad del Mar (Puerto Escondido and Huatulco, Oaxaca) and with the support of the Chacahua Lagoons National Park. The objective of this project is to regularly measure the level of water and tichinda contamination in different areas of the lagoon. This project originally set out to combine empirical-scientific information in order to develop a management manual. The monitoring was developed and led by the women of the cooperative in two monthly sessions, one per day, from August to December 2019. The *tichinda* collection was carried out from the banks located in mangrove roots, from whose roots the women extracted the samples without the need to cut them. On my last visit in December 2019, the Management Plan was already prepared, although analyses of the level of cleanliness or contamination of the *tichindas* had not yet been carried out.

The project has also taught women how to collect and analyse data: they have learned to measure the *tichinda* and understand its degree of contamination.

FIGURE 5.3 Fisherwoman cleaning *tichindas*
SOURCE: NURIA JIMÉNEZ GARCÍA

Since they have learned these important skills, they can continue monitoring the lagoon once the project is over. The fisherwomen are concerned because the analysis of the *tichindas* has not yet been done. This is one of the aspects of the project that most interests these women since it is part of the daily diet of the area. Typical dishes of the area are made with this mollusc since it has always been found easily and abundantly (in the roots of the mangroves) (see Figure 5.3).

The challenges for the cooperative are many, but what most caught my attention was that, despite the obstacles and difficulties (external and internal to the group), the remaining members continue to do what they believe is fair and good for them as well as the entire community by promoting projects and initiatives that men's cooperatives, in decades of existence, never intended to do. Women combine these tasks with the gender-specific obligations and duties that are expected of them within their communities. Sometimes, these demands overload them and they are forced to constantly negotiate their participation in the cooperative with the expectations of their families and the community. However, it also fills them with pride. As they say, they have achieved something that had not been done before; they have made visible and brought recognition to their invaluable contribution to local fishing practices and the sustainability of the ecosystem. In turn, this has provided them with increased power and influence.

8 Conclusions

Throughout this text, an attempt has been made to present the situation, work, obstacles and achievements of women – companions, and family members of fishers, who for years have participated in the work of their husbands, without recognition and without salary. On the contrary, their work was perceived as help in times of crisis or a way to avoid having to hire more people. Even women themselves did not perceive what they were doing as work since it was considered an activity to help meet family needs or even because, in many cases, these activities were carried out in the domestic space. After the constitution of the *Mujeres pescadoras del Manglar* cooperative, all this began to change. As the association was built, an empowerment process began, in which these women began to establish resource governance. The formation of the cooperative contributed to changes in both the natural and institutional systems. They transformed their informal activity into a professional one.

This entire process, with all of its "joys and sorrows", has led these women to understand that they should unite their efforts rather than compete for resources. In turn, it has made them aware of and helped them to understand the discrimination to which they have been subjected and which they still have to face because they are women. Women who are engaged in fishing, both in the capture phase and in the subsequent phase of sale and marketing, make their own unique spaces through the control of specific women networks, which empowers them in their practices. These practices are sustained through continuous cooperation, which allows women who generate more networks of solidarity and mutual collaboration to have greater support vis-à-vis society than those who remain in the domestic sphere and are under greater vigilance and control (Jiménez , 2015, p. 190).

Having the right of access to the resources of the ecosystem in which they live, and in particular, to fishing vessels, has allowed women to be in contact with other spheres of power and information. It has also paved the way for spaces linked to decision-making, which can impact community resource management (Savard and Fraga, 2005; Meinzen-Dick et al., 1997; Kleiber, 2014). This, in turn, has had a great impact on their economies, leading them to acquire economic autonomy, which, in turn, gives them greater independence of movement and control over their lives. They have begun to understand the world and its role in the community in a different way, showing other women "that yes, you can". The participation of women as fisherwomen, on equal terms with men in the fishing sector, has significant effects on nutrition and the standard of living of households. If women have access to fishing, they can contribute to gender equality and promote the participation of more women as active agents of change in the sector (Liguori, 2005). Likewise, until now, they had not been involved in the decision-making process or in positions of responsibility (Salas et al., 2006), which has been changing. Although the positions of responsibility and decision-making at the community level continue to be occupied by men, the women of the community, especially those who make up the fishermen's cooperative, have already begun to be taken into consideration, both in the meetings of fishing cooperatives, as well as in the institutional ones and in relation to environmental issues and public works.

I am interested in highlighting the community role of these women in the defence and rescue of the lagoon system; requesting aid from institutions; and engaging in workshops and projects for the benefit of the community, their families and themselves. On the contrary, men have always shown great disinterest in new forms of learning through the support of biologists or participation in workshops related to artisanal fishing. These women have come to initiate projects, as shown in the text, to rescue the lagoon system, in which they have promoted the involvement of different members of the community, giving jobs to men and women.

As a final reflection, the participation of women in positions that allow them access to decision-making must start from the political leadership of women and their participation, but it is also about a change in self-esteem and self-care. The empowerment intervention is based on this leadership to equally appreciate the perspective and skills of women in their institutional arrangements.

References

Alfaro, M. y Escalona, I. (2002). "El proceso de colonización: poblamiento y formación de localidades", In M. Alfaro, G. Sánchez (eds.) *Chacahua: Reflejos de un Parque*, CONANP/PNUD/SEMARNART/Plaza y Váde, (pp. 87–113), México

Agarwal, B. (1995). *A Field of One's Own: Gender and Property in South Asia*. Cambridge, Cambridge University Press

Agarwal, Bina. (1997). "Bargaining" and gender relations: within and beyond the household. *Feminist Economics*, 1(3), 1–51.

Alcalá (2011). *Pescadores en América Latina y El Caribe: espacio, población, producción y política*, Vol. I y II, UNAM-Facultad de Ciencias y Unidad Multidisciplinaria de Docencia e Investigación Social-SISAL, Yucatán.

Arizpe, L. (1993). *Cultura y cambio global: Percepciones sociales sobre la deforestación en la Selva Lacandona*. México: Centro Regional de Investigaciones Multidísciplinarías, Universidad Nacional Autónoma de Mexico.

Bailey, G., Parkington, J. (1988). The archaeology of prehistoric coastlines: An introduction. En G. Bailey, J.Parkington (eds). *The Archaeology of Prehistoric Coastlines*, (pp. 1–10). New York: Cambridge University Press.

Bedoya, E., Martínez, S. (2000). De la economía política a la ecología política: Balance global del ecomarxismo y la crítica al desarrollo. In Viola, A. (ed). *Antropología del desarrollo, teoría y estudios etnográficos en América Latina*. (pp. 129–168). Barcelona, Paidós

Blaikie, P. (1996). Understanding environmental issues. In Morse, S.,Stocking, M. (eds). *People and enviroment*. (pp. 1–30). Vancuver, UBC Press, University of British Columbia

Crean K., Symes, D. (Eds.). (1996). *Fisheries Management in crisis*. Oxford: Blackwell Sciencie. Fishing New Books.

Escalona, I., Alvarado, N., Sadìvar, E. (2018). *Racismo ambiental/institucional en México: el caso de las comunidades del sistema laguna Chacahua-Pastorìa en Oaxaca*. Copera, Ciudad de México.

FAO (2000). *El Estado mundial de la pesca y la acuicultura*. Roma, Italia.

FAO (2002). *Uso de medidas técnicas en la pesca responsable: regulación de artes de pesca*. Roma, Italia.

FAO (2004). *Women in the fisheries sector of Argentina, Uruguay and Southern Brazil*. Roma, Italia. Retrieved from: http://www.fao.org/DOCREP/006/J0964E/J0964E00.htm.

Fraga, J. (1999). *Política ambiental y relaciones de género en un área natural protegida: las dimensiones locales de la globalidad en Río Lagartos, México*. Quebec, Laval

Jiménez, N. (2015). Solidaridades femeninas y espacios comunitarios: prácticas femeninas en la Costa Chica de Oaxaca. *ILUMINURAS. Vidas rurais, contextos agrários, paisagens interioranas: desafíos para uma antropología com imagens*, 16(40), 184–217.

Jiménez, N. (2016). Espacios y luchas femeninas. Usos y apropiaciones espaciales en la Costa Chica. In *Revista de Estudios de Género. La Ventana*, v (44), 142–186

Kleiber, D. (2014). *Gender and small-scale fisheries in the Central Philippines*. Vancouver, Canada: The University of British Columbia.

Leach, M., Joekes, S., Green, C. (1995). Editorial: Gender Relations and Environmental Change. *International Development Studies Bulletin*, 26(1).

Liguori, L. A. (2005). *The role of women in the social and ecological resilience of San Felipe's fisheries*. (Master of Arts). University of British Columbia.

López-Ercilla, I. N. S. (2019). *Participación de las mujeres en la cadena de valor de tres pesquerías ribereñas en México*. https://doi.org/10.13022/M33357

Marín, G. (2007). Pesca artesanal, comunidad y administración de recursos pesqueros. Experiencias en la costa de Michoacán, México. *Gazeta Antropológica*, 27, Universidad de Granada, España.

McGoodwin, R. (1990). *Crisis in the world's fisheries*. Stanford University Press, Stanford.

Meinzen-Dick, R. S., Brown, L.R., Sims Feldstein, H., Quisumbing, A.R. (1997). Gender, property rights, and natural resources. World Development, 25(8).

Mijangos, R.O. (2017). *Medios de vida y vulnerabilidad de la comunidad pesquera del área natural protegida Parque Nacional Lagunas de Chacahua*. Puerto Ángel: Universidad del Mar.

Munguía, M. T., Méndez, G., Soares, D. (2013). Condiciones de Vulnerabilidad de Género en la Crisis Ambiental y el Cambio Climático en Yucatán, México. In López Castellano, F. (ed.). *Medio Ambiente y Desarrollo. Miradas Feministas Desde Ambos Hemisferios, España*. (pp. 289–312). Universidad de Granada y Fundación IPADE

Trujillo, N., Lorena, M., Pineda Ramírez, C. E. (2009). Luchas socioambientales en América Latina y México. Nuevas subjetividades y radicalidades en movimiento. *Bajo el Volcán*, 14(8), 81–104

Parra-Sosa, B., Martínez-Corona, B., Herrera-Cabrera, E., Fernández-Crispín, A. (2007). Reproducción campesina, recursos naturales y género en una comunidad campesina en Puebla, México. *Agricultura, sociedad y desarrollo*, 4(1): 53–67. Retrieved from: http://www.scielo.org.mx/scielo.php?script=sci_arttext&pid=S187054722007000100004&lng=es&tlng=es.

Perez Orozco, A. (2011). Crisis multidimensional y sostenibilidad de la vida. *Investigaciones feministas*, 11, 29–53

Pedroza, C. (2018). El rol de las mujeres en la pesca en México. *Foro Económico de Pesca y Acuicultura*, CONAPESCA.

Rosas Narvaez, S. (2017). *Anàlisis socio-ambiental de los factores de estés del Parque Nacional Lagunas de Chacahua, Oaxaca, México*. Puerto Ángel, México.

Salas, S., Mexicano-Cíntora, G., Cabrera, M. A. (2006). *Hacia donde van las pesquerías en Yucatán?: tendencias, retos y perspectivas*: Cinvestav Mérida.

Salazar, R., Salazar, H., Rodríguez, B., Rodríguez, M. (2012). *Agenda de género y agua en Iztapalapa: acciones para el disfrute del derecho humano al agua.* México: Mujer y Medio Ambiente A.C. y Gobierno de la Ciudad de México.

Sartini, I. (2019). *Cooperativismo femenino como herramienta para el empoderamiento de las mujeres: la cooperativa Mujeres Pescadoras del Manglar en la costa de Oaxaca*, M.A. Thesis, Leiden University.

Savard, K., Fraga, J. (2005). A bottom-up Approach to the Creation of a Marine Protected Area in San Felipe, Mexico. Gender Relations, Governance Mechanisms and Globalization. In: Neis, B., Binkley, M., Gerrard, S., Maneschy, M.C. (eds). *Changing Tides. Gender, Fisheries and Globalization.* (pp. 169–181). Halifax, Canadá, Fernwood Publishing.

Stott, P., S. Sullivan, ED. (2000). *Political ecology. Science, myth and power.* London, Arnold

Uc-Espadas, M.; Molina-Rosales, D.; Vázquez-García, V.; Pérez-Jiménez, C., Gurri-García, F. (2017). Permisos de pesca y relaciones de género en isla Arena, Campeche. *Agricultura, sociedad y desarrollo*, 383–404.

Velázquez, M. (1996). *Género y ambiente en Latinoamérica.* Cuernavaca, Morelos: CRIM, UNAM.

Vázquez García, V.; Godínez, L.; Ortiz, A. S., Montes, M. (2004). Uncultivated Foods in Southern Veracruz, México: Establishing the Links between Ecosystems Health, Food Availability, and Human Nutrition, *Ecohealth* 1(2).

Yesner, D. (1980). Nutrition and Cultural Anthropology. In Jerome, N. W., Kandel, R. F., Pelto, G. H. (Eds.). *Nutritional Anthropology.* (pp. 85–116). Redgrave, Pleasantville, New York.

CHAPTER 6

The Fishing Profession in Quebec (Canada): Structure, Origins and Development of a "Typically Male" Sector

Marco Alberio

1 Introduction

Fishing is traditionally regarded as a male profession. Due to a strong gendered division of labour, women have mainly held supporting roles within family-based catching enterprises and more broadly in the fishing industry, for example, in the fish processing sector. As Couliou (2010) explains for the French case, "the organisation of work during fishing activities is at the root of the challenges linked to the temporalities of the job. Absence for several days and weeks can itself be experienced as a hardship by fishers and their families" (cited in Alberio & Tremblay, 2020, p. 91, our translation).[1] For these reasons, the spouses of captain-owners have historically played, and often continue to play, an essential supportive role within family fishing enterprises. They have historically taken care of preparing meals for fishing excursions, as well as the accounting and administration of the business, which some spouses continue to do today. However, especially among the newer generation, women are not always involved in family fishing businesses (Alberio & Tremblay, 2020). As will be observed in this chapter, this lack of participation in the sector may be a choice. Although, it may also depend on the structure of the industry which, because of inherent characteristics, is unable to integrate women, and especially to integrate them into important roles and functions (captains, business owners, etc.). A perspective focusing on social times, work rhythms and, more generally, life courses will enable a more comprehensive understanding of the specificities of this profession and its activities, as well as of its professional identity and ethos. Such an approach will enable us to grasp the various tensions and a relationship to time that has become more and more complex over the years with the struggle between tradition (including

1 "L'organisation du travail à la pêche est au fondement de pénibilités liées aux temporalités du métier. L'absence pour plusieurs jours et semaines elle-même peut être vécue comme pénible par les pêcheurs et leur famille."

 | DOI:10.1163/9789004518841_008

fairly traditional and stereotyped gender roles) and the need to adapt to the changes in the labour market and more broadly in society.

In this chapter, we will focus in particular on the gendered dimensions of the fishing industry, specifically the catching sector, by trying to answer, at least in part, the following questions: what are the representations of fishers, both inside and outside the professional community, that reproduce it as a predominantly male occupation? How do the social mechanisms of professional selection affect the structuring of fishing activities as predominantly male? What role do, for example, gender stereotypes, family socialisation, economic and social gendered inequalities, and the current organisational model play in the professional selection and reproduction of this profession?

2 A Relatively Traditional Sector Subjected to Transformations and in Need of Adaptation

Fishing is a mature economic sector, but one that is currently undergoing change. This transformation allows us to analyse the effects of economic, social, political, environmental, technological and organisational changes on work activities, on the relationship to work, on the temporalities related to work, on the careers of fishers and, more broadly, on all the social temporalities associated with this very particular economic activity. These transformations are also shaping the configuration of the different actors involved, with the relations between the state, the market and families/communities changing at different levels (Alberio, 2020). For example, these transformations can change traditional configurations at the family, local and regional levels, and shape new relationships structured within social spheres – families and communities, markets, and political institutions – and their intersections. Changes in socioeconomic regulation, fluctuations in the profitability of this economic activity, as well as variations in the abundance or scarcity of the resource due to environmental factors can influence family (Alberio & Tremblay, 2020) and community (Alberio, 2020) relationships. The family and the community are central to this activity, which is by nature rooted in its territory (Alberio, 2020). Within this territory takes place the extraction of a natural resource (i.e., fish), but also the social regulation of the fishing occupation and its activities, including gendered socialisation, at several levels. This complexity exacerbates an already challenging demographic situation within the labour and employment market.

This situation requires that the commercial fishing sector be highly adaptive and capable of innovation (not only technological but also social) and of assuring its professional succession. However, as we shall see in this chapter, the fishing sector still seems, at least in part, reluctant to allow women into the profession and imposes (albeit indirectly) several obstacles to them. As a result, women fishers, and especially women captain-owner entrepreneurs, are still very rare.

3 A Brief Overview of Quebec and Gaspésie Fishers

This section (and the respective tables and charts in the appendix), based on our original analysis of Canadian census data[2] from 1986, 1991, 1996, 2001, 2006, 2011 (National Household Survey – NHS[3]) and 2016, will focus on the socioeconomic and sociodemographic characteristics of workers and entrepreneurs in this industry. The Census Program distinguishes three categories of fishers, based on the National Occupational Classification (NOC): fishing vessel masters and officers; self-employed fishers;[4] and fishing vessel deckhands.[5] The captain-owners who participated in our qualitative study may fall in either the first or the second category. In this section, the term "fishers" will be used to refer to individuals from all three of these categories.

In Quebec, the total number of people working in the catching sector of the fishing industry has decreased from 4,585 individuals in 1986 to 2,615 in 2016, a decline of 43% (Please see Table 6.1 and Figure 6.1 below).

2 We would like to extend a special thanks to the Quebec inter-University Centre for Social Statistics (QICSS) at the Université Laval for giving us access to this census data. We would also like to thank Hubert Doyon and Baptiste Beck for their assistance in processing and analysing the census data, and Emanuele Lucia for his work as a research assistant during the last year of the project.

3 In 2011, the Canadian Census Program consisted of a mandatory short form census questionnaire and a voluntary National Household Survey (NHS), instead of a mandatory short and long form census questionnaires like the previous years. The NHS program was later dismissed, and the 2016 census included once again both mandatory short and mandatory long form census questionnaires.

4 Following the Canadian Revenu Agency thereare several types of fishers. "Type 1" fisher – a) a member of the crew who either: owns or leases the boat or specialised fishing gear used to make a catch b)employs other persons under a contract of service to make a catch. "Type 2" fisher – any self-employed fisher who is not considered "type 1." This category includes a single fisher who borrows a boat and specialised fishing gear and has no employees. https://www.canada.ca/en/revenue-agency/services/forms-publications/publications/t4005/fishers-employment-insurance.html.

5 In French, in the everyday language of the fishing sector, these workers are commonly referred to as hommes de pont. The use of the term "homme", which means "man" in English, shows the clear predominance of men occupying this function.

TABLE 6.1 Number of individuals and proportions by type of occupation in the catching sector in Quebec and Gaspésie between 1986 and 2016

	Type of occupation	1986	1991	1996	2001	2006	2011	2016
Quebec	Masters and officers[a]	450 *9,8%*	380 *10,3%*	390 *11,7%*	365 *10,6%*	370 *10,5%*	375 *13,1%*	395 *15,1%*
	Independent fishers[b]	3 250 *70,9%*	2 405 *65,2%*	2 200 *66,1%*	2 210 *64,2%*	2 125 *60,5%*	1 710 *59,7%*	1 325 *50,7%*
	Deckhands[c]	885 *19,3%*	905 *24,5%*	740 *22,2%*	870 *25,3%*	1 020 *29,0%*	780 *27,2%*	895 *34,2%*
	Total	4 585 *100%*	3 690 *100%*	3 330 *100%*	3 445 *100%*	3 515 *100%*	2 865 *100%*	2 615 *100%*
Gaspésie	Masters and officers[a]	235 *12,5%*	140 *9,6%*	140 *11,0%*	150 *11,7%*	160 *12,2%*	185 *15,7%*	140 *16,2%*
	Independent fishers[b]	1 295 *68,7%*	870 *59,8%*	835 *65,7%*	810 *63,3%*	795 *60,7%*	690 *58,5%*	420 *48,6%*
	Deckhands[c]	355 *18,8%*	445 *30,6%*	295 *23,2%*	320 *25,0%*	355 *27,1%*	305 *25,8%*	305 *35,3%*
	Total	1 885 *100%*	1 455 *100%*	1 270 *100%*	1 280 *100%*	1 310 *100%*	1 180 *100%*	865 *100%*

a Fishing vessel masters and officers;
b Independent fishermen/women;
c Fishing vessel deckhands.

SOURCES: 1986, 1991, 1996, 2001, 2006, 2011 (NHS) ET 2016 CANADIAN CENSUSES

The decline has been erratic, with two specific periods showing a more pronounced decrease. The decline in cod fishing stocks between 1986 and 1991, and the subsequent moratorium on this fishery in the early 1990s, seem to have affected the total number of fishers in the province. In 1991, there were 895 fewer fishers in Quebec than in 1986. Another significant decrease took place between 2006 and 2011, a period that saw several changes in the regulation of the sector, with a reduction of 650 fishers. This decrease in workers is slightly more significant in the Gaspésie region, with a decline of 54% of fishers between 1986 and 2016.

When comparing the different subgroups, fishing vessel masters and officers tend to have a higher average age than other fishers. This is not surprising given that generally only more experienced fishers tend to become vessel

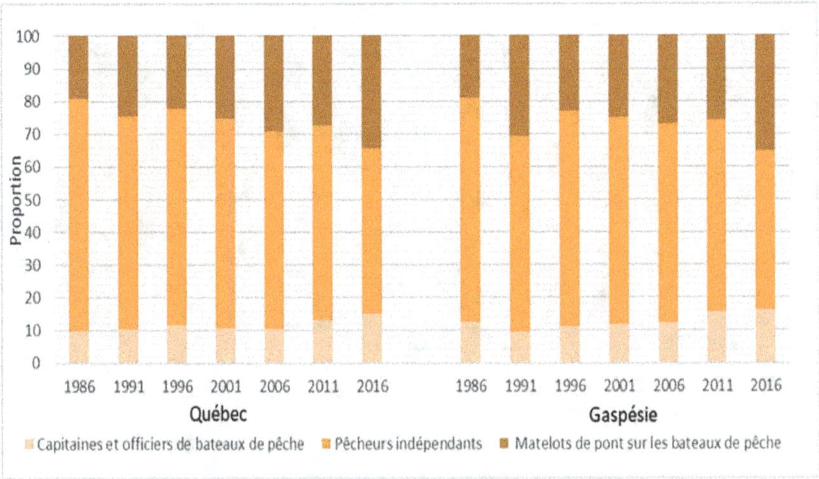

FIGURE 6.1 Distribution of individuals by type of occupation in the catching sector in Quebec and Gaspésie between 1986 and 2016

SOURCES: 1986, 1991, 1996, 2001, 2006, 2011 (NHS) ET 2016 CANADIAN CENSUSES.

captains and that, to be a captain-owner more specifically, one needs financial capital that generally is developed over the life course. The average age of independent fishers is also higher than that of fishing vessel deckhands. However, the proportion of those aged 45 and over has increased for each category throughout the different censuses. In 1986, in Quebec, the share of fishers aged 45 and over was 30% for masters and officers, 20% for independent fishers and 22% for deckhands (Please see Figure 6.2 below).

In 2016, the share of those aged 45 and over was 62% for masters and officers, 66% for independent fishers and 54% for deckhands. Both in Quebec and in Gaspésie, we can observe a generalised ageing of masters and officers, independent fishers and deckhands over time. While only less than a third of masters and officers were aged 45 years and over (30%) in Quebec in 1986, that proportion rose to more than two thirds (71%) in 2011. This trend is also apparent among independent fishers and deckhands.

In Quebec, between 1986 and 2016, the proportion of women working as masters and officers, self-employed fishers and deckhands has ranged between 8 and 15% (see Figure 6.3).

Both in Quebec and Gaspésie, women's presence in the catching sector reached its peak in 2006 when close to 15% in Quebec and 13% in Gaspésie of fishers were women. In other years, the proportion of women in the Gaspésie catching sector is closer to 10%. Moreover, it should be noted that the number

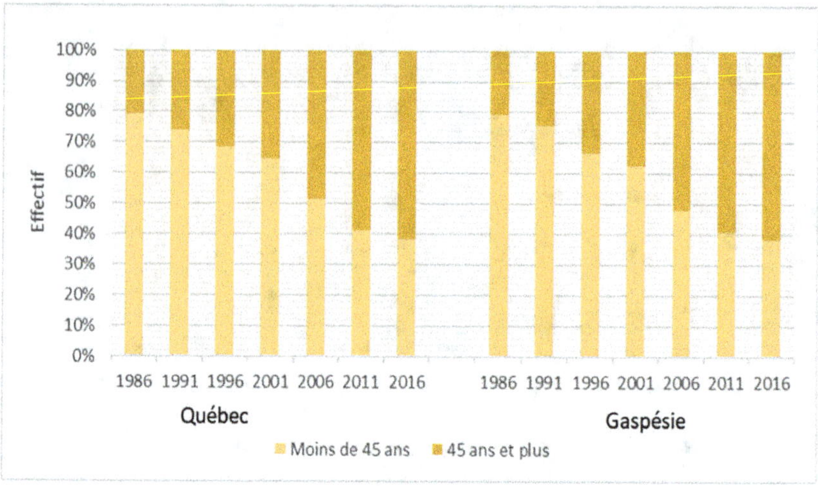

FIGURE 6.2 Distribution of individuals by age group in the catching sector in Quebec and Gaspésie between 1986 and 2016

SOURCES: 1986, 1991, 1996, 2001, 2006, 2011 (NHS) ET 2016 CANADIAN CENSUSES.

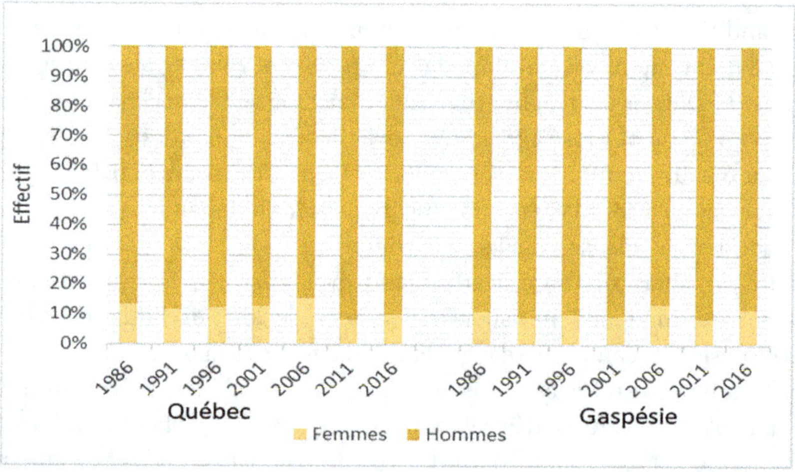

FIGURE 6.3 Distribution of individuals by gender in the catching sector in Quebec and Gaspésie between 1986 and 2016

SOURCES: 1986, 1991, 1996, 2001, 2006, 2011 (NHS) ET 2016 CANADIAN CENSUSES.

of female masters and officers is below the threshold set by Statistics Canada for each of the censuses, except in 1991, when there were 35 women masters and officers in Quebec (Please see Table 6.2 below).

TABLE 6.2 Number of individuals and proportions by gender and by type of occupation in the catching sector in Quebec and Gaspésie between 1986 and 2016

		Quebec			Gaspésie		
		Women	**Men**	**Total**	**Women**	**Men**	**Total**
1986	Masters and officers[a]	X	X	X	X	X	X
	Independent fishers[b]	240 *7,38%*	3010 *92,62%*	3 250 *100,00%*	65 *5,04%*	1225 *94,96%*	1 290 *100,00%*
	Deckhands[c]	310 *35,03%*	575 *64,97%*	885 *100,00%*	115 *32,39%*	240 *67,61%*	355 *100,00%*
	Total	550 *13,30%*	3585 *86,70%*	4 135 *100,00%*	180 *10,94%*	1465 *89,06%*	1 645 *100,00%*
1991	Masters and officers[a]	35 *9,21%*	345 *90,79%*	380 *100,00%*	X	X	X
	Independent fishers[b]	195 *8,11%*	2210 *91,89%*	2 405 *100,00%*	30 *3,43%*	845 *96,57%*	875 *100,00%*
	Deckhands[c]	205 *22,65%*	700 *77,35%*	905 *100,00%*	85 *19,10%*	360 *80,90%*	445 *100,00%*
	Total	435 11,79%	3255 88,21%	3 690 100,00%	115 8,71%	1205 91,29%	1 320 100,00%
1996	Masters and officers[a]	X	X	X	X	X	X
	Independent fishers[b]	180 *8,18%*	2020 *91,82%*	2 200 *100,00%*	60 *7,19%*	775 *92,81%*	835 *100,00%*
	Deckhands[c]	185 *24,83%*	560 *75,17%*	745 *100,00%*	50 *16,95%*	245 *83,05%*	295 *100,00%*
	Total	365 *12,39%*	2 580 *87,61%*	2 945 *100,00%*	110 *9,73%*	1020 *90,27%*	1 130 *100,00%*
2001	Masters and officers[a]	X	X	X	X	X	X
	Independent fishers[b]	240 *10,86%*	1970 *89,14%*	2 210 *100,00%*	65 *7,98%*	750 *92,02%*	815 *100,00%*
	Deckhands[c]	145 *16,67%*	725 *83,33%*	870 *100,00%*	40 *12,50%*	280 *87,50%*	320 *100,00%*
	Total	385 *12,50%*	2 695 *87,50%*	3 080 *100,00%*	105 *9,25%*	1030 *90,75%*	1 135 *100,00%*

TABLE 6.2 Number of individuals and proportions by gender and by type of occupation in the catching sector in Quebec and Gaspésie between 1986 and 2016 (*Cont.*)

		Quebec			Gaspésie		
		Women	Men	Total	Women	Men	Total
2006	Masters and officers[a]	X	X	X	X	X	X
	Independent fishers[b]	295 *13,88%*	1 830 *86,12%*	2 125 *100,00%*	110 *13,75%*	690 *86,25%*	800 *100,00%*
	Deckhands[c]	190 *18,72%*	825 *81,28%*	1 015 *100,00%*	45 *12,68%*	310 *87,32%*	355 *100,00%*
	Total	485 *15,45%*	2 655 *84,55%*	3 140 *100,00%*	155 *13,42%*	1000 *86,58%*	1 155 *100,00%*
2011	Masters and officers[a]	X	X	X	X	X	X
	Independent fishers[b]	155 *9,06%*	1 555 *90,94%*	1 710 *100,00%*	70 *10,14%*	620 *89,86%*	690 *100,00%*
	Deckhands[c]	45 *5,77%*	735 *94,23%*	780 *100,00%*	15 *4,92%*	290 *95,08%*	305 *100,00%*
	Total	200 8,03%	2 290 91,97%	2 490 100,00%	85 8,54%	910 91,46%	995 100,00%
2016	Masters and officers[a]	20 *5,06%*	375 *94,94%*	395 *100,00%*	X	X	X
	Independent fishers[b]	130 *9,81%*	1195 *90,19%*	1 325 *100,00%*	50 *11,90%*	370 *88,10%*	420 *100,00%*
	Deckhands[c]	110 *12,29%*	785 *87,71%*	895 *100,00%*	35 *11,48%*	270 *88,52%*	305 *100,00%*
	Total	260 *9,94%*	2 355 *90,06%*	2 615 *100,00%*	85 *11,72%*	640 *88,28%*	725 *100,00%*

a Fishing vessel masters and officers;
b Independent fishermen/women;
c Fishing vessel deckhands.

SOURCES: 1986, 1991, 1996, 2001, 2006, 2011 (NHS) ET 2016 CANADIAN CENSUSES

The proportion of women tends to be highest amongst deckhands (see Figure 6.4): the lowest paid and least qualified of the three occupations.

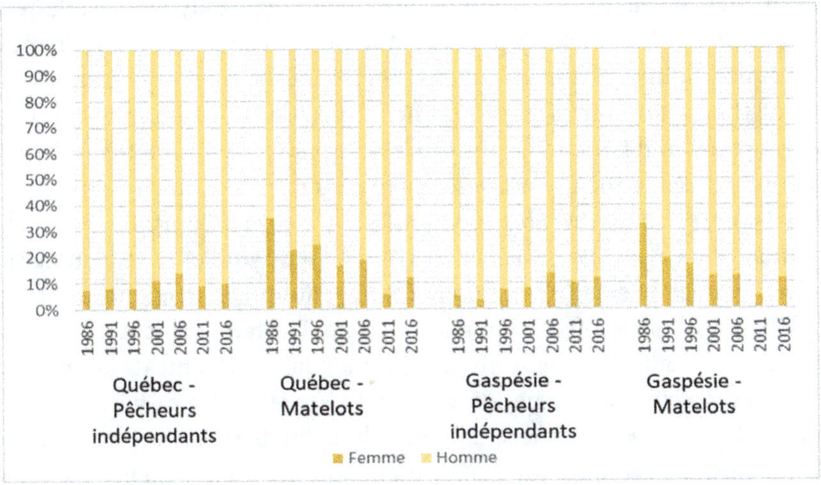

FIGURE 6.4 Distribution of workers in the fishing industry by gender and by type of occupation in the catching sector in Quebec and Gaspésie between 1986 and 2016

SOURCES: 1986, 1991, 1996, 2001, 2006, 2011 (NHS) ET 2016 CANADIAN CENSUSES.

This data indicates a certain segmentation of women in the catching labour market.[6]

The number of women masters and officers being too low for statistical analysis, we can only grasp trends in the gendered distribution of the workforce among independent fishers and deckhands. At the provincial level, the proportion of women among independent fishers is around 10% between 1986 and 2016, with a peak of 13% in 2006. The proportion of women among independent fishers in Gaspésie is lower than that of Quebec until 2006 but is then slightly higher than that of Quebec after 2006.

4 Women and Fishing: A Review of Scientific Literature

Although studies on the role of women in the fishing industry are relatively limited and tend over a very wide range of countries, there seems to be a

6 Our focus is on the catching sector of the fishing industry, therefore excluding the processing sector where women represent the majority of the workforce, but where wages are generally lower (CSMOPM, 2018).

consensus that women play an important albeit a generally less visible role in the industry. Fishing is characterised, at least formally, as a predominantly male occupation in which men not only represent the majority of the workforce, but they also occupy more significant positions. Women mostly hold supporting roles and tend to occupy the lowest-paid positions in the industry. Internationally, scientific literature tends to characterise women in the commercial fishing sector as invisible (Bennett, 2005; Deb et al., 2015; Harper et al., 2017; Koralagama et al., 2017; Zhao et al., 2013). Several studies have focused on the role of women in small-scale family fishing enterprises in countries of the "Global South" where, unlike in Canada and other Western countries, fishing is predominantly traditional and artisanal. Women in these contexts are mainly involved in the activities surrounding fishing, i.e. pre- and post-harvest activities, as well as in the domestic sphere of fishing families. In the case of West Africa, Bennet (2005) observes that "women are involved in many complex networks and alliances that enable them to negotiate access to fish and market successfully. There is thus a symbiotic relationship between the women and men in the fishing industry: neither could survive without the other" (Bennett, 2005, p. 453). Women are the main actors in the processing and marketing of maritime resources and, since they control these sectors, they have privileged access to credit to finance fishing activities (Bennett, 2005). In this context, fishing activities tend to be pre-financed by women. In India, on the island of Vypeenkara, a similar situation exists. Women have historically been responsible for processing, which includes sorting, butchering, salting and transporting catches, and selling the resource in local markets (post-harvest), but also for the acquisition and maintenance of some fishing equipment, such as making nets (pre-harvest) (Srinath, 1987). In a recent study on artisanal fisheries in Bangladesh, Deb and colleagues (2015) highlight a gendered division of labour in the fishing sector along water and land: women's contribution is on land, while men's contribution is mainly on the water (Deb et al., 2015). A similar gender division of labour is found in Mexico, Peru, Senegal, South Africa and Vietnam (Harper et al., 2017).

In the context of market globalisation, commercial fishing is increasingly part of global value chains, even in the countries of the "Global South". Harper and colleagues (2017), for example, highlight the vulnerability of women to these changes.

> This shift toward a global seafood market has potentially significant implications for women who have traditionally dominated small-scale fish processing and trade for local markets. With fish being increasingly processed and shipped abroad, women fish processors and traders have taken

> a considerable financial hit, as they are often unable to access these markets to sell their fish. (Wade et al., 1997, cited in Harper et al., 2017, p. 97).

As commercial fishing becomes more integrated into global markets, women seem to lose the primary role they used to play in more traditional and artisanal fisheries. There is a progressive exclusion or segmentation of women in specific occupations or labour markets where technology and/or capital are increasingly important. For example, in the case of fish processing (which we did not consider in our analysis), Harper et al. (2017) highlight how offshoring and automation in processing plants disproportionately affect women since they constitute the majority of the workforce in small local plants. Critical studies of globalisation processes have demonstrated how these structural economic changes (related to globalisation) affect women (Falquet, 2008; Falquet et al., 2010). Globalisation tends to transform gender relations and reinforce inequalities in particular sectors or contexts, for example, by pushing women into "care" related occupations (Lautier, 2006). However, evidence shows that women play an important role in new global economic structures, but that their work tends to be devalued. "Through their work, both in global cities and in circuits of survival, women, often devalued as economic actors, occupy crucial positions in the construction of new economies and the development of existing ones." (Sassen, 2003 cited in Hirata, 2005, p. 398, our translation)[7]

In countries of the "Global North", women's contribution to commercial fishing also tends to be defined as invisible or undervalued (Calhoun et al., 2016; Zhao et al., 2013), although the modalities of the division of labour may be different from those in the "Global South". In the "Global North", studies have focused mainly on women's contribution to the domestic sphere within fishing families. Research in "Global North" countries often focuses on small commercial fishing family enterprises, as in the case we studied in the Gaspésie region of the province of Quebec. Women's contribution in this sector is still mainly through the domestic sphere.

> The role of fisherman's wife in the home, taking care of the family and maritime household, is perhaps the most recognized role of women in the fishing sector. Although this role too has changed over time, in duties and precedence, one fisherman's wife claims, "The fundamentals of being a fisherman's wife have not changed." (Calhoun et al., 2016, p. 3)

---

7 "Par leur travail, tant dans les villes globales que dans les circuits de survie, les femmes, si souvent dévalorisées en tant qu'acteurs économiques, occupent des positions cruciales dans la construction des nouvelles économies et dans le développement de celles existantes."

Through the domestic sphere, women may be responsible for certain logistical activities, such as preparing meals for the fishing crew, distributing paycheques and transporting mechanical or technical equipment, as well as the accounting and administration of the fishing enterprise (Calhoun et al., 2016). These are all elements that we also found in our research in Gaspésie (Alberio, 2020; Alberio & Tremblay, 2020). Women's involvement in small fishing enterprises is often seen as an extension of their domestic responsibilities. They often do not have a formal employment status, even though they are responsible for specific tasks within the family business, such as accounting and administration, preparing meals for the crew and participating in official meetings on behalf of the fisher (Zhao et al., 2013, p. 73).

The restructuring of the fishing industry of several countries in recent decades, including the rationalisation of fishing fleets and the introduction of individual fishing quotas, has had a significant impact on small family enterprises, and, by extension, on the women who contribute to them (Davis & Gerrard, 2000; Neis et al., 2005), particularly by pushing women to seek formal employment to contribute financially to the family (and the enterprise).

> While money derived from catching and landing from the sea dwindled, many families had to seek a second income, in most cases, in shore-based sectors of the fisheries such as processing and trading, to make ends meet. As a result, many wives and partners have become significant second, or even first bread winners in the households (Zhao et al., 2013, p. 73).

As in countries of the "Global South", where women historically "can exhibit enabling and empowering roles, and be supportive of livelihood functions" (Deb et al., 2015, p. 3), the financial contribution of women in fishing families of the "Global North" is increasingly present and necessary (Alberio & Tremblay 2020). The contribution of women (and youth) is increasingly related to their influence on the dynamics of fishing businesses and their opportunities for employment and access to wealth from outside the business, affecting the resilience and sustainability of small-scale fishing enterprises (Neis et al., 2013). Furthermore, the search for more stable and "interesting" employment for a fisher's spouse can sometimes bring a fishing family to relocate (Gerrard, 2013), thus influencing local fishing territories and communities. Organising small fishing enterprises around the family and the domestic sphere, with the involvement of spouses (and children), offers a certain resilience to these enterprises. Structural changes in the industry pushing women (and children) to work outside the family enterprise affects their resilience (Neis et al., 2013; Alberio, 2020).

Changes in the fishing profession and the fishing industry more broadly have, to a certain extent, pushed away women from the catching sector, rather than formalising their role. It is therefore understandable that the fishing sector, whether in the "Global South" or the "Global North", still shows a significantly gendered division of labour. Men still almost exclusively undertake fishing activities at sea, while women's contribution is on land and still tends to be informal and less visible. Some researchers have tried to identify some of the barriers preventing women from becoming more directly involved in catching activities. Mertens de Wilmars (2017) gives the example of a small fishing community in Spain where fishing permits were explicitly reserved exclusively for men until the early 2000s, where the right to fish was transferred from father to son, de facto excluded women. Even if in most cases, such as in Canada, this kind of formal exclusion of daughters in the succession of family fishing rights does not exist, in practice, as we will observe in our case study, a model of succession from father to son seems to prevail. Mertens de Wilmars (2017) acknowledges "the persistence of material and symbolic male power" that affects the social structure and power relations within the fishing community he studied (Mertens de Wilmars, 2017, p. 74, our translation).[8]

The main obstacles that women face in the catching sector are related to finding a first boat to work on, the lack of appropriate infrastructure for women on boats, intimidation and harassment from other workers, and the persistence of cultural taboos (Zhao et al., 2013). Living and working conditions on fishing vessels are, as we will also observe in our case study, structured around a male-dominated workforce. Women must, therefore, show a high degree of flexibility and adapting to these conditions is a sort of "test" for women who wish to enter this occupation (Zhao et al., 2013). A common example is the sharing of a single sleeping quarter for all crew members, whether male or female. Men tend to explain women's withdrawal from this type of work with the fact that it is physically demanding. However, women's experiences tend to point to the conditions on board fishing vessels and the negative attitudes and behaviours caused by a male-dominated culture. Women may be subject to sexual harassment and cultural taboos on board. They may also face intimidation from their male colleagues or be the subject of jokes and sarcasm (Zhao et al., 2013). Finally, the lack of recognition by public policies of the systemic exclusion of women from the catching sector reinforces acts as an additional challenge (Harper et al., 2017; Koralagama et al., 2017; Zhao et al., 2013). "An overall lack of attention to gender dimensions in fisheries policy

8 "la persistance d'un pouvoir masculin de nature matérielle et symbolique"

and management may be compromising the outcomes of valuable efforts to rebuild fisheries and to improve the livelihoods and well-being of all those in fishing communities." (Harper et al., 2017, p. 92) The structure and model for public consultations within fisheries are so that they are mainly directed at men in the catching sector or the management of the industry. Women's voices are not taken into account in these consultations, and by extension, are not reflected in public policy (Zhao et al., 2013).

Women involved in family fishing businesses generally take care of very specific tasks, such as the accounting and administration of the business (e.g., making sure the business respects the regulations put forth by regulatory bodies, etc.). Given the increase in regulation in the industry in recent years (Alberio, 2020; Alberio & Lucia, in press; Alberio & Tremblay, 2020), their role is increasingly important, although not always recognised. Despite making an important contribution to the sector through their involvement in these fishing enterprises, their decision-making power is often limited.

Studies in the "Global North" have also raised the issue of women's presence in the fishing industry outside the catching sector (Neis et al., 2013; Calhoun et al., 2016). Women are active in the processing sector and, increasingly, in other high skilled fishing sectors. Some women from fishing families who decide to become involved in the fishing sector may not necessarily go into the catching sector, but rather seek jobs in management, training, marketing and research (Neis et al., 2013; Calhoun et al., 2016). In territorial contexts characterised by the mono-industry of fishing, young women who decide to make their way in the field often do so in sectors other than catching. However, their decision-making power is still limited. For example, in the seafood sales sector:

> More women are found holding administrative positions, some as office administrators with significant responsibilities in helping the daily operation of the organisations, and some responsible for data entry and other clerical tasks. Compared with managers and directors, these women have less influence in policy making (Zhao et al., 2013, p. 74).

5 Methodology

The empirical research underlying this article was conducted using qualitative methods, specifically semi-structured interviews and focus groups. Semi-structured interviews make it possible to collect data on professional experiences and practices from a micro-sociological perspective. We used a comprehensive approach (Gherghel, 2013; Grossetti, 2006; Demazière, 1995), without limiting our questions to retrospection (the past). Our questions were also related to present and future experiences.

Our methodological objective was to analyse the careers of captain-owners, taking as a starting point the experiences of the individuals themselves (Dubet, 1995). An interview grid organised around different themes, formulated as general questions, was used to conduct the interviews. If necessary, we guided the discussion with more specific questions to focus on the key elements and moments in the captain-owner's career, professional practices and enterprise.

We interviewed more than 40 captain-owners and fishing vessel captains. Please note that their citations are indicated as CP which stands for the French work "Capitaine propriétaire" (Captain owner). The selection of participants was carried out using multi-case sampling within micro-social units. This form of sampling is appropriate for research on life experiences, institutions and social practices. In this case, we wanted to understand actors' positions, roles and the functioning of an institution (the family fishing enterprise), through narratives on individual experiences (Pirès, 1997). Two fundamental criteria also guided our sampling: diversification and saturation (Bertaux, 1980; Pirès, 1997). In our case, we looked for intra-group diversification. We aimed to understand the experiences of a small and relatively homogeneous group, that of fishing captain-owners. The sample was diversified based on age (45 and under, 46 to 55, 56 and over), length of fishing experience (under and over 15 years of experience), gender (although the majority of the sample is made up of men), geographical position (municipality of residence), family status (in a stable relationship or single, with or without children) and type of fishery (crab, shrimp and groundfish).[9]

When spouses and/or children were also involved in the fishing enterprise, individual interviews were also conducted with them. We interviewed a total of 25 spouses (whose citations are indicated as C which stands for "conjoint", meaning spouse in French) and 20 sons and daughters, mostly sons (whose citations are identified with a R which stands for "Relève" that means successor in French).

The more than 85 interviews were transcribed verbatim in order to carry out thematic content analysis. We then ranked and classified each interview fragment within our central themes, or within related, complementary or

9 We selected captain-owners in the crab, shrimp and/or groundfish fisheries. These fisheries differ from one another in terms of economic profitability, as well as technical (type of fishing equipment, type of fishing vessel, fishing techniques, etc.) and temporal characteristics (duration of fishing trips, durations of fishing season, etc.).

divergent themes (Paillé & Mucchielli, 2012, p. 237). This analysis led to identifying different trajectories and experiences and relating them to overlying macro-level structures and issues (e.g., cultural, social, political, environmental, etc.).

Before conducting individual interviews, we conducted two focus groups with approximately ten participants each: three stakeholders at the institutional level (a representative of the *Association des capitaines-propriétaires de la Gaspésie* (ACPG) [The Gaspésie captain-owners' association] and two government representatives from Quebec's *Ministère de l'Agriculture, des Pêcheries et de l'Alimentation* (MAPAQ) [Ministry of Agriculture, Fisheries and Food] and Fisheries and Oceans Canada (DFO)); three experts, for example researchers from the DFO's Maurice Lamontagne Institute; and three captain-owners. These focus groups allowed us to identify macro-level elements (institutional, legal, economic, social, environmental, etc.) likely to influence captain-owners' careers, practices and professional status.

6 "A Country for (old) Men"? Representations of the Required Skills

6.1 *Ambition, Growth and Overcoming Challenges*

Among captain-owners, and more broadly among fishers, the collective imaginary and the representations of the skills necessary for fishing are built around certain values and stereotypes traditionally associated with men. Even if today fishing is no longer as competitive as it was in the past, mainly because of the allocation of individual fishing quotas which means that fishers do not have to compete with each other for a part of the global fishing quota,[10] there is still a competitive spirit among fishers. Participants in our interviews often defined a "good" fishing captain as ambitious. A good fishing captain lands

10 "The principle of Total Allowable Catches (TACs or global quotas), which defines the total volume of catches that can be landed within a specific fishery, has existed for several years. One of the first measures consisted in limiting access to the resource through fishing licences. This measure limited fishing effort and reduced competition. The second major transformation was the introduction, in the 1980s, of individual allocations (or "individual quotas"), where each licence holder is allocated a portion of the TAC. The aim was to reduce catching over capacity and eliminate the "race for fish". Individual allocation of groundfish quotas in the Atlantic region were based on principles of equity, proximity to the resource (coastal communities), the relative dependence of communities on the fishery, profitability and fleet mobility. The distribution of individual allocations among fishers within the fishery is usually a reflection of the fisher's historical volume of catches." (Alberio & Brêthes, in press, our translation)

large quantities at a time and fishes his quota quickly. Some referred to a sense of satisfaction when their boat is filled with fish. Although the official discourse of the industry focuses on sustainable fishing and a decrease in quantity in favour of a better quality of the product, the narrative of accumulation and quantity is still very much present among fishing captains when defining their profession.

> That's it, you're ambitious. And yes, we have individual quotas and all that, but it's our ambition that drives us to bring back fish. When you come back with your boat, with the hold full, you're happy. (R15)[11]
>
> Like it or not, the job of a fisher is... You have to go and you have to put as much as you can in the hold, so we're driven by ambition all the time. It's not like the one who works, let's say in an office, he's paid from 8 to 4, he gets his salary, when he's done his week, he has something to provide at the end of the week. But when we leave land, it's not from 8 to 4, it's for 24 hours a day, for 16 days at a time. (CP18)

Many captains highlight the challenge of catching fish as one of the dimensions of the job that they appreciate the most. They describe a sense of "hunting" for fish, especially in the groundfish and cod fisheries. They feel a sense of excitement when they see fish appear in their sonar after having chased it.

> Especially when fishing with the longline, for example, when fishing halibut [Atlantic halibut], I would say that it is my favourite type of fishing. It is really challenging. You mount the fish one by one on the boat. You see them come up one by one. It's motivating. (R22)
>
> There's no feeling in the world like when you're trawling and you're chasing fish, and you finally see fish on the sonar, so you know that you're finally in the right place. You know what time of day it is, you've still got a couple of days to go, or a couple of hours to go ... All these calculations, it's a challenge. You've understood or figured out something that others haven't. And it's not written anywhere, but it's there, you've figured it out, and you pass it on to your son. It gives you pleasure. I'm telling you, it's huge, it's a huge feeling! (CP07)

Ambition in terms of catching fish is not enough. Captain-owners also highlight the importance of entrepreneurial ambition (the desire to expand their

11 All interviews were conducted in French. The citations in this article were originally in French, but translated to English for the purpose of this article.

business). For some captain-owners, such an entrepreneurial vision takes precedence over that of the fisher. Several captains use the metaphor of the marine ecosystem to describe the business or industry ecosystem; bigger and stronger businesses thrive, while smaller and weaker business slowly disappear, just like bigger fish feed on smaller fish in the ocean. It should be noted that objectively, the catching sector in Eastern Quebec is still predominantly made up of small or medium-sized family businesses with an allocated individual fishing quota. "The boats [enterprises] that survive, it's because they merge with another business or because they expand. Fishing is increasingly harder, as a business either you get bigger, or you are eaten up. It's going to be one of the two." (R02)

This type of discourse based on competition is more typical of male sectors, for example, in finance. There is no consensus in research on the existence of gender-differentiated management practices. However, some research seems to show that in certain sectors, or in particular contexts, men and women will have different attitudes towards their profession. Constantinidis (2010), who studied women business managers in France, identified four typologies. Of these four typologies of women entrepreneurs, two show entrepreneurial attitudes that differ more from their male counterparts. For example, concerning business growth and expansion, which we discuss here, some women entrepreneurs claim that they have "more limited growth objectives, would develop better relations with their staff and clients, [and] would be more oriented towards the administrative management of the business" (Constantinidis, 2010, p. 134, our translation).[12] Some women also claim to be

> more creative, more conciliatory in their relationships, closer to their employees and customers, more cautious in their decision making, and more focused on taking pleasure in their work rather than the growth of the business. Alternatively, they see male entrepreneurs as more hierarchal in relation to their employees, more direct and aggressive in their relations with customers and suppliers, taking more risks and favouring business development and profit." (Constantinidis, 2010, pp. 136–137, our translation)[13]

12 "des objectifs de croissance plus limités, développeraient de meilleures relations avec leur personnel et leurs clients, seraient plus tournées vers la gestion administrative de l'entreprise"

13 "plus créatives, plus conciliantes dans leurs relations, plus proches de leurs employés et de leurs clients, plus prudentes dans la prise de décision, et privilégiant le plaisir de travailler plutôt que la croissance de l'entreprise. Alternativement, elles voient les hommes entrepreneurs comme plus directifs par rapport à leurs employés, plus incisifs et agressifs dans

Similar observations have been made in the "Global South", where female entrepreneurship is based on economic activities of subsistence (Vossenberg, 2013) embedded in local communities. In these activities, women acknowledge that they have a responsibility towards their local living environment (Guérin, 2002), which mitigates the entrepreneurial spirit of growth. One could argue that such a phenomenon might also be found in the local economies of the "Global North".

Another important challenge faced by fishers is the unpredictability of the ocean, the resource, the industry, etc. Each fishing trip and even each workday can be very different from the previous one. Work rhythm is often dictated by nature (e.g., storms and bad weather) but also by institutional decisions and regulations (e.g., fishing area closures, etc.).

> We never know what's happening. It's never the same. There's never an hour that's the same as the hour before it. (R10.2)
>
> I wouldn't be able to work on land, it's hard working 40 hours a week all year round. We're in nature, on the water. We never have the same day twice. We never know what to expect, and that's the "fun". (R31)

Fishers and fishing captains seem to appreciate unpredictability in their work since it is an additional challenge to overcome, but this forces wives(women) to play a decisive role in facing the unexpected and being resilient. Although the situation has changed, with a generally more equitable sharing of domestic labour within young families, spouses still seem to bear more of the burden of family organisation and domestic labour than their husbands in fishing families (Alberio & Tremblay, 2020). For a woman fisher wanting to reconcile family and work today, the challenges related to unpredictability are an important issue. The unpredictability of the occupation is, therefore, a structural obstacle for women fishers, rather than a positive characteristic that makes the work less routine, as presented to us by the current male captains and fishers.

6.2 *Courage*

The captain-owners and fishing captains we met also emphasised courage as a necessary characteristic in their work. For example, courage is necessary when making choices related to the business, but also when facing bad weather and storms when at sea. Captains have a responsibility towards their crew. They have to protect their crew and keep their composure while making sure that the

leurs relations avec les clients et fournisseurs, prenant plus de risques et privilégiant le développement de l'entreprise et le profit."

boat will return to the dock with enough catch for the fishing trip to have been profitable. The captain is the ultimate authority on board the fishing vessel and is responsible for the safety and protection of the crew. According to the narratives collected, a "good" captain looks after the well-being of "his men".

> A good captain-owner is someone who brings his men back to shore safe and sound. Their safety is very important. I often say that my most important cargo on board is my men. It's not the fish. When I leave the quay with my men, I have to be able to bring them back to shore. (CP16)
>
> I went into Anticosti [Island] at one point with my boat. We were hit by a storm, it was a storm that hit us hard. We went into a kind of small bay that was behind us, in a corner of the island. One of my men was crying, "what if we get lost". I said, "Don't worry, we won't get lost. I know where to go". We went inside the boat, we dropped anchor, and waited. [...] You have to still like the job during these situations. At the fishing school, the teachers showed us how to manage these situations. But you still have to have this instinct inside of you. (CP17)

The captain-owner and fishing captain is represented as a business and professional figure in the industry and on the boat. He also must have humane skills to manage every type of situation that may arise while at sea. Following these discourses, he has to show strength, confidence, but also calm. Captain-owners, especially those part of the older generation, evoke the image of the "good father" responsible for the protection of his family in their narratives. In the event of a crisis, he must remain calm and react thoughtfully to solve the problem. He should never be impulsive. "Calmness, I think that is the basis for being a good captain. Or at least give the impression of calmness and of being in control of the situation when there is a problem. Apart from that, it's like any other job. But calmness is key" (R16).

We are not suggesting that women do not have the qualities and characteristics, such as calmness, required to be a "good" captain-owner. We do however want to highlight how the narratives on how to be a good fishing captain are still structured around qualities and characteristics traditionally associated with men, based on male stereotypes, like ambition, calmness, courage, quick decision-making and physical strength.

6.3 *Physical Strength*

Finally, physical strength is very common in the narratives on the qualities and characteristics needed to become a captain-owner. Many captains consider fishing too physically difficult of an occupation for women. However, there have been some changes over the generations. Younger fishing captains are, at least they claim to be, more open to the idea that their daughters may one day become captains and take over their fishing business. Captains also point out that some fisheries may be more "adapted" to women. For example, they suggest that lobster or crab fishing might be more appropriate for women since they tend to be less physically demanding and are closer to shore (requiring shorter fishing trips, usually less than 24h), yet remain highly profitable and show no sign of a decline in stocks.

> My daughters, they never considered going into fishing. In those days, it was rare to see women on board a boat. Today, boats are better equipped. There is a shower, there's everything on board. Then there's the new technology. As a captain, you sit there and you control everything from your cabin. Even a woman can do that. I don't want to come off as backward thinking but working on the deck is more physical. You have to go into the hold. We might catch a thousand pounds of fish, and two hours later catch another thousand pounds of fish. On deck, you have to work with the fish, pick it up, then offload it at the port. Some women can do it, but some wouldn't like it. Nowadays, we can no longer say that a woman won't be able to do this job physically. If she can steer a boat, if she knows the boat, and is not sick at sea, she can do this job. I don't see why she shouldn't be able to. (CP31)
>
> Well, we see it more and more in our industry, a daughter who took over the business of her father. I think it's beautiful. It means that there are boats, there are several boats, that women captain or fish on. Maybe not that many still, but compared to before … (CP8)

6.4 *A Feeling of Freedom* (*and Its Limits*)

Another valued characteristic of the profession is the feeling of freedom at sea. "For me, being at sea is a quest for freedom. A lot of fishers like that feeling of freedom, feeling the clean air and the great outdoors" (CP05). Going out to sea is often described as a way of isolating oneself, escaping the accelerated pace of life in society on land and taking refuge in nature and its wide-open spaces (Alberio & Lucia, 2020). Fishers also highlight how the rhythm of the sea shapes their professional practices. When they are at sea, the sea imposes its rhythm. This narrative seems to portray stereotypical images of fishing in the same way the profession might have been portrayed in film and literature.

> My God! Yes! Yes! On land, we are in a world where everything is fast [...]. When we let go our lines from the quay, we take a big sigh of relief and leave! It's not the same on water, it's not the same rhythm of life. On the water, it's calm, it's a kind of freedom. (CP25)

Captains also mention being free of all social relationships once they are on the water. At sea, captains are alone with their crew on a fishing vessel. They feel a sense of freedom within that solitude. "It's a freedom that you can't experience anywhere else. There's no one to watch us. That's what I like" (CP8).

This vision contrasts, at least in part, with the reality within the catching sector, with significant obstacles and constraints imposed by nature and the environment (e.g., storms, weather conditions, protected wildlife) and regulatory institutions (e.g., regulations, surveillance, administrative and bureaucratic requirements). These obstacles and constraints weigh heavily on the careers and professional experiences of captain-owners both on board the ship and on land (Alberio, 2020; Alberio & Lucia, 2020; Alberio & Tremblay, 2020). When digging deeper into this narrative of freedom while at sea, it becomes clear that this divide between work and life at sea and on land is less clear-cut than originally described. Captains recognise that administrative business requirements and increasing institutional regulation and control are ever more central to their work and the enterprise in general, both at sea and on land.

The contribution of spouses is often essential for overcoming these obstacles and fulfilling these requirements. A captain's wife says:

> When you work full time, but you have a thick pile of papers waiting for you on your desk when you get home at night, it's not always fun. Or for my family to see me working on a Saturday, taking care of all that paperwork, updating the books, sending reports, make sure that suppliers are paid, make sure that taxes are paid, that payroll is done on time... It has an impact on the family. (C18)

These tasks and skills (e.g., accounting, administrative) are essential for fishing enterprises but are seldom mentioned as characteristics required to be a "good" fishing captain. As seen in the scientific literature on the subject, these tasks, related to the business, are often performed by women (mainly spouses) as an extension of the domestic responsibilities and tasks (Alberio & Tremblay, 2020). Since these tasks are generally carried out by women, they are not part of the narratives on the skills needed to be a captain-owner or fishing captain. The support of spouses within family fishing enterprises becomes, paradoxically, one of the barriers preventing them from becoming captains. Women's skills and characteristics, although necessary in the sector, never become an integral and valued part of the narrative on the skills required to be a "good" captain, because spouses, in any case, consistently provide them informally. In affirming this, however, we want to reject any approach that blames women themselves for this situation.[14]

7 Is Access to the Profession More Difficult for Women?[15]

One of the themes explored in this project was career choice (i.e., the mechanisms leading fishers and captains to choose a career in fishing). Fishing is less often described as a choice, but more as an innate calling. Many describe a deep desire to be on the water that dates back to birth and childhood. This feeling of innateness is linked to the nature of family fishing enterprises and the socialisation of children (mainly sons) in these families to fishing life (Alberio, 2020). However, this process of socialisation is taking place at a later age among the younger generation. For example, captains currently retired (aged between 60 and 70) might have been introduced to the fishing trade around the ages of 8–10, but they introduced their own children to fishing at a later age, around the beginning of adolescence. One young captain-owner says: "Fishing always "matched" for me. In high school, even in elementary school, I used to go on fishing trips. After high school, I went to fishing school. Whether to become a fisher or not was a question I never asked myself, becoming a fisher was simply the way that it was" (R2.2). Furthermore, in a context where certified vocational training is increasingly valued (and sometimes mandatory) for practising this trade, the age of socialisation into the fishing trade tends to increase with future generations.

If socialisation into fishing life from a young age plays a fundamental role in choosing this profession, not all the children (and more specifically sons) of a captain-owners become fishers. "My sons have tried fishing. One fished for one year, one summer, and realised he didn't like it" (C17).

Women have been, and often still are, discouraged by family members from becoming fishers, even though as children they may have been socialised to fishing life through their upbringing and by accompanying their fathers on fishing trips. In many families, women are still strongly associated with the

---

14 Some feminist theory cautions against holding women themselves responsible for their predicament, or "blaming the victim".

15 Some of the citations and paragraphs in this section were taken from Alberio (2020).

role of motherhood, and the fishing profession is described as being difficult to reconcile with the traditional role of motherhood. A captain-owner's spouse relates what her husband used to say to their daughter (now in her thirties): "It's hard, dear, it's hard for a girl to fish. You always say that I was never around when you were young. How are you going to feel when you have children of your own, it will be the same problem" (C24).

In cases when more than one child wishes to take over the fishing business, the decision of which child will take over the business is often made by the family as a whole. It is rarely the captain-owner himself who makes this decision on his own. There is often a family discussion, and the decision might depend on the family's particular situation or other external factors:

> [One of my sons] had tried to buy a boat from a guy who was selling his business, but finally, an already established captain-owner who was "bigger" than him [with an already established business and access to more capital] outbid him. So he said, "Dad, you've got to sell me the boat!" The other brothers all agreed that I should sell it to him. (CP29)

Daughters tend to be excluded or to exclude themselves from this negotiation within the family because they are generally less socialised into fishing as a career, even if they were brought up in a fishing household and introduced to fishing activities as children just like their brothers. Some daughters of fishers might continue to contribute to their father's or their spouse's fishing business in the same way that they would have seen their mom do in the past (e.g., accounting and administrative tasks). Daughters might be more socialised into taking on this type of role, more than that of fisher or captain-owner.

There were three women fishers in our sample: two were spouses that started fishing with their husbands who were captain-owners, one of which ended up buying a boat of her own and becoming captain-owner, and a third who was a daughter of a captain-owner and succeeded her father in the family business. Although the women fishers we interviewed did not speak of hostility as such, they pointed out a certain lack of openness on behalf of their male colleagues to accept them: "There are some men who cannot accept that there is a woman on board. [...] A woman should be home cooking your eggs, your bacon, cleaning the house" (R42, a woman captain-owner).

As with newcomers in general in the industry (fishers not born into fishing families), female captains and fishers are changing the status quo. Their arrival and presence creates tensions and brings changes to the social fishing system. Fishers and captains are adaptive, because of the nature of the industry, and open to technical and technological innovations. However, they seem generally reluctant to changes in social and professional norms.

> When I bought my first boat, most people I talked to said: "You're going to fall and break your face!" [...] Well, it was true. I had a lot of hardship, some of it was just "bad luck". I even thought of stopping sometimes. But, no, I didn't! There was always a voice inside of me telling me: "Look, you've got nothing to lose by continuing!" I kept on going, and over the years the situation stabilised itself. The company got stronger and more stable. (CP1)

The importance of family socialisation into fishing makes it difficult for newcomers to access the field, and to thrive once they are in it. In fact, all of the newcomers that we met, although their fathers weren't fishers, had at least one family member or very close acquaintance working as a fisher or a captain (e.g., an uncle, a grandfather, a close neighbour, a spouse) leading to a form of socialisation into the profession, albeit to a lesser extent than if their fathers were fishers.

Even if today the industry is more open to newcomers than it might have been in the past, a lack of socialisation into the trade is still an important barrier. The profession of captain-owner specifically is still primarily passed on from father to son, and any form of deviation from this model is still perceived and felt as a disruption of the norm.

Like the male newcomer to the industry, the female fisher or captain disrupts the status quo and "has to prove herself" before being taken seriously by her counterparts. Following this discourse, she must take her place and prove that she has the necessary skills and physical capacity to do the job. The female fisher or captain does not only have to demonstrate that she has the skills and the capacity to do the job like any other fisher. She also needs to prove and show, more generally, that women have their place on a boat. She is put to the test even more so than her male counterparts because of her gender. The young female captain-owner we interviewed relates her experience when succeeding her father in the fishing business:

> Maybe it was more difficult because I am a woman. Or maybe it was because other captains would have liked to buy dad's fishing licence to expand their own business, they would have liked to get rid of my dad's business altogether. But I was already in the industry, fishing with my

> dad. I decided to go straight ahead, to continue. It hasn't always been a pretty picture. (R42)

Women captain-owners are less likely to be taken seriously by their male counterparts at the beginning of their careers. For example, their voice and opinion might not be taken as seriously during captain-owners' association meetings or consultation committees. A captain-owner's spouse who went on to becoming a captain-owner of her own relates:

> The hardest part was during meetings, during consultation committees. You get a funny look from the other. You know that they're thinking: "She's only there because she's an informal licence holder for her husband. He already had too many licences, so she put her name on this new licence. She's nothing more than a figurehead." [...] I was seen like that. When you're feeling embarrassed, you don't talk too much at these meetings. It took a while before it came out in my case. It took another captain to push me, he said: "Hey, if you don't talk, no one is going to talk for you. Take your place!" So I took my place! (CP38)

Regulation of fishing licences makes access to the profession of captain-owner even more difficult16. When a spouse becomes herself a captain-owner, the presumption within the professional community (and within the local community of small fishing villages in general) is that she is nothing more than a figurehead so that her spouse can access licences that he would have otherwise been prohibited from buying himself because of current regulations. The reactions can be harsh and may have a significant impact on the professional experiences of these women, especially in the first years as captain, which are fundamental for establishing the business.

> In that meeting where I finally took my place and spoke, I was no longer perceived as the woman who was there simply as a figurehead for her husband's licences. I had proven that I was the true operator of the licences, that I was a real captain, and that I spoke in my own name. (CP38)

In the original French version, this citation shows even more, by the use of masculine nouns, how this woman identifies herself as captain in masculine terms.

When considering social relations in this profession, it is important to look at informal socialisation and moments of camaraderie between captains and between captains and their crew. Although ships are more comfortable today, for example, in newer boats, captains often have their own sleeping quarter that is separate from that of the crew, space is still limited on a boat, and crew members and the captain tend to share tight living spaces (e.g., for showering, for eating, for resting, for socialising). During fishing trips, crewmembers and the captain are not only work colleagues, but they also live together. A captain-owner describes the living situation on board and some of the changes he has made so that crewmembers are more comfortable:

> This is the new and improved kitchen that we renovated. The guys sleep over there. That used to be a shared room for all of us, but I now have my own room on the deck. It's comfortable, and it's bigger than some other boats. But believe me, after a month and a half, it feels very small! (R07)

A fishing crew shares a very small space (that of the fishing boat) for several days, sometimes weeks. If not adequately adapted, it could be difficult to share such a restricted space with individuals of the opposite sex. Previous studies have shown how the lack of adaptation of the physical infrastructure is an important obstacle to the integration of women on fishing boats (Zhao et al., 2013).

Moreover, in this context of physical proximity between individuals on board, a certain camaraderie forms over time. "We do about 50 hours of work per week because we don't work in the evenings. In the afternoon, we stop working. We take a shower and then play videogames together in the evening" (CP40).

This type of informal sociability is inevitable when sharing such a tight work and living space. One could argue that it makes the situation, living and working on a boat, more bearable. Many captain-owners highlighted how they aim to make sure that all crew members have a good time together and get along when on the boat, both while working and outside of work, because everything else would make the situation unbearable. However, this traditionally male camaraderie, which is typical of the fishing trade, might act as a barrier for women wanted to enter the trade. It might be difficult for a woman to penetrate and integrate this informal male camaraderie, consequently preventing her from integrating the profession in general.

8 Conclusion

The aim of this book chapter was to show the mechanisms at play in the catching sector of the fishing industry that tend to undervalue women's work, assigning them secondary and often invisible roles, and that act as barriers to women's access to other roles. Our analysis is based on a review of the international scientific literature and our own original data (both quantitative and qualitative) from a research project in Gaspésie, Quebec. Previous studies on the role of women in the fishing industry describe an involvement that is often less formally recognised than that of their male counterparts, but still fundamental for the industry on several levels. Women are present in the sector, but their contribution is less visible or valued. Scientific literature, specifically focusing on countries of the "Global North", emphasises women's involvement in the sector through their contribution in small family fishing enterprises (which represent the majority of fishing enterprises in Gaspésie) which are often perceived as an extension of the domestic sphere. Our statistical data on fishers in Gaspésie and Quebec, in general, shows that women are marginal in the formal labour market in the catching sector.

Our qualitative analysis of the narrative around what it means to be a "good" captain-owner shows that the main values and skills identified as necessary tend to correspond to traditionally male stereotypes, such as ambition, calmness, courage, quick decision-making and physical strength. Cultural "taboos" on what it means to be a woman or a man and the current representation of what it means to be a "good" captain in the collective professional imaginary act as obstacles to gender diversity on fishing boats. Furthermore, when describing their occupation, fishers and captains refer to the unpredictability of daily life on the water and unpredictability in the fishing industry in general. While this unpredictability is often perceived as a positive and attractive feature of the job by current male fisher and captains, it may make it more difficult for newcomers to the trade, especially women, to balance work and family life. This unpredictability acts as another barrier for women. Finally, the catching sector and the fishing industry in small fishing communities tend to be particularly "insular". The traditional model of transmission from father to son is still the norm, and any form of deviation from this model is sometimes perceived as a disruption or rupture. Just like the male newcomer in the industry, who does not come from a fishing family, women entering the field change the status quo.

The need to "prove oneself" towards colleagues and to gain experience over time is typical for any trade. However, in the catching sector, sons of fishers seem to boaster inherent credibility within the professional community, due to the heritage left to them by their fathers, whereas newcomers and women tend to undergo more scrutiny on behalf of their colleagues. Furthermore, the size of the environment (generally small fishing villages) influences, both positively and negatively, these social relations. "Everyone knows everyone", so when a newcomer or a woman enters the fishery, others find about it, they might have an opinion of that person, and might scrutinise that person's work more easily. Taking one's place and proving they have the necessary skills to carry out the trade is therefore not always easy for young fishers and captains, especially when they are women. This context within the professional community and fishing communities acts as an additional barrier for women. As other authors have also pointed out, the recognition of these structural barriers by public policy officials and local development actors would be the first step towards gender diversification on fishing boats.

References

Alberio, M., & Brêthes, J.-C. (submitted). La gestion des pêches au Canada: un état de l'art [Fisheries management in Canada: a state of the art]. *Interventions économiques/Papers in Political Economy.*

Alberio, M., & Lucia, E. (in press). Ricerca del profitto e protezione dell'ambiente. Un binomio possibile? Il caso delle piccole imprese del settore della pesca in Québec, Canada [Seeking profit and protecting the environment. A possible combination? The case of small fishing enterprises in Quebec, Canada]. *Meridiana*, 98.

Alberio, M. (2020). Un métier en transformation, mais encore significatif dans la ruralité côtière québécoise : le cas de la pêche et de sa relève en Gaspésie [An occupation undergoing transformations, but still significant in Quebec's rural coastal regions: the case of the fishing industry and its succession in Gaspésie]. *Revue Organisations & Territoires*, 29(1), 53–64. https://doi.org/10.1522/revueot.v29n1.1126

Alberio, M., & Tremblay, D.-G. (2020). Conciliation travail-famille dans un secteur mature mais en transformation. Le cas de la pêche dans l'Est du Québec [Work-family balance in a mature but changing sector. The case of the fishing sector in Eastern Quebec]. In D.-G. Tremblay & S. Soussi (Eds.), *Le travail à l'épreuve des nouvelles temporalités* (pp. 83–118). Québec: Presses de l'Université du Québec.

Bennett, E. (2005). Gender, fisheries and development. *Marine Policy*, 29(5), 451–459. https://doi.org/10.1016/j.marpol.2004.07.003

Bertaux, D. (1980). L'approche biographique, sa validité méthodologique, ses potentialités [The biographical approach, its methodological validity, its potentiality]. *Cahiers internationaux de sociologie*, LXIX(2), 198–225.

Calhoun, S., Conway, F., & Russell, S. (2016). Acknowledging the voice of women: implications for fisheries management and policy. *Marine Policy*, 74, 292–299. https://doi.org/10.1016/j.marpol.2016.04.033

Constantinidis, C. (2010). Représentations sur le genre et réseaux d'affaires chez les femmes entrepreneures [Gender Representations and Business Networks among

Women Entrepreneurs]. *Revue française de gestion*, 202(3), 127–143. https://doi.org/10.3166/RFG.202.127-143

CSMOPM – Comité sectoriel de main-d'œuvre des pêches maritimes. (2018). *Diagnostic sectoriel dans l'industrie des pêches et de l'aquaculture au Québec* [Sectoral analysis of the fishing and aquaculture industry in Quebec]. Québec: Comité sectoriel de main-d'œuvre des pêches maritimes, 109 p.

Davis, D., & Gerrard, S. (2000). Introduction: Gender and resource crisis in the North Atlantic fisheries. *Women's Studies International Forum*, 23(3), 279–286. https://doi.org/10.1016/S0277-5395(00)00086-8

Deb, A. K., Haque, C. E., & Thompson, S. (2015). 'Man can't give birth, woman can't fish': gender dynamics in the small-scale fisheries of Bangladesh. *Gender, Place & Culture*, 22(3), 305–324. https://doi.org/10.1080/0966369X.2013.855626

Demazière, D. (2003). Matériaux qualitatifs et perspective longitudinale. La temporalité des parcours professionnels saisis par les entretiens biographiques [Qualitative data and a longitudinal perspective. The temporality of the career paths captured by the biographical interviews]. In *10es journées d'étude du Céreq: «Les données longitudinales dans l'analyse du marché du travail»* (pp. 75–89). Caen: LASMAS-CEREQ.

Dubet, F. (1994). *Sociologie de l'expérience*. Paris: Seuil.

Falquet, J. (2008). *De gré ou de force. Les femmes dans la mondialisation*. Paris: La Dispute.

Falquet, J., Hirata, H., Kergoat, D., Labari, B., Le Feuvre, N., & Sow, F. (2010). *Le sexe de la mondialisation. Genre, classe, race et nouvelle division du travail*. Paris: Les Presses de Sciences Po.

Gerrard, S. (2013). Mobilities, materialities, and masculinities: Interconnected mobility practices in Norwegian coastal fisheries. *Norsk Geografisk Tidsskrift/Norwegian Journal of Geography*, 67(5), 312–319. https://doi.org/10.1080/00291951.2013.847482

Gherghel, A. (2013). *La Théorie du parcours de vie*. Québec: Presses de l'Université Laval.

Grossetti, M. (2011). L'espace à trois dimensions des phénomènes sociaux. Échelles d'action et d'analyse [The three dimensional space of social phenomena. Scales of action and analysis]. *SociologieS* [Online]. http://sociologies.revues.org/3466

Guérin, I. (2002). Les pratiques financières des femmes entrepreneurs. Exemples sénégalais [Financial practices of women entrepreneurs. Senegalese examples]. Revue Tiers Monde, 43(172), 809–828. http://www.jstor.org/stable/23594061

Harper, S., Grubb, C., Stiles, M., & Sumaila, U. R. (2017). Contributions by Women to Fisheries Economies: Insights from Five Maritime Countries. *Coastal Management*, 45(2), 91–106. https://doi.org/10.1080/08920753.2017.1278143

Hirata, H. (2005). Femmes et mondialisation [Women and globalisation]. In M. Maruani (Ed.), *Femmes, genre et sociétés* (pp. 398–405). Paris: La Découverte.

Koralagama, D., Gupta, J., & Pouw, N. (2017). Inclusive development from a gender perspective in small scale fisheries. *Current Opinion in Environmental Sustainability*, 24, 1–6. https://doi.org/10.1016/j.cosust.2016.09.002

Lautier, B. (2006). Mondialisation, travail et genre: une dialectique qui s'épuise [Globalisation, work and gender: a fading dialectic]. *Cahiers du Genre*, 40(1), 39–65. https://doi.org/10.3917/cdge.040.0039

Mertens de Wilmars, F. (2017). L'exclusion des femmes d'une communauté de pêcheurs espagnols. "Qui a un fils a une propriété, qui a des filles n'a rien" [The Exclusion of Women from a Community of Spanish Fishermen. "He who has a son has property, he who has daughters has nothing"]. *Cahiers du Genre*, 62(1), 61–75. https://doi.org/10.3917/cdge.062.0061

Neis, B., Binkley, M., Gerrard, S., & Maneschy, C. (2005). *Changing tides: gender, fisheries and globalization*. Halifax: Fernwood.

Neis, B., Gerrard, S., & Power, N. G. (2013). Women and Children First: the Gendered and generational Social-ecology of Smaller-scale Fisheries in Newfoundland and Labrador and Northern Norway. *Ecology and Society* [Online], 18(4). http://www.ecologyandsociety.org/vol18/iss4/art64/

Paillé, P., & Mucchielli, A. (2012). *L'analyse qualitative en sciences humaines et sociales* [Qualitative analysis in the humanities and social sciences]. Paris: Armand Colin.

Pirès, A. (1997). Échantillonnage et recherche qualitative : essai théorique et méthodologique [Sampling and qualitative research: theoretical and methodological essay]. In Poupart, Deslauriers, Groulx, Laperrière, Mayer & Pirès (Eds.), *La recherche qualitative. Enjeux épistémologiques et méthodologiques* (pp. 113–169). Montreal: Gaëtan Morin.

Srinath, K. (1987). Role of women in small scale fisheries – a case study. *Marine Fisheries Information Service, Technical and Extension Series*, (72), 12–17. http://eprints.cmfri.org.in/3973/

Vossenberg, S. (2013). *Women Entrepreneurship Promotion in Developing Countries: What explains the gender gap in entrepreneurship and how to close it?*. Maastricht: Maastricht School of Management.

Zhao, M., Tyzack, M., Anderson, R., & Onoakpovike, E. (2013). Women as visible and invisible workers in fisheries: A case study of Northern England. *Marine Policy*, 37, 69–76. https://doi.org/10.1016/j.marpol.2012.04.013

PART 3

Micro-Sociological Approaches

CHAPTER 7

"Team Play": Seafarers' Strategies for Coping with Job Demands of Short Sea Cargo Shipping Lines

Birgit Pauksztat

> Well I see it more like team play here. Because everyone participates. Especially in the ports, when there is a lot of discharging and loading now, then the AB and the boatswain and everyone participates. [...] So it is coordinated, and more of a team play here.

•••

> If you don't work together with everyone on board, then it doesn't work.

∴

1 Introduction

Job demands in seafaring have been associated with negative consequences for seafarers' health and well-being, job attitudes, and retention (Caesar et al., 2015; Oldenburg et al., 2013; Poulsen et al., 2014; Project Horizon, 2012); they also contribute to accidents that can endanger the safety of vessels and crew (Williamson et al., 2011). Short sea shipping, in particular, has been associated with high workloads and high levels of stress and fatigue (Kahveci, 1999; Pauksztat, 2017a, b; Shan & Neis, 2020; Wadsworth et al., 2008). In this context, the ability to cope with job demands may be especially important. Nevertheless, little attention has been paid to seafarers' strategies for coping with job demands.

To date, research on job demands has typically adopted an individualistic perspective; that is, studies have examined how job demands affect individuals, focusing on individuals' fatigue, health and well-being (Oldenburg et al., 2013; Poulsen et al., 2014; Stannard et al., 2015). With regard to factors that influence job demands and their effects, the focus has been on industry-level and organisational factors, notably work hour regulations, crewing levels, and

 | DOI:10.1163/9789004518841_009

workload (e.g., Grech, 2016; Österman & Hult, 2016). More recently, individual characteristics, such as personality traits, psychological capital or "hardiness" (e.g., Doyle et al., 2016; Hystad & Eid, 2016; Slišković, this volume), have been considered as well. While existing studies on job demands in seafaring have done much to enhance our understanding of the institutional framework and the role of individual characteristics, they have paid less attention to social interactions among crew members, and to the strategies that crew members use in order to cope with job demands.

The lack of attention to social interactions on board in research on job demands contrasts with seafarers' own emphasis on the importance of teamwork, as well as with early sociological analyses of ships as social systems. As illustrated in the opening quotes, to seafarers, the importance of teamwork seems self-evident – the crew is not a set of individuals, but a team where everyone works together (Antonsen, 2009; Knudsen, 2004). Similarly, early sociologists (e.g., Aubert & Arner, 1959; Homans, 1946) highlighted the interdependencies between seafarers occupying different roles in a hierarchically ordered system, examining social norms as well as formal and informal relationships. However, these insights about the ship as a social system are not reflected in research on job demands.

Moreover, there has been little research on the strategies used by seafarers for coping with job demands. Ethnographies and interview studies (e.g., Antonsen, 2009; Karjalainen, 2007; Knudsen, 2004; Østreng, 2007; Sampson, 2013) provide occasional glimpses of seafarers' coping strategies; however these are mentioned in passing in connection with other topics, rather than being the topic of explicit discussion. Survey studies (Andrei et al., 2020; Pauksztat, 2017a; Wadsworth et al., 2008) suggest that social support plays a role, but it remains unclear how exactly social support relates to particular coping strategies. To date, only three empirical studies focused specifically on coping strategies in the context of seafaring. Two concerned strategies used by Australian maritime pilots for coping with sleepiness (Chambers & Main, 2015; Ferguson et al., 2008), while the third examined officers' strategies for coping with reduced crewing levels (Ljung & Lützhöft, 2014). Given the focus of these studies, the strategies identified may comprise a relatively narrow set. Thus, a more comprehensive approach is needed.

Extending previous research, the purpose of this chapter is to identify strategies used by seafarers for coping with job demands of short sea cargo shipping lines, i.e., demands associated with a ship's schedule and characteristics of the ports and sea routes it includes. Further, this chapter explores the constraints and resources that limit or enable the availability and effectiveness of these coping strategies. In doing so, this study goes beyond existing research in two ways: first, by taking a social perspective that emphasises the social aspects of interactions on board, and second, by highlighting the strategies that seafarers use to actively deal with job demands.

2 Job Demands, Resources and Coping Strategies: An Overview

To provide a framework for the discussion, this section integrates insights from the Job Demands-Resources (JD-R) model (Bakker et al., 2014; Demerouti et al., 2001), Conservation of Resources (COR) theory (Hobfoll, 1989) and Lazarus and Folkman's (1984) Transactional Model to introduce key concepts, i.e., job demands, resources, and coping strategies, together with findings from previous studies in the context of seafaring.

2.1 *Job Demands*

Job demands are "physical, social, or organizational aspects of the job that require sustained physical or mental effort and are therefore associated with certain physiological and psychological costs (e.g., exhaustion)" (Demerouti et al., 2001, p. 501). In the context of seafaring, job demands include demands related to separation from friends and family ashore (Thomas et al., 2003) as well as demands related to the work itself. Here, the focus is on work-related demands.

As in other workplaces (Bowling et al., 2015), arguably the most significant demand is the workload, i.e., the number of work hours and the amount or intensity of the work (Andrei et al., 2020; Oldenburg et al., 2013; Pauksztat, 2017b). This includes routine work necessary for the functioning of the vessel, such as maintenance or administrative work, as well as work related to cargo operations. Other demands include the difficulty of the work, the disturbance of circadian rhythms through shift work and irregular work hours, lack of predictability, and interference from third parties (Knudsen, 2004; Pauksztat, 2017b; Project Horizon, 2012; Sampson et al., 2016).

As illustrated in Figure 1, previous studies have documented how job demands, notably workload and circadian disturbance, affect fatigue (Arendt,

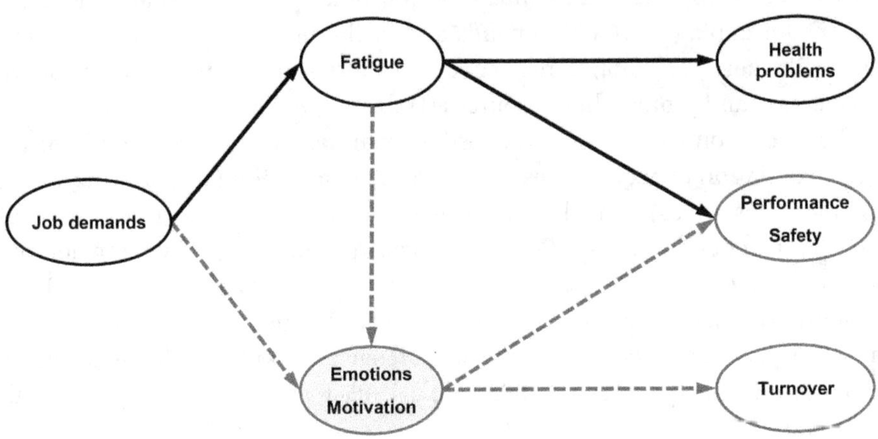

FIGURE 7.1 **Effects of job demands in the context of seafaring**

2010; Oldenburg et al., 2013; Project Horizon, 2012). Fatigue, in turn, has been associated with reduced levels of health and well-being (Bloor et al., 2000; Wadsworth et al., 2008), lower levels of performance in reaction time studies (Arunalandam & Tsing, 2009; Project Horizon 2012; van Leeuwen et al., 2013) and higher risks for accidents (Akhtar & Utne, 2015; Williamson et al., 2011).

More recently, studies have started to explore the effects of job demands on emotions and motivation (Gu et al., 2020; Pauksztat, 2017b; Pekcan, 2017), indicated by the broken arrows in Figure 1. Interviews with seafarers (Pauksztat, 2017b) suggest that job demands can be associated with negative emotions, such as frustration, annoyance, or anger; this is exacerbated by fatigue. Emotional reactions and motivation matter because, first of all, they reflect individuals' wellbeing. Moreover, they can affect individuals' safety and performance. Frustration, anger, and annoyance can affect concentration, leading to carelessness and increasing the risk of unsafe behaviours (Pekcan, 2017). Negative emotions also contribute to conflicts, thus eroding the basis for good collaboration (Pauksztat, 2017b). Third, emotions, specifically whether the work itself is considered interesting or "fun", can be a consideration in individuals' decision to quit (Gu et al., 2020; Pauksztat, 2017b). Finally, emotions are critical because they affect not only individuals, but may spread to other crew members (Knudsen 2004; Pauksztat, 2017b; Sampson 2013) through processes of contagion or collective sensemaking (Menges & Kilduff, 2015).

Taken together, this suggests that job demands present a double challenge: seafarers do not only need to cope with job demands (such as workload) and their effects (notably fatigue), as highlighted in numerous studies to date, but also with the negative emotional and motivational effects of job demands.

2.2 *Resources*

Resources are aspects of the context, the job, or the individual that provide the means for coping with job demands and facilitate the achievement of work goals (Bakker et al., 2014; Demerouti et al., 2001). Individuals, therefore, strive to increase and protect their resources (Hobfoll, 1989).

For crews on cargo ships, key resources are associated with the industry (e.g., legislation concerning rest hours), the organisation (e.g., crewing levels, financial resources), and the vessel (e.g., facilities, equipment, and state of repair) (Gander et al., 2011; Østreng, 2007; Sampson, 2013). They provide the context that enables and constrains everyday coping strategies on board. Other resources are more directly controlled by the crew, such as a good working climate or personal resources such as knowledge and skills (Andrei et al., 2020; Knudsen, 2004; Ljung & Lützhöft, 2014; Pauksztat, 2017a, 2021; Wadsworth et al., 2008).

2.3 *Coping Strategies*

Coping strategies are "cognitive and behavioral efforts to manage external and/or internal demands that are appraised as taxing or exceeding the resources of the person" (Lazarus & Folkman, 1984, p. 141). This can include individual strategies, i.e., strategies used by individuals acting on their own, as well as collective or communal strategies (Lyons et al., 1998; Rodriguez et al., 2019). Collective strategies are coordinated actions of two or more individuals who pool their resources and efforts in order to address a shared stressor. They may be especially relevant in work contexts characterised by task interdependence and shared demands and/or resources (Barnes et al., 2008; Lyons et al., 1998), such as seafaring.

Coping strategies are commonly divided into problem-focused and emotion-focused strategies, depending on their purpose (Folkman & Moskowitz, 2004). Problem-focused strategies are "directed at managing or altering the problem causing the distress" (Lazarus & Folkman, 1984, p. 150). Emotion-focused strategies are "directed at regulating emotional responses to the problem" (Lazarus & Folkman, 1984, p. 150).

Because they address the problem directly, problem-focused strategies are generally considered more effective than emotion-focused strategies (e.g., Boyd et al., 2009; Brown et al., 2005). For the latter, effectiveness may depend on whether they promote positive or negative emotions. Whereas negative emotions may distract from problem-solving and increase stress, positive emotions can be beneficial (Folkman & Moskowitz, 2004; Menges & Kilduff, 2015). They support problem-solving by promoting flexibility, creativity, and optimism. They can also provide a "psychological break", allowing individuals to replenish their resources and thus supporting continued coping efforts. Thus, positive emotions provide "emotional capital", an important resource for individuals and for groups (Bakker et al., 2014; Menges & Kilduff, 2015). Individual strategies for regulating emotions, such as focusing on positive aspects or benefits of the situation (Lazarus & Folkman, 1984), are well documented (Folkman & Moskowitz, 2004). By contrast, little is known about collective strategies for regulating emotions, although emotion contagion or convergence of emotions in groups is a well-known phenomenon (Menges & Kilduff, 2015).

As noted above, in the context of seafaring, only three empirical studies have focused specifically on coping strategies. Two of them concerned strategies used by Australian pilots for coping with sleepiness on long pilotage passages (Chambers & Main, 2015; Ferguson et al., 2008). They found that pilots relied largely on individual strategies, notably opportunistic napping, being "as organised as possible", and keeping "busy and active". A third study (Ljung & Lützhöft, 2014) explored how officers coped with reduced crewing levels, identifying a flexible division of work and adjustments of work hours as key strategies. However, given the focus of these studies, this may comprise only a small subset of the strategies used by seafarers.

3 Methods

To explore seafarers' strategies for coping with job demands in short sea cargo shipping, I draw on 54 semi-structured interviews with 46 seafarers on five cargo ships in 2013–14. All interviewees were men, and most (94 per cent) were European nationals. They were between 20 and 63 years old. Both officers and ratings from different departments (deck, engine, galley) were included. More information is provided in Paukszta (2017b).

Interviews during the last six months of the study focused specifically on seafarers' perceptions of job demands of shipping lines, and their strategies for coping. To provide information on the context and as a starting point for the discussion, interviewees were asked to identify the job demands they faced (a detailed analysis of this part of the interviews can be found in Paukszta, 2017b). Then, to explore coping strategies, interviewees were asked how they dealt with the demands they had described. In addition, coping strategies were mentioned in other parts of the interviews, especially in connection with collaboration and the working climate on board.

The interviews were analysed inductively in two steps (Bernard & Ryan, 2010), using NVivo 11 (QSR International, 2015). First, themes were identified through open coding; constant comparison between statements in the text and emerging themes helped to clarify and demarcate the themes. In the second step, themes were grouped into larger categories. The findings are presented in the next section.

4 Coping Strategies in Short Sea Cargo Shipping

In the interviews, seafarers mentioned a range of coping strategies. Most aimed directly at dealing with job demands. Others aimed at managing emotions, or at protecting resources.

4.1 *Strategies for Dealing with Job Demands*

Strategies for spreading tasks over a larger number of individuals and/or over time were most frequently mentioned. Individuals or teams could make day-to-day adjustments in the division of tasks – "helping" and "delegating" – to deal with high workloads and ensure a minimum number of rest hours.

Helping, i.e., involving more people and dividing the work between them, was common within departments. This sometimes, but not necessarily, involved the adjustment of work hours (see below). For instance, several deck officers and crew could be involved during cargo operations:

> [When we are in port] I can go there and help out, I can drive the forklift. And the deck crew, they are very happy [when I say] "okay, who wants to go on a coffee break? I can drive." [...] So there is a rotation around coffee time, even if we have a lot of cargo. Because I can drive, and the chief officer can drive, [so we can say] "okay, who wants to go for coffee?" We have very good ... what we call "seamanship".

To assist others, individuals might go beyond their formal duties. For instance, masters might prepare the paperwork for port calls beyond the crew change day, or boatswains might take on more responsibility in planning maintenance work. One boatswain explained:

> Usually, it's the chief officer who assigns the work to us, even at sea. But now, with this line, he's very busy. He has to make the cargo plans as well, and so on. So I and [the other boatswain] now manage that ourselves somehow.

Although helping was usually mentioned in relation to practical tasks, it could also take the form of supporting others in monitoring the situation, identifying problems, and finding solutions. This provided a way of coping with complex or difficult tasks, as well as with forgetting and mistakes due to fatigue. A master explained:

> Well, of course I have always said, or, I have said several times, that "if you think that I do something stupid, or that I am forgetting something, then tell me." Like I often forget things, I write down everything nowadays.

Delegating, i.e., entrusting tasks to subordinates to complete without close supervision, reduced the workloads of those at higher hierarchical levels. However, as this strategy was based on trust in others' competence, it was not used when others' competence was unknown or considered insufficient - "if I have someone who is new, who is really new to the job, then I am down there [in the engine room] all the time", a chief engineer explained.

Temporary adjustments to work and rest hours were common, such that crew members worked when they were needed (e.g., during arrivals and departures, cargo operations, or in emergencies), and rested during less busy periods.

Adjustments to work hours were also used to ensure that a sufficient number of people were available when needed:

> When we were in [port], we were loading non-stop for 36 hours. [...] So we made two shifts: the chief officer and the boatswain and the OS worked for six hours. And then came the officer and the two other OS and worked for six hours. So that three slept, and three worked. That was the only way.

More medium- and long-term changes were made as well. For instance, introducing or adjusting the watch system could be a way of coping with the workload on a particular line and complying with legal requirements for rest hours. On one vessel, dividing the watches between the first and second officer in a 6 hours on/6 hours off system freed the chief officer to focus on supervising cargo operations, and ensured that an additional deck officer was available to support the chief officer in port. Moreover, by providing regularity, watch systems were considered helpful for planning rest hours and avoiding the circadian disturbance caused by irregular work hours. Thus, in one case, a 6 hours on/6 hours off watch system was introduced for the first and second engineer when arrival and departure times became unpredictable.

In making adjustments, careful *planning* helped to optimise the use of the available time and personnel. Planning was used to spread out tasks more evenly over a given period of time (e.g., using longer sea voyages for routine tasks and paperwork). Planning was also important for coping with constraints imposed on work in the engine room by the duration of port calls and sea voyages, and by certain ports' restrictions on the type of work that could be carried out:

> [In the engine room] it's not affecting us so much, but ... I mean, you just have to plan it more carefully, a little bit, now. Like how to do it, and when to do it. But it's not affecting us so much; I mean, we can do what we want to do, and what we have to do, so it's not such a big deal.

Another strategy involving planning was to prepare things in advance as far as possible. "I usually see to it that I am one step ahead, or two steps ahead. Then you are in control of the situation", one interviewee explained. For instance, masters might use days at sea to complete the paperwork for several upcoming ports, or the deck crew might use the waiting time at a lock to get equipment ready for use during cargo operations in port.

Prioritising, a last resort when it was considered impossible to complete all tasks with the time and crew available, involved deciding which tasks to complete, and how much time to spend on each. This could mean omitting tasks that were considered non-essential (e.g., dusting in shared living areas), or doing tasks "quickly and in a rush, in the easiest way". It could also mean postponing less urgent tasks; maintenance work was a frequently mentioned example:

> [At that time] the deck crew worked so long days that all the maintenance work was left undone, because nobody had time for that. Fortunately that wasn't a long period. Now it is more quiet again, so we can catch up and start doing things at the normal pace again, so to speak.

"Technical" solutions, i.e., using or adapting tools and equipment, were mentioned as well, such as using written handover reports when there was no time for meeting face-to-face. Some solutions were more long-term, such as setting up software to reduce administrative work.

4.2 *Strategies for Managing Emotions and Motivation*

Individuals' attitudes and "mental strategies", such as trying to "keep a level head" in stressful situations, flexibility, and persistence, were considered important for dealing with negative emotions, maintaining motivation, and preventing potentially dangerous situations. Talking about interactions with shore-side personnel, one interviewee described the mental strategy he used:

> You have to get into a kind of "never mind" feeling, and ... go into your bubble. And when there are 40 guys shouting at you, then just let them shout. Just do your work. And it can be quite stressful and quite hard, if you don't get that bubble around you to protect you.

Flexibility and the ability to improvise were needed when planning was not possible, for instance when the crew had not received a cargo list: "In [port] and [port], I have no idea what kind of cargo we will get. So there you just have to load as you go along, so to speak."

Persistence ("gritting your teeth"), adjusting performance goals and standards ("take one day at a time and do the best we can"), as well as a "positive attitude" and humour were ways of coping with situations beyond the control of the crew. This included weather conditions as well as apparently unreasonable demands from shipping companies, high workloads, and unpredictable or inefficient organisation of work in port. "What can we do? – Just work", one man explained, and another said, "well, mostly, you just laugh about it. Because there is nothing you can do about it."

These strategies were not only important for those individuals who experienced negative emotions. Avoiding, handling, or (if that was not possible) hiding negative emotions also helped to prevent their spreading to others. Thus individuals' ability to manage stress and negative emotions was noted approvingly: "We are trying not to stress. Of course, there are ... maybe the captain is stressed, but he knows how to hide it. So that affects the crew, so the crew don't have so much stress either."

While negative emotions and motivation could spread through social interactions, social interactions could also have positive effects. First, having "normal" conversations with colleagues helped to take one's mind off negative or frustrating experiences:

> But then I really started to feel like "what the f.. am I doing here", like "now it's really time to go home." Like you start waiting for ... that you can go on leave. So there is this annoyance, you know, you don't joke amongst each other. But then, he [the master] often comes up to the bridge, then you can sit there and chat about everyday stuff, you can make jokes, you can ... like people hang out with each other, you have like normal, social interactions.

Second, many highlighted the importance of humour and joking together:

> Yes, we have a lot of fun, among the deck crew. If we look at the whole workday, there is a lot of joking and things like that, it's not like ... we are not just sitting there quietly and just look at each other, but it's like ... we talk and joke around. So it's really enjoyable.

In this way, talking to others created positive experiences that could counterbalance negative emotions. In addition, social interactions could transform negative experiences into something positive: laughing about frustrating or annoying events together with others provided a way to discuss such events without dwelling on negative emotions. Instead, negative experiences were transformed into "something new to talk about". In this way, rather than leading to heightened levels of frustration and tensions, negative experiences and the stories they provided contributed to positive interactions and a good working climate.

Finally, like the use of humour, getting others to see the positive aspects of a situation could be a deliberate strategy for improving their mood:

> You always have to find something positive. If there is a storm, you can think "well, at least there is no ice", or something like that. There is always something positive in everything. [...] You have to use a little humour, and joke about everything. Even if you are delayed, and you know that "now we will get home a day later", then you have to come up with something why that could be a good thing.

4.3 *Strategies for Protecting Resources*

Some of the strategies discussed in the interviews may be best understood as ways of protecting resources, notably rest hours. Ensuring a sufficient number of rest hours was not only a formal matter of compliance with legal requirements, but was considered essential for reducing fatigue. On busy lines, crew members used every opportunity to catch up on sleep, so that "everyone sleeps as soon as they get the chance".

Making day-to-day adjustments to work and rest hours or revising the watch system were key strategies for keeping work and rest hours within legal and sustainable limits. In addition, shared social norms and values helped to minimise interruptions during rest hours, and thus enhanced the quality of the rest. This included norms against disturbing colleagues who were resting ("we usually let the person sleep who is off duty"), as well as norms prescribing to "do your own job", i.e., being self-reliant and completing one's tasks independently ("It's a little like that at sea, that you mustn't ask, but you are supposed to know, or to solve everything on your own."). One interviewee observed:

> During loading and discharging, it's chief officer who is in charge. Of course, sometimes we have a question for the captain. But not so often. And that's good. We try to disturb the captain as little as possible.

These norms were supported by values emphasising self-reliance and endurance; "there is a certain pride in that as well, that you can manage such setbacks and difficulties".

Violating these norms could lead to informal sanctions, ranging from raised eyebrows and subtle hints ("he has hinted a bit that one shouldn't ask for help all the time") to strong disapproval and conflicts:

> If someone doesn't do his part and does his job, then others have to cover for him, and work harder, and work more. And in the end, this would mean that we get paid the same, but we don't do the same amount of work. That also creates conflicts, like "I work so hard for my money every month, and that person only does *half* of what I'm doing, and still gets paid the same".

It is important to note that these norms – completing one's tasks independently and not disturbing colleagues during their rest hours – were based on the premise that other crew members had the skills and competence to carry out their tasks unaided. Consequently, these norms could put additional pressure on less experienced crew members when they were faced with a situation they felt unable to resolve on their own: "That's a stressful situation in itself, to ask someone for help who will only be able to sleep for four hours in 48 hours. To ... well, to force them to get up."

4.4 *Changing Constraints*

The strategies discussed so far operate within the constraints set by shipping lines, shipping companies, and international and national legislation. These constraints affected not only job demands, but also the strategies and resources available for coping with these demands.

First, shipping lines limited the availability and effectiveness of coping strategies. Strategies based on dividing tasks among crew members or spreading tasks over time were effective only up to a point: when workloads were high for everyone over long time periods, spreading tasks over more people or over time was not possible. Further, the unpredictability of the schedule and/or work in port could undermine coping strategies that were based on the ability to plan, as in this example:

> That's the bad thing in [port] right now, that *sometimes* they [the stevedores] work during the night, and sometimes they don't. But they give us the information usually only about one hour before the shift ends or starts. So it's very, very hard for us to plan how to work, when to have our rest hours, if you don't know how *they* will work.

Second, shipping lines and external constraints affected resources, and thus, indirectly, coping strategies. For instance, time to rest was affected by international and national regulations, crew size, and workload. Rest hours meant time to "recharge your batteries" for individual crew members, as well as time for joint leisure activities, which contributed to a good working climate (Kahveci, 1999; Pauksztat, 2017b). A good working climate, characterised by a positive atmosphere, good personal relationships and a sense of 'team play', with colleagues being helpful and approachable, was important because it supported many of the coping strategies discussed above. A positive atmosphere, with humour and joking, could help to counteract negative emotions, while good personal relations and 'team play' provided the foundation for collaboration and open communication:

> I think the atmosphere on board is good. I think ... well, what can I say. I think people are friendly, people are helpful. If there is something that ... if you have a question, you can always ask.

> When we have some problem, for example on deck or something, they [the deck crew] can go and ask us [the engine crew] – no problem! We fix it. And then, you know ... I mean, we don't have problems between the departments, like between the deck department and the engine room. So

> ... if somebody sees something somewhere, we always ... we can solve it without any ... without starting to discuss whose job it is.

Similarly, competence levels were affected by company policies for recruitment and training, as well as by the time available for training on board (Knudsen, 2004). A busy schedule often left little time for on-the-job training of new and less experienced crew members. This, in turn, could affect crew members' competence levels and hence the availability of coping strategies that depended on others' competence, such as dividing work and protecting rest hours.

Consequently, in the interviews, changing the constraints within which the crew operated was sometimes described as an effective way of managing job demands and resources, e.g., by arranging to load only two rather than three decks simultaneously (thus spreading the work over time) or by increasing the number of crew on board. Changing constraints could also enable coping strategies. For instance, obtaining accurate and timely information about the schedule, the cargo, or about stevedores' work hours made it possible to use strategies that involved planning.

However, attempts to change constraints were often considered futile due to the opposition expected from other parties. In general, crew members considered it unlikely that it would be possible to influence them. One interviewee explained:

> But with the lashing, we don't say anything. There is no point. It doesn't help. But instead, when they [the stevedores] are done, we wait two hours until departure, and check all the lashings and improve them before departure, when all the stevedores are gone. Because in [port], or in [country] in general, especially [port], the stevedores' unions are very strong. They are very powerful. So you can't argue with them and say, "you are doing this badly" and "do it better!" Then they can get angry, and maybe they do it even more badly, or they just go home.

Exceptions were those cases where changing constraints was considered the only way to ensure minimum legal standards of health and safety and/or minimum rest hours.

5 Discussion

5.1 *Collective Coping Strategies in Seafaring*

Coping strategies mentioned in the interviews included strategies aimed at mitigating job demands and fatigue, maintaining positive emotions and motivation, and protecting rest hours. Whereas previous research distinguished between emotion- and problem-focused strategies (Lazarus & Folkman, 1984), here this distinction was blurred. This was because negative emotions could become a problem in themselves as they could exacerbate the problems caused by job demands and undermine resources.

Some of the strategies discussed in the interviews have been mentioned in previous research on seafaring, notably temporary adjustments to work hours, improvisation, technical solutions and emotion-focused strategies such as joking and humour (Bhattacharya & Tang, 2012; Karjalainen, 2007; Knudsen, 2004; Ljung & Lützhöft, 2014; Østreng, 2007; Sampson et al., 2016). Other strategies, including key strategies related to planning and prioritising, have not been considered in connection with coping or were interpreted in a different light. For instance, in contrast to previous research (Project Horizon, 2012), watch systems were presented not so much as a stressor, but as a way of coping with unpredictable and/or irregular timing of the work (Arendt, 2010).

While many of the strategies mentioned in the interviews seem familiar from previous research on coping strategies, existing research has focused on *individuals'* coping with job demands. By contrast, this study's findings pointed to coping as a *collective* endeavour, reflecting a strong sense of interdependence among the crew. Thus, many of the problem-focused strategies mentioned were collective strategies, such as strategies concerning the division of work or protecting rest hours. Other strategies (e.g., adjusting work hours; planning; prioritising; technical solutions) could be either individual or collective, depending on the extent of someone's interdependence with others. For instance, adjusting work hours could be an individual strategy for a master or a chief engineer, or a collective strategy when work hours had to be coordinated with others (e.g., for watchkeepers). Even emotion-focused strategies, such as maintaining a positive attitude, had a collective element, as a way of preventing that negative emotions spread or affected others.

In line with this, the interviews highlighted the pivotal role of a good working climate. Whereas previous research on seafaring emphasised social support from family and friends ashore (Sampson & Thomas, 2003), the interviews showed *that* and *how* social interactions on board could support coping. A good working climate, characterised by a positive atmosphere, good personal relationships and a sense of "team play", provided a source of "emotional capital" (Menges & Kilduff, 2015) and a basis for mutual trust and open communication (Pauksztat, 2021). It also increased crew members' motivation and willingness to collaborate. In this way, the working climate was not only essential for individuals' well-being, job satisfaction, and turnover (Andrei et al., 2020; Caesar et al., 2015; Gu et al., 2020; Pauksztat, 2017b; Wadsworth et al., 2008); it also enabled coping strategies that required coordination and collaboration, and strategies for coping with negative emotions.

5.2 *Limitations of Coping Strategies*

The findings also indicated that job demands could limit the availability and effectiveness of coping strategies. First, the nature of the job demands could rule out certain problem-focused coping strategies. For instance, strategies that involved planning were ruled out when work was unpredictable. Thus, the unpredictability of the schedule or the work in port was not only a job demand but also ruled out a key set of coping strategies.

In addition, the effectiveness of coping strategies could diminish as job demands increased. Strategies that involved distributing work across more persons and/or longer time periods became ineffective when the overall workload remained high for all crew members over a longer period of time. This might explain why the effect of supportive social interactions on fatigue was found to become weaker as the workload increased (Pauksztat, 2017a).

In such situations, strategies that reduced job demands (e.g., introducing or adjusting the watch system to reduce circadian disturbance; adopting technical solutions or prioritising to reduce the workload) could become more important. "Crew negligence", a factor described as contributing to accidents (Allianz Global Corporate & Specialty, 2015), could perhaps be seen in this context, i.e., not as wilful "negligence" but as the result of a prioritisation strategy used as a last resort for coping with exceedingly high workloads. Importantly, however, the extent to which it is possible to postpone or omit tasks is limited by the need to ensure the safety of the vessel and the crew, and by legal constraints. Although questions about illegal practices were avoided in the current study, such practices have been documented elsewhere (Baumler et al., 2021; Bhattacharya & Tang, 2012).

When problem-focused strategies become unfeasible or ineffective, emotion-focused strategies may still be effective. However, as discussed above, emotion-focused strategies may be indirectly undermined by job demands as well. Hence, when coping strategies operating within existing constraints reach their limit, attempts to change organisational or industry constraints (e.g., crewing levels) could become the last resort, although, in practice, such attempts were often considered futile by interviewees, a view that may be widely shared by seafarers (cf. Baumler et al., 2021; Ljung & Lützhöft, 2014; Sampson, 2013). In line with other studies (e.g., Gander et al., 2011; Grech, 2016; Project Horizon, 2012), these findings draw attention to the constraints set by legislation as well as by industry and organisational practices for managing job demands and their effects.

5.3 *Practical Implications*

While the findings suggest that crews may be able to cope with temporarily high levels of job demands, coping strategies may become ineffective when job demands remain high over extended time periods. Consequently, for long-term sustainability, the available resources (e.g., crewing levels) need to be sufficient to meet job demands (e.g., workload, work hours). To support the crew in coping with temporarily high job demands, schedules should be designed for predictability as well as taking into account workload and work hours. Importantly, also, non-work hours should not only be designed to provide a minimum amount of sleep but also provide sufficient leisure time to encourage the development of a good working climate on board (Andrei et al., 2020; Pauksztat, 2017b). Finally, HR policies should be designed with a view to stable crews (Andrei et al., 2020; Pauksztat, 2017b) and to ensure high levels of competence among the crew (Knudsen, 2004; Ljung & Lützhöft, 2014).

6 Conclusion

Taking an interview-based approach, this study revealed a broad set of strategies used by seafarers for coping with the job demands of short sea cargo shipping lines and their effects. The study extended previous research on coping by highlighting collective aspects of coping strategies, as well as the pivotal role of the working climate on board in enabling such strategies. However, the findings also indicated that seafarers may not only need to cope with job demands but also with threats to valued resources. In addition, job demands and external constraints could undermine the availability and effectiveness of coping strategies.

Taken together, the interviews suggest that crews take an active role in managing job demands by working together as a team. However, the constraints set by organisational and industry practices and regulations and the characteristics of the shipping line cannot be ignored.

Acknowledgements

Data collection was supported by the Hanken Foundation and the Dr. h.c. Marcus Wallenberg Foundation for Promoting Research in Business Administration. Earlier versions of this chapter were presented at the *International Conference on Maritime Policy, Technology and Education* (ICMPTE), Southampton, UK, 7 June 2017, and at the Kalmar Maritime Academy, Kalmar, Sweden, 8 May 2019. I would like to thank those who provided comments on earlier versions of this chapter, as well as Jannika Lassus for her support with data collection. Special thanks to the masters and crews of the ships who participated in this study for their hospitality, and to the office personnel for their help with practical matters. Most of all, I would like to thank all who participated in the interviews and shared their views and experiences.

References

Akhtar, M.J., & Utne, I.B. (2015). Common patterns in aggregated accident analysis charts from human fatigue-related groundings and collisions at sea. *Maritime Policy & Management*, 42(2), 186–206. doi: 10.1080/03088839.2014.926032

Allianz Global Corporate & Specialty (2015). *Safety and shipping review 2015: An annual review of trends and developments in shipping losses and safety.* Munich, Allianz Global Corporate & Specialty AG. Retrieved from http://www.agcs.allianz.com/insights/white-papers-and-case-studies/safety-and-shipping-review-2015

Andrei, D. M., Griffin, M. A., Grech, M., & Neal, A. (2020). How demands and resources impact chronic fatigue in the maritime industry: The mediating effect of acute fatigue, sleep quality and recovery. *Safety Science*, 121, 362–372. doi: 10.1016/j.ssci.2019.09.019

Antonsen, S. (2009). The relationship between culture and safety on offshore supply vessels. *Safety Science*, 47(8), 1118–1128. doi: 10.1016/j.ssci.2008.12.006

Arendt, J. (2010). Shift work: Coping with the biological clock. *Occupational Medicine*, 60, 10–20. doi: 10.1093/occmed/kqp162

Arulanandam, S., & Tsing, G. C. C. (2009). Comparison of alertness levels in ship crew: An experiment on rotating versus fixed watch schedules. *International Maritime Health*, 60(1–2), 6–9

Aubert, V., & Arner, O. (1959). On the social structure of the ship. *Acta Sociologica* 3(4), 200–219. doi: https://www.jstor.org/stable/4193493

Bakker, A. B., Demerouti, E., & Sanz-Vergel, A. I. (2014). Burnout and work engagement: The JD-R approach. *Annual Review of Organizational Psychology and Organizational Behavior*, 1, 389–411. doi: 10.1146/annurev-orgpsych-031413-091235

Barnes, C. M., Hollenbeck, J. R., Wagner, D. T., DeRue, D. S., Nahrgang, J. D., & Schwind, K. M. (2008). Harmful help: The costs of backing-up behavior in teams. *Journal of Applied Psychology*, 93, 529–539. doi: 10.1037/0021-9010.93.3.529

Baumler, R., Bhatia, B. S., & Kitada, M. (2021). Ship first: Seafarers' adjustment of records on work and rest hours. *Marine Policy*, 130, 104186. doi: 10.1016/j.marpol.2020.104186

Bernard, H. R., & Ryan, G. W. (2010). *Analyzing qualitative data: Systematic approaches*. Los Angeles, CA, Sage

Bhattacharya, S., & Tang, L. (2012). Fatigued for safety? Supply chain occupational health and safety initiatives in shipping. *Economic and Industrial Democracy*, 34, 383–399. doi: 10.1177/0143831X12439760

Bloor, M., Thomas, M., & Lane, T. (2000). Health risks in the global shipping industry: An overview. *Health, Risk and Society*, 2(3), 329–340. doi: 10.1080/713670163

Bowling, N. A., Alarcon, G. M., Bragg, C. B., & Hartman, M. J. (2015). A meta-analytic examination of the potential correlates and consequences of workload. *Work & Stress*, 29(2), 95–113. doi: 10.1080/02678373.2015.1033037

Boyd, N., Lewin, J. E., & Sager, J. K. (2009). A model of stress and coping and their influence on individual and organizational outcomes. *Journal of Vocational Behavior*, 75, 197–211. doi: 10.1016/j.jvb.2009.03.010

Brown, S. P., Westbrook, R. A., & Challagalla, G. (2005). Good cope, bad cope: Adaptive and maladaptive coping strategies following a critical negative work event. *Journal of Applied Psychology*, 90(4), 792–798. doi: 10.1037/0021-9010.90.4.792

Caesar, L. D., Cahoon, S., & Fei, J. (2015). Exploring the range of retention issues for seafarers in global shipping: Opportunities for further research. *WMU Journal of Maritime Affairs*, 14, 141–157. doi: 10.1007/s13437-015-0078-0

Chambers, T. P., & Main, L. C. (2015). Symptoms of fatigue and coping strategies in maritime pilotage. *International Maritime Health*, 66, 43–48. doi: 10.5603/IMH.2015.0011

Demerouti, E., Bakker, A. B., Nachreiner, F., & Schaufeli, W. B. (2001). The Job Demands-Resources model of burnout. *Journal of Applied Psychology*, 86, 499–512. doi: 10.1037/0021-9010.86.3.499

Doyle, N., MacLachlan, M., Fraser, A., Stilz, R., Lismont, K., Cox, H., & McVeigh, J. (2016). Resilience and well-being amongst seafarers: Cross-sectional study of crew across 51 ships. *International Archives of Occupational and Environmental Health*, 89, 199–209. doi: 10.1007/s00420-015-1063-9

Ferguson, S. A., Lamond, N, Kandelaars, K., Jay, S. M., & Dawson, D. (2008). The impact of short, irregular sleep opportunities at sea on the alertness of marine pilots working extended hours. *Chronobiology International*, 25, 399–411. doi: 10.1080/07420520802106819

Folkman, S., & Moskowitz, J. T. (2004). Coping: Pitfalls and promise. *Annual Review of Psychology*, 55, 745–774. doi: 10.1146/annurev.psych.55.090902.141456

Gander, P., Hartley, L., Powell, D., Cabon, P., Hitchcock, E., Mills, A., & Popkin, S. (2011). Fatigue risk management: Organizational factors at the regulatory and industry/company level. *Accident Analysis & Prevention*, 43, 573–590. doi: 10.1016/j.aap.2009.11.007

Grech, M. (2016). Fatigue risk management: A maritime framework. *International Journal of Environmental Research and Public Health*, 13(2), 175. doi: 10.3390/ijerph13020175

Gu, Y., Liu, D., Zheng, G., Yang, C., Dong, Z., & Tee, E.Y.I. (2020). The effects of Chinese seafarers' job demands on turnover intention: The role of fun at work. *International Journal of Environmental Research and Public Health*, 17, 5247. doi: 10.3390/ijerph17145247

Hobfoll, S. E. (1989). Conservation of resources: A new attempt at conceptualizing stress. *American Psychologist*, 44, 513–524. doi: 10.1037/0003-066X.44.3.513

Homans, G.C. (1946). The small warship. *American Sociological Review* 11(3), 294–300

Hystad, S. W., & Eid, J. (2016). Sleep and fatigue among seafarers: The role of environmental stressors, duration at sea and psychological capital. *Safety and Health at Work*, 7, 363–371. doi: 10.1016/j.shaw.2016.05.006

Kahveci, E. (1999). *Fast turnaround ships and their impact on crews*. Cardiff, Seafarers International Centre. Retrieved from http://www.sirc.cf.ac.uk/SIRC_Free_Online_Reports.aspx

Karjalainen, M. (2007). *In the shadow of freedom: Life on board the oil tanker*. Commentationes Scientiarum Socialium 69. Helsinki, Finnish Society of Sciences and Letters

Knudsen, F. (2004). *"If you are a good leader I am a good follower", Working and leisure relations between Danes and Filipinos on board Danish vessels*. Arbejds- og Maritimmedicinsk Publicationsserie, Report No. 9. Retrieved from http://static.sdu.dk/mediafiles/Files/Om_SDU/Institutter/Ist/MaritimSundhed/Rapporter/report92004.pdf

Lazarus, R. S., & Folkman, S. (1984). *Stress, appraisal and coping*. New York, NY: Springer

Ljung, M., & Lützhöft, M. (2014). Functions, performances and perceptions of work on ships. *WMU Journal of Maritime Affairs*, 13, 231–250. doi: 10.1007/s13437-014-0057-x

Lyons, R. F., Mickelson, K., Sullivan, J. L., & Coyne, J. C. (1998). Coping as a communal process. *Journal of Social and Personal Relationships*, 15, 579–607. doi: 10.1177/0265407598155001

Menges, J. I., & Kilduff, M. (2015). Group emotions: Cutting the Gordian knots concerning terms, levels of analysis, and processes. *Academy of Management Annals*, 9, 845–928. doi: 10.1080/19416520.2015.1033148

Oldenburg, M., Hogan, B., & Jensen, H.-J. (2013). Systematic review of maritime field studies about stress and strain in seafaring. *International Archives of Occupational and Environmental Health*, 86, 1–15. doi: 10.1007/s00420-012-0801-5

Österman, C., & Hult, C. (2016). Administrative burdens and over-exertion in Swedish short sea shipping. *Maritime Policy & Management*, 43(5), 569–579. doi: 10.1080/03088839.2016.1154994

Østreng, D. (2007). *I samme båt: Forholdet mellom sjøfolk på multinasjonale skip* (PhD dissertation). Institutt for sosiologi og samfunnsgeografi, Universitetet i Oslo, Oslo

Pauksztat, B. (2017a). Effects of job demands and social interactions on fatigue in short sea cargo shipping. *Maritime Policy & Management*, 44(5), 623–640. doi: 10.1080/03088839.2017.1298868

Pauksztat, B. (2017b). 'Only work and sleep': Seafarers' perceptions of job demands of short sea cargo shipping lines and their effects on work and life on board. *Maritime Policy & Management*, 44(7), 899–915. doi: 10.1080/03088839.2017.1371347

Pauksztat, B. (2021). Informal relations and communication about work-related problems in two multilingual crews. *Marine Policy*, 130, 103767. doi: 10.1016/j.marpol.2019.103767

Pekcan, C. H. (2017). *Safety at sea: understanding the role of the psychological contract in seafarers' safe and unsafe behaviour using affective events and ego depletion theories* (PhD dissertation). Royal Holloway, University of London, London

Poulsen, T. R., Burr, H., Larsen, H. L., & Jepsen, J. R. (2014). Health of Danish seafarers and fishermen 1970–2010: What have register-based studies found? *Scandinavian Journal of Public Health*, 42, 534–545. doi: 10.1177/1403494814534538

Project Horizon. (2012). *Project Horizon: A wake-up call. Research into the effects of sleepiness on the cognitive performance of maritime watchkeepers under different watch patterns, using ships' bridge, engine and liquid cargo handling simulators*. Research Report. Retrieved from www.project-horizon.eu

QSR International. (2015). *NVivo qualitative data analysis software*, version 11. Doncaster, VIC, Australia, QSR International Pty Ltd

Rodriguez, I., Kozusznik, M. W., Peiró, J. M., & Tordera, N. (2019). Individual, co-active and collective coping and organizational stress: A longitudinal study. *European Management Review*, 37, 86–98. doi: 10.1016/j.emj.2018.06.002

Sampson, H. (2013). *International seafarers and transnationalism in the twenty-first century*. Manchester, Manchester University Press

Sampson, H., Acejo, I., Ellis, N., Tang, L., & Turgo, N. (2016). *The relationships between seafarers and shore-side personnel: An outline report based on research undertaken in the period 2012–2016*. Cardiff, Seafarers International Research Centre, Cardiff University. Retrieved from http://orca.cf.ac.uk/92378/

Sampson, H., & Thomas, M. (2003). The social isolation of seafarers: Causes, effects, and remedies. *International Maritime Health*, 54, 58–67

Shan, D., & Neis, B. (2020). Employment-related mobility, regulatory weakness and potential fatigue-related safety concerns in short-sea seafaring on Canada's Great Lakes and St. Lawrence Seaway: Canadian seafarers' experiences. *Safety Science*, 121, 165–176. doi: 10.1016/j.ssci.2019.08.017

Stannard, S., Vaughan, C., Swift, O., Robinson, G., Altaf, S.A., & McGarry, A. (2015). Women seafarers' health and welfare survey. *International Maritime Health*, 66(3), 123–138

Thomas, M., Sampson, H., & Zhao, M. (2003). Finding a balance: Companies, seafarers, and family life. *Maritime Policy & Management*, 30, 59–76. doi: 10.1080/0308883032000051630

Van Leeuwen, W. M. A., Kircher, A., Dahlgren, A., Lützhöft, M., Barnett, M., Kecklund, G., & Åkerstedt, T. (2013). Sleep, sleepiness, and neurobehavioral performance while on watch in a simulated 4 hours on/8 hours off maritime watch system. *Chronobiology International*, 30(9), 1108–1115. doi: 10.3109/07420528.2013.800874

Wadsworth, E. J. K., Allen, P. H., McNamara, R. L., & Smith, A. P. (2008). Fatigue and health in a seafaring population. *Occupational Medicine*, 58, 198–204. doi: 10.1093/occmed/kqn008

Williamson, A., Lombardi, D. A., Folkard, S., Stutts, J., Courtney, T. K., & Connor, J. L. (2011). The link between fatigue and safety. *Accident Analysis & Prevention*, 43, 498–515. doi: 10.1016/j.aap.2009.11.011

CHAPTER 8

The Role of Personality Traits, Work Motivation and Job Satisfaction in the Explanation of Seafarers' Well-being

Ana Slišković

1 Introduction

Previous research addressed seafaring as a highly demanding, risk and stressful occupation that may lead to the negative effects on the seafarers' health, safety and well-being (Oldenburg & Jensen, 2019; Slišković, 2017; Slišković & Penezić, 2015a). Until recently, most of the research in this area was focused on consequences of stress on safety and/or physical health of seafarers (e.g. Chung et al., 2017; Kaerlev et al., 2005; Oldenburg et al., 2010; Oldenburg, 2014; Jepsen et al., 2015; Roberts, 2005; Roberts, 2008; Roberts & Marlow, 2005; Slišković & Penezić, 2017), while psychological functioning of seafarers attracted fewer research papers (MacLachlan et al., 2012). However, during the last decade seafarers' psychological well-being and mental health became important topics (Iversen, 2012; Jagosh et al., 2017; McVeigh et al., 2019a; McVeigh & MacLachlan, 2019). Implications of different lines of studies in this area showed that promotion of the seafarers' well-being should be based on improving work and psychosocial conditions in the maritime sector (Slišković & Penezić, 2015b; Slišković & Penezić, 2016), and on strengthening seafarers' psychological capital and resilience (Hystad & Eid, 2016; McVeigh et al., 2017).

Still, a thorough study of antecedents of well-being in seafarers represents a gap in the scientific literature. While the job satisfaction is recognised as an essential factor in determining seafarers' well-being (Slišković, 2017), the role of more stable individual differences in personality and motivation in the explanation of the well-being of the employees (Sulsky & Smith, 2005; Ryan & Deci, 2000) was rarely studied among seafarers (Slišković, 2017). Therefore, this study aimed at testing the role of *personality traits, work motivation*, and *satisfaction with seafaring jobs* in the explanation of different aspects of seafarers' well-being.

Researchers most often use ***subjective*** (or *hedonic*) conceptualisation of well-being, according to which well-being is a multidimensional construct that implies "person's cognitive and affective evaluations of his or her life" (Diener

 | DOI:10.1163/9789004518841_010

et al., 2002, p. 63). While ***cognitive aspect*** refers to what one thinks about his/her life satisfaction (satisfaction with life as a whole or satisfaction in specific areas, such as work, relationships etc.), the ***affective aspect*** refers to emotions, moods and feelings, whereby affect is classified as a positive (pleasant) or negative (unpleasant). Besides cognitive and affective measures of subjective well-being, Diener et al. (2010) developed a measure of **social - psychological** (or *eudemonic*) well-being, named the *Flourishing scale*. It focuses on core aspects of social-psychological functioning, such as relationships, self-esteem, self-realisation, purpose, meaning and optimism. Creating scale items to measure the essential components of *social-psychological* well-being was driven by different psychological perspectives on well-being (Diener et al., 2010). This includes theories of universal human psychological needs, theories of "psychological capital" (the importance of 'flow', interest, and engagement), as well as different theories of "social capital" relating both to support from others and helping others. In addition, the development of *Flourishing scale* was also based on previous theoretical and empirical knowledge on the roles of *purpose* and *meaning*, as well as the *optimism*, to successful human functioning. Considering that hedonic and eudemonic dimensions represent mutually related, but distinct concepts (Vanhoutte, 2015), in this study multiple perspectives on well-being, i.e. assessments of **cognitive, affective** and **social-psychological well-being**, are used.

Job satisfaction is mostly defined as a positive emotional state resulting from the appraisal of job experiences (Judge & Klinger, 2008). The significant role of job satisfaction in the determination of well-being is well documented in the general population (e.g. Sironi, 2019) and seafarers (e.g. McVeigh et al., 2019b). Studies among seafarers furtherly showed that job performance may be predicted on the basis of job satisfaction (An et al., 2020; Yuen et al., 2018). In spite of the great number of valid and reliable measures of *general job satisfaction* in the literature (see Judge & Klinger, 2008), there is a noted absence of valid and reliable measure which would cover satisfaction by specific working conditions in seafaring. Therefore, in testing the contribution of job satisfaction to the explanation of well-being dimensions, this study used the newly developed measure of job satisfaction in the seafaring (see description and psychometric properties in Method section). Its development was driven by the results of the descriptive qualitative study of seafarers' satisfaction (Slišković & Penezić, 2015b), and theoretical consideration based on a review of occupational sources of stress in seafaring (Slišković, 2017). Accordingly, it was assumed (**H1**) that job satisfaction will have a significant positive contribution to the explanation of three dimensions of the seafarers' well-being.

Previous research that included testing the role of **personality traits** in the explanation of work-related well-being of seafarers indicated the importance of personal hardiness (Doyle et al., 2016) and *psychological capital* (Hystad & Eid, 2016). Since both noted traits are considered as meta-constructs, this study aimed at the attempt of the explanation of seafarers' well-being by more fundamental personality traits described in *Big Five model of personality* (Goldberg, 1993; McCrae & Costa, 1987), which reflect relatively stable individual differences in patterns of behaviour, emotion, and cognition. Big Five model, consisting of five personality traits: *extraversion, agreeableness, conscientiousness, emotional stability* (or opposite pole: neuroticism), and *openness to experience* (also named intellect/imagination), is the most empirically accepted model that describe individual differences in personality (Johnson, 2017). The role of the Big Five personality traits in the explanation of different dimensions of well-being is confirmed in many studies in the general population (e.g. Cosentino & Castro Solanom 2017; Gutiérrez et al., 2005; Siegler & Brummett, 2000; Strickhouser et al., 2017). However, relations of the Big Five personality traits with seafarers' well-being represent a new research question, considering the fact that the Big Five model of personality is rarely used in studies on seafarers (exception may be found in Jeżewska et al., 2013; Lipowski et al., 2014). Still, on the basis of previous theoretical and empirical knowledge in the broader area which shows possible mechanisms of links between personality traits and life outcomes (Soto et al., 2016; Strickhouser et al., 2017), particularly related to the well-being in occupational settings (Sulsky & Smith, 2005), it was hypothesised (**H2**) that Big Five personality traits will provide a significant contribution to the explanation of the well-being dimensions in seafarers. Precisely, positive relations between positive poles of five traits - extraversion, agreeableness, conscientiousness, emotional stability, and intellect/imagination (Goldberg, 1992), with cognitive, affective, and social-psychological well-being, were expected.

Finally, this study included ***work motivation*** as a theoretically important factor that possibly may provide an additional contribution to explaining seafarers' well-being. The relation between work motivation and well-being of seafarers was rarely in the focus of scientific research. On the other side, seafarers' work motivation is addressed in the vast number of recent studies, which are understandably considering the available statistics (BIMCO/ISF, 2015; European Maritime Safety Agency, 2019; McLaughlin, 2012) that show a decrease in the number of seafarers from developed countries. Some of the most crucial research questions include attraction, recruitment and retention in the seafaring occupation, underlying intrinsic and extrinsic motivational factors, and the links of motivation with safety and efficiency in the maritime sector (e.g.

Haka et al., 2011; Kanev et al., 2017; Mitroussi & Notteboom, 2015; Nielsen et al., 2013; Pauksztat, 2017; Slišković et al., 2021; Tsai & Liou, 2017). *Work motivation* in this study is conceptualised through the level of ***work self-determination*** (Tremblay et al., 2009), theoretically grounded in Self-determination Theory (Deci & Ryan, 1985; Deci & Ryan, 2000; Ryan & Deci, 2000). Self-determination theory (SDT) is a broad theory of personality, behaviour, and motivation that explains the achievement of autonomously regulated motivation as an internalisation process during which three universal human needs are satisfied; the need for autonomy, competence and relatedness. SDT explains an individual's behaviour through six levels of autonomous regulation or self-determination. At the low-end of the continuum lies *amotivation*, which implies the lack of the intention to act, or passive behaviour. The next two category levels include *externally regulated motivation* (fully controlled regulation; behaviour is a reflection of satisfying external demands - rewards or punishments), and *introjected regulation* (assuming the regulation of behaviour through self-worth contingencies, e.g., self-esteem or guilt, whereby the regulation is not fully accepted as personal). The following level at the continuum refers to *identified regulation* and implies doing an activity because one identifies with its value or meaning. Penult level is *integrated regulation*. It alludes complete internalisation of regulation of behaviour. It is similar to the *intrinsic motivation* that is at the high-end of the continuum. However, the goal of the integrated regulation of behaviour is to achieve specific outcomes, while intrinsic motivation is based on achieving internal satisfaction from particular behaviour or activity. Considering the theoretical assumptions of SDT, according to which individuals with higher levels of self-determinate motivation have higher levels of satisfaction of three innate psychological needs (Ryan & Deci, 2000), it was assumed (**H3**) that *self-determination index of motivation* (Tremblay et al., 2009) will have significant positive contribution in the explanation of different aspects of seafarers' well-being (Ryan & Deci, 2001).

2 Method

2.1 *Sample*

The convenience sample consisted of 286 Croatian male seafarers, ranging from 18 to 65 years (M = 37.39, SD = 10.28 years). Their average working experience in seafaring was 12.46 years (SD = 9.94). Majority seafarers in the sample work in international/deep-sea shipping (88.81%), and they are mostly employed in foreign maritime companies (81.10%). The largest number of participants work on cargo ships (near 61%), including mostly oil and oil products tankers, LNG and LPG ships, chemicals, containers, and general cargo ships. About 20% of participants work at passenger ships (e.g. cruises, ferries, yachts). Near 14% of participants work at special-purpose ships (e.g. dredgers, tugs, research ships). The rest of the participants (about 5%) reported "other" types (e.g. offshore platforms, fishing ships). Regarding the work position on board, the sample mostly included higher ranks. More precisely, the study included masters (12.24%), chief engineers (6.64%), deck officers (33.57%), engine officers (20.98%), electricians (4.20%), deck and engine cadets (10.84%), deck crew members (4.89%), engine crew members (2.20%), members of Stewart department (1.40%), and other positions (3.15%). Regarding the level of education, most of the participants have completed high school (46.50 %) or Bachelor's college (41.96 %), while about 11.19 % of participants hold a Master's degree. About half of participants are married (52.44%), followed by participants living in a domestic partnership (16.78%), single (25.52%), divorced and separated (3.85%), and widowed (1.05%). Having children was reported by 53.85% of participants, with two children on average (M = 1.8, D = 2).

2.2 *Measures*

The used questionnaire consisted of relevant socio-demographic questions (gender, age, working experience in seafaring, type of ship, work position, level of education, marital status and number of children), and a set of measures of the well-being, personality traits, work motivation, and job satisfaction. All used measures had satisfactory internal reliability (Cronbach alpha coefficients are shown in Table 8.2).

Satisfaction with Life Scale (SWLS; Diener et al., 1985; Komšo & Burić, 2016) consists of five items that measure global cognitive assessment of satisfaction with one's life. Respondents express a degree of agreement with each item statement using a 7-point scale (from 1 = strongly disagree to 7 = strongly agree). Examples of the items: In most ways, my life is close to my ideal; The conditions of my life are excellent. The total score is formed by summing the answers to all five items, with a higher score indicating higher life satisfaction.

Scale of Positive and Negative Experience (SPANE; Diener et al., 2010; Komšo & Burić, 2016) consists of 12 items, whereby six items relate to the experience of positive affect (e.g. pleasant, happy, contented), and the remaining six items relate to the negative affect (e.g. unpleasant, sad, angry). Respondents' task is to evaluate their experiences in the last four weeks on a 5-point scale (from 1 = very rarely or never to 5 = very often or always). The total scores for two subscales; Positive affect (SPANE-P) and Negative affect (SPANE-N), are formed by summing the results for each subscale separately. An overall affect balance score (SPANE-B) is derived by subtracting negative affect score from the positive affect score. The resultant difference score can vary from -24 to 24, whereby 24 implies highest affect balance possible.

Flourishing Scale (FS; Diener et al. 2010; Komšo & Burić, 2016) is a brief 8-items measure that provides a single psychological well-being score, which is defined as social-psychological prosperity. The scale measures respondents' self-perceived success in essential areas such as relationships, self-esteem, purpose, and optimism. It includes three items on social relationships (having supportive and rewarding relationships, contributing to the happiness of others, and being respected by others). The rest of the items relate to the self-assessment of having a purposeful and meaningful life, being engaged and interested in one's activities, feeling competent and capable in the activities that are important to the respondent, self-respect, and optimism regarding future. Respondents express a degree of agreement with each item statement by using a 7-point scale (from 1 = strongly disagree to 7 = strongly agree). The total score is formed by summing the answers to all items, with a higher score indicating a higher level of social-psychological prosperity.

IPIP Big-Five factor markers (Mlačić & Goldberg, 2007) consists of five subscales measuring the Big-five personality traits. Each trait or factor is represented by ten items; Extraversion (e.g. I am the life of the party); Agreeableness (e.g. I sympathise with others' feelings); Conscientiousness (e.g. I get chores done right away); Emotional Stability (e.g. I get irritated easily; note: the item in this example is reverse scored); Intellect/Imagination (e.g. I am quick to understand things). The task of respondents is to describe themselves, i.e. to indicate the accuracy of each statement using a 5-point scale (from 1 = very inaccurate to 5 = very accurate). After using a standardised scoring system for IPIP, including reversed scoring of part of items, the total score for each of the five subscales is formed by summing the results of the specific subscale's items. A higher score on subscales reflects a higher level of self-assessed personality dimensions.

The Work Extrinsic and Intrinsic Motivation Scale (WEIMS; Tremblay et al., 2009) was translated into Croatian for the purpose of this study (using expert back-to-back translation procedure). It consists of 18 items divided into six subscales, which corresponds to the six types of motivation postulated by Self-determination Theory. The each of the subscales consists of three items; Intrinsic motivation (IM; e.g. For the satisfaction I experience from taking on interesting challenges); Integrated regulation (INTEG; e.g. Because it is part of the way in which I have chosen to live my life); Identified regulation (IDENT; e.g. Because it is the type of work I have chosen to attain certain important objectives); Introjected regulation (INTRO; e.g. Because I want to be very good at this work; otherwise I would be very disappointed); External regulation (EXT;

e.g. For the income it provides me); Amotivation (AMO; e.g. I do not know why we are provided with unrealistic working conditions). The task of respondents is to assess to what extent each of the items corresponds to the reasons why they are presently involved in their work, by using a 7-point scale (from 1 = does not correspond at all to 7 = corresponds exactly). The score of each subscale is generated using the mean score of the three items within the subscale. The total score on the WEIMS scale is expressed as the Work Self-Determination Index (W-SDI), which is obtained by using the scores of each of the subscales through the following formula W–SDI = (+3 x IM) + (+2 x INTEG) + (+1 x IDEN) + (-1 x INTRO) + (-2 x EXT) + (-3 x AMO). W-SDI score reflects individuals' relative level of self-determination. The possible W-SDI score ranges from -36 to 36; whereby a positive score indicates a self-determined profile, while the negative score suggests a non-self-determined profile.

The Seafarer's Job satisfaction Scale (SJS) is developed for the purpose of this study, whereby the choice of the items was strongly based on the results of the descriptive qualitative study of job satisfaction among seafarers (Slišković & Penezić, 2015b). The purpose of developing this measure, which consists of 18 items, was to tackle specific aspects of seafarers' job satisfaction. The task of the respondents was to evaluate their satisfaction with each of the aspects, using the 7-point scale (from 1 = completely dissatisfied to 7 = completely satisfied), having in mind their current or last work contract. Obtained results on SJS scale were analysed using Maximum likelihood factor analysis, which showed a one-factor solution, and explained 48% of the variance. All items had satisfactory factor loadings (Table 8.1), and Cronbach alpha reliability coefficient was high (Table 8.2).

2.3 *Procedure*

The study was conducted in the spring of 2019. Two forms of content-identical questionnaires were used in the study; traditional paper-pencil and online electronic form. About half of the sample (50.70%) completed the traditional, while 49.30% of the sample completed the online form of the questionnaire. Participation in the study was completely voluntary and anonymous. The traditional form of the questionnaire was administrated at several maritime educational institutions in Croatia with the help of teachers at various training sessions that seafarers attended. Sampling the participants for the online form of the questionnaire was based on the help of several maritime educational and/or crewing organisations who advertised the invitation to the study via social media. In both cases, the contact information of the researcher was provided to ensure that participants had opportunities for questions, comments and/or requests for feedback.

TABLE 8.1 Results of factor analysis of SJS items (N = 286)

	Items	Factor Loadings
1	Organisation of work on board.	.77
2	Your workload on board.	.73
3	Respect for working and non-working periods on board.	.75
4	Amount of overtime hours on board.	.68
5	Adherence to safety standards on board.	.76
6	Working conditions on board.	.85
7	Knowledge, skills and competencies of onboard employees.	.67
8	Interpersonal relations on board.	.63
9	Opportunities for leisure time on board (availability of sport, recreational and social facilities and activities).	.68
10	The quality, preparation and variety of food on board.	.66
11	Opportunities and cost of internet access on board.	.48
12	Relations with your land based company representatives.	.66
13	The way your company executives manage the business.	.74
14	Fair treatment of employees by the company.	.78
15	Your contract in terms of the amount of time on board and at home.	.62
16	Respect for the contracted periods on board / at home.	.66
17	Your income.	.62
18	Other material benefits from the company (bonuses, health insurance, pension fund, payment for trainings, etc.)	.63
Eigenvalue		8.63
Proportion of explained variance		.48

3 Results

According to descriptive statistics of the used measures (Table 8.2) seafarers' well-being in the sample under investigation is in average good (moderate level of cognitive, and relatively higher levels of affective and social-psychological well-being). Assessments of personality show that participants' Big Five personality traits are in average moderate (exception is *agreeableness* with somewhat higher average value). Regarding work motivation dimensions, it is interesting that the highest average value is obtained on the *external regulation* subscale. However, reports on all three self-determinate subscales of

TABLE 8.2 Descriptive statistics for personality traits, extrinsic and intrinsic work motivation measures, job satisfaction, and well-being measures (N = 286)

Measures	Items number	Cronbach alpha	Theoretical range	Obtained range	M	SD	Skewness	Kurtosis
Personality traits								
Extraversion	10	.78	10–50	18–48	33.39	5.60	0.11	0.05
Agreeable-ness	10	.77	10–50	33–50	45.04	4.65	0.12	-0.19
Conscien-tiousness	10	.80	10–50	19–50	38.63	5.56	-0.35	-0.11
Emotional Stability	10	.86	10–50	14–49	36.53	6.58	-0.35	-0.01
Intellect/ Imagination	10	.75	10–50	23–50	35.50	5.09	0.36	0.10
WEIMS scale								
IM - Intrinsic motivation	3	84	1–7	1–7	4.41	1.53	-0.30	-0.59
INTEG - Integrated regulation	3	.81	1–7	1–7	4.35	1.59	-0.29	-0.67
IDENT - Identified regulation	3	.75	1–7	1–7	4.66	1.45	-0.37	-0.48
INTRO - Introjected regulation	3	.82	1–7	1–7	3.82	1.68	0.03	-0.83
EXT - External regulation	3	.66	1–7	1–7	5.37	1.12	-0.53	0.12
AMO - Amotivation	3	.76	1–7	1–7	2.89	1.54	0.62	-0.39
W–SDI	18	-	-36–36	-22–21	3.37	7.62	-0.13	-0.02
SJS scale								
Seafarer Job Satisfaction	18	.94	18–126	18–126	87.42	20.96	-0.65	0.31

TABLE 8.2 Descriptive statistics for personality traits, extrinsic and intrinsic work motivation measures, job satisfaction, and well-being measures (N = 286) (*Cont.*)

Measures	Items number	Cronbach alpha	Theoretical range	Obtained range	M	SD	Skewness	Kurtosis
Well-being measures								
Life satisfaction	5	.87	5–35	5–35	21.54	6.56	-0.25	-0.40
Flourishing	8	.91	8–56	16–56	42.61	7.85	-0.74	0.55
SPANE - Positive	6	.89	6–30	6–30	23.32	3.71	-0.68	1.47
SPANE - Negative	6	.89	6–30	6–30	13.28	4.70	0.86	1.17
SPANE – Balance	12	.90	-24–24	-24–24	10.04	7.29	-0.76	1.61

Note: W–SDI = Work Self-Determination Index

motivation are above the average, which, in forming total score, resulted in a positive value of the *work self-determination* index. Finally, the average value of job satisfaction of the tested sample may be described as relatively high, considering the theoretical range.

Before performing the main analyses related to research aim (hierarchical regression analyses on criterion variables), bivariate correlations between predictor variables (work experience in seafaring, five personality traits, work self-determination index, and job satisfaction) and criterion variables (three well-being dimensions), as well as intercorrelations between all predictors, were tested. Bivariate correlations between used predictors and well-being measures were, as expected, mostly significant and positive, while their magnitude is low to moderate (Table 8.3). Work experience in seafaring, which was used as controlling demographic variable, was negatively related to life satisfaction and flourishing ($p<.05$).

Hierarchical regression analyses on three dimensions of well-being were performed in four identical steps (Tables 8.4, 8.5 and 8.6), with theory-driven order. Work experience in seafaring is included in the first step as the only demographic controlling variable used (correlation between age and seafaring experience was .84. Therefore, it was redundant to include age into regression analyses). Personality traits, as most stable characteristics, were included in the second step, and work self-determinate index was included

TABLE 8.3 Pearson coefficients of correlation between predictors and criterion variables (N = 286)

	Measure	2	3	4	5	6	7	8	9	10	11
1	Work experience in seafaring	-.00	.03	.02	.02	-.09	-.02	-.03	-.12*	-.12*	.02
2	Extraversion	-	.36**	.26**	.36**	.40**	.17**	.15*	.28**	.34**	.39**
3	Agreeableness		-	.37**	.26**	.39**	.04	.12*	.10	.37**	.21**
4	Conscientiousness			-	.49**	.35**	.17**	.16**	.20**	.41**	.33**
5	Emotional Stability				-	.22**	.21**	.21**	.24**	.40**	.60**
6	Intellect/ Imagination					-	.21**	.01	.16**	.32**	.13**
7	W-SDI						-	.28**	.29**	.23**	.27**
8	Job Satisfaction							-	.43**	.39**	.39**
9	Life satisfaction								-	.56**	.43**
10	Flourishing									-	.44**
11	SPANE-B										-

Note: *p<.05, **p<.01

TABLE 8.4 Hierarchical regression analysis of predictors of life satisfaction (N = 286)

	Step 1 β	Step 2 β	Step 3 β	Step 4 β
Step 1				
Work exp.in seaf. (years)	-.12*	-.12*	-.12*	-.10
Step 2				
Extraversion		.21**	.20**	.17**
Agreeableness		-.05	-.02	-.06
Conscientiousness		.10	.09	.07
Emotional Stability		.12	.09	.05
Intellect/Imagination		.03	-.01	.05
Step 3				
W-SDI			.23**	.13*
Step 4				
Job Satisfaction				.35**
Adjusted R2	.01*	.10**	.15**	.25**

Note: *p<.05, **p<.01

TABLE 8.5 Hierarchical regression analysis of predictors of flourishing (N = 286)

	Step 1 β	Step 2 β	Step 3 β	Step 4 β
Step 1				
Work exp.in seaf. (years)	-.12*	-.12*	-.12*	-.11*
Step 2				
Extraversion		.13*	.12*	.09
Agreeableness		.17**	.18**	.16**
Conscientiousness		.19**	.19**	.17**
Emotional Stability		.21**	.19**	.16**
Intellect/Imagination		.08	.06	.10
Step 3				
W-SDI			.12*	.05
Step 4				
Job Satisfaction				.28**
Adjusted R2	.01*	.29**	.30**	.37**

Note: *p<.05, **p<.01

TABLE 8.6 Hierarchical regression analysis of predictors of SPANE-balance (N = 286)

	Step 1 β	Step 2 β	Step 3 β	Step 4 β
Step 1				
Work exp.in seaf. (years)	.02	-.00	.00	.01
Step 2				
Extraversion		.23**	.22**	.20**
Agreeableness		.01	.03	.00
Conscientiousness		.06	.05	.03
Emotional Stability		.51**	.49**	.46**
Intellect/Imagination		-.09	-.12*	-.08
Step 3				
W-SDI			.14**	.08
Step 4				
Job Satisfaction				.24**
Adjusted R2	.00	.39**	.40**	.46**

Note: *p<.05, **p<.01

in the third step. Finally, job satisfaction (related to the current or last work contract) was included in the fourth step.

As shown in Tables 8.4, 8.5 and 8.6, used predictors explained significant proportions of variances of well-being measures. However, the total explained variances varied among three measures (25% for cognitive, 37% of the variance for social-psychological and 46% for affective dimension). According to the last steps of regression analyses, personality traits and job satisfaction are significant predictors of all three used dimensions of well-being, while results differ with regard to the role of work motivation. Precisely, work self-determination index remained significant only in the explanation of life satisfaction (at a lower significance level of $p<.05$). Additionally, the explanation of three dimensions of well-being by Big Five personality traits results also differ. More precisely, *extraversion* is a significant predictor of cognitive and affective, but not social-psychological well-being; *emotional stability* is a significant predictor of affective and social-psychological well-being, but not the cognitive dimension, and *agreeableness* is an additional significant predictor of social-psychological well-being.

4 Discussion

The aim of this study was to examine the independent contributions of the Big Five personality traits, the level of self-determined work motivation, and job satisfaction in the explanation of three aspects of seafarers' well-being (cognitive, affective, and social-psychological dimension), while controlling for working experience in seafaring.

The contributions of Big Five personality traits in the explanation of three aspects of well-being proved to be significant, thus confirming H2. However, according to the percentages of explained variances of the three well-being dimensions by the personality traits, it may be said that the personality traits (primarily *emotional stability* and *extraversion*) have the highest contribution in the explanation of the *affective well-being* (39%). The *cognitive dimension of well-being* (life satisfaction) is less explained by personality traits (9%), and *extraversion* was shown as the only significant predictor of life satisfaction. Finally, personality traits of seafarers explained 28% of the variance of *social-psychological* well-being. The obtained results of additional significant predictors (agreeableness, and conscientiousness) in the explanation of this eudemonic dimension of well-being, additionally proved the need of multidimensional approach to the well-being (Vanhoutte, 2015). However, although the results of the performed multivariate analyses show that some of the Big

Five personality did not reach the significance level in the explanation of the different dimensions of well-being, it is important to note that correlation analyses on the bivariate level confirmed the theoretical assumption of a significant positive relation between Big Five personality traits and well-being in seafarers. The following text based on a theoretical review (Soto et al., 2016; Strickhouser et al., 2017; Sulsky & Smith, 2005) brings a deeper view on the possible mechanisms of links between personality traits and well-being. *Extraversion* (reflecting sociability, assertiveness, and activity) generally predicts positive interpersonal outcome (e.g. friendship, partnership, social status, more likelihoods for leadership positions in workplace settings, etc.). It is also linked to higher self-esteem, more frequent and intense positive affect, a higher level of emotional resilience, and adaptable strategies of coping. Extraverts also tend to seek social support in facing stressful situations, explaining thus additionally their generally higher levels of well-being. *Agreeableness* relates to social behaviour, i.e. to the extent to which individual behaves prosocial toward others and maintains pleasant and harmonious interpersonal relations. It is considered, like extraversion, as an important predictor of social outcomes and better performance in collaborative work environments. *Conscientiousness* (with key facets including orderliness, self-discipline, and reliability) describes a person's ability to engage in goal-directed behaviours, and exert control over their impulses, which explains the relation of conscientiousness with work productivity. In addition, individuals high on conscientiousness use problem-focused strategies in coping with sources of stress more often and consequently experience less negative stress outcomes in work settings. *Emotional stability* is also a desirable trait. Emotional stable individuals remain calm and optimistic in difficult situations and find it easier to regulate their emotions. On the other hand, the effect of *neuroticism* (negative pole of emotional stability) is shown on the perception of stressful events, unadaptable ways of coping with stress, and dissatisfaction with social support, explaining thus the negative contribution of neuroticism to the explanations of well-being and overall health. Finally, *intellect/imagination* is a trait that describes a person's level of creativity and curiosity. Individuals who score high on this trait tend to have a broad range of interests; they enjoy learning new things and prefer novelty and variety. In contrast, individuals with a low score in this trait are uncomfortable with change, explaining thus differences in facing novel and demanding situations in the work context.

Although correlations between work self-determination index (WSD) and three dimensions of well-being proved as significant and positive, the contributions of WSD to the explanations of the variances of three well-being dimensions above the personality traits were relatively small (ranging from 1 to 5%). In addition, according to the last steps of hierarchical regression analyses, this predictor remained significant after including job satisfaction, only in the explanation of the cognitive aspect of well-being, i.e. life satisfaction, confirming thus H3 only partially. Additional studies are needed to furtherly assess the usefulness of WSD index (Tremblay et al. 2009) and SDT (Deci & Ryan, 1985; Decy & Ryan, 2000; Ryan & Deci, 2000) in seafarers well-being. According to SDT, at the continuum from *amotivation* to *intrinsic motivation*, there are four different types of extrinsically regulated motivation that vary depending on the level of autonomy (*external regulation, introjection, identification*, and *integration*). The first three levels (*amotivation, external regulation*, and *introjection*) are categorised as non-self-determined motivations, while *identification, integration*, and *intrinsic motivation* are the prototype of self-determined motivations, which according to SDT leads to higher well-being. Although the basic assumption of positive relations WSD index and well-being is confirmed, results show that among three tested sets of predictors, WSD had the relatively smallest role in the determination of seafarers' well-being. The obtained results may be partially explained with the fact that external regulation (payment) strongly determines Croatian seafarers' job satisfaction and work-related well-being (Slišković & Penezić, 2015b). This explanation is supported by descriptive values (Table 8.2) which show the highest average value for external regulation.

Finally, results fully supported H1, showing the significant contribution of seafarers' job satisfaction in the explanation of well-being, whereby percentages of explained variance for three dimensions of well-being (above the contributions of more stable differences in personality and motivation) range from 6% to 10%. Besides confirming theoretical assumptions of the importance of work conditions in seafaring for work-related well-being of seafarers (Slišković, 2017), it is safe to say that obtained results also showed on initial confirmation of criterion validity of this newly constructed measure.

In considering the obtained results, it is important to have in mind several methodological limitations, primarily related to the use of convenience sample and cross-sectional design that does not allow a conclusion about causal relations between used constructs. However, noted limitations do not diminish the fact that this is the first study that considers the role of basic personality traits and self-determinate work motivation in the explanation of three conceptually distinct dimensions of seafarers' well-being. Obtained results in general confirmed assumptions of the importance of individual differences in personality and work motivation, and job satisfaction, in the explanation of seafarers' subjective and social-psychological well-being. Further studies in this area, as well as practical interventions aimed at promoting well-being among seafarers, should simultaneously focus on satisfaction by work conditions in seafaring and individual differences in personality and work motivation.

References

An, J., Liu, Y., Sun, Y., & Liu, C. (2020). Impact of work–family conflict, job stress and job satisfaction on seafarer performance. *International Journal of Environmental Research and Public Health* 17, 2191. https://doi.org/10.3390/ijerph17072191

BIMCO/ISF (2015). *Manpower Report: The global supply and demand for seafarers in 2015*. Dalian Maritime University / Dearsley Maritime Consulting Ltd.

Chung, Y., Lee, P. T., & Lee, J. (2017). Burnout in seafarers: its antecedents and effects on incidents at sea. *Maritime Policy & Management*, 44(7), 916–931. https://doi.org/10.1080/03088839.2017.1366672

Cosentino, A. C., & Castro Solano, A. (2017). The High Five: Associations of the Five Positive Factors with the Big Five and well-being. *Frontiers in psychology*, 8, 1250. https://doi.org/10.3389/fpsyg.2017.01250

Deci, E. L., & Ryan, R. M. (1985). Intrinsic motivation and self-determination in human behavior. Plenum.

Deci, E. L., & Ryan, R. M. (2000). The "what" and "why" of goal pursuits: Human needs and the self-determination of behavior. *Psychological Inquiry*, 11(4), 227–268. https://doi.org/10.1207/S15327965PLI1104_01

Diener, E., Emmons, R. A., Larsen, R. J., & Griffin, S. (1985). The Satisfaction with Life Scale. *Journal of Personality Assessment*, 49(1), 71–75. https://doi.org/10.1207/s15327752jpa4901_13

Diener, E., Oishi, S., & Lucas, & R. E. (2002). Subjective well-being: The science of happiness and life satisfaction. In C. R. Snyder & S. J. Lopez (Eds.), *Handbook of Positive Psychology* (pp. 187–194). Oxford University Press.

Diener, E., Wirtz, D., Tov, W., Kim-Prieto, C., Choi, D., Oishi, S., & Biswass-Diener, R. (2010). New well-being measures: Short scales to assess flourishing and positive and negative feeling. *Social Indicators Research*, 97, 143–156. https://doi.org/10.1007/s11205-009-9493-y.

Doyle, N., MacLachlan, M., Fraser, A., Stilz, R., Lismont, K., Cox, H., & McVeigh, J. (2016). Resilience and well-being amongst seafarers: Cross-sectional study of crew across 51 ships. *International Archives of Occupational and Environmental Health*, 89(2), 199–209. https://doi.org/10.1007/s00420-015-1063-9

European Maritime Safety Agency (2019). *Seafarers Statistics in EU. Statistical review* (2017 data – STCW-IS).

Goldberg, L. R. (1992). The development of markers for the Big-Five factor structure. *Psychological Assessment*, 4(1), 26–42. https://doi.org/10.1037/1040-3590.4.1.26

Goldberg, L. R. (1993). The structure of phenotypic personality traits. *American Psychologist*, 48, 26–34. https://doi.org/10.1037/0003-066X.48.1.26

Gutiérrez, J. L. G., Jiménez, B. M., Hernández, E. G., & Puente, C. P. (2005). Personality and subjective well-being: Big five correlates and demographic variables. *Personality and Individual Differences*, 38(7), 1561–1569. https://doi.org/10.1016/j.paid.2004.09.015

Haka, M., Borch, D. F., Jensen, C., & Leppin, A. (2011). Should I stay or should I go? Motivational profiles of Danish seafaring officers and non-officers. *International Maritime Health*, 63(1), 20–30.

Hystad, S.W., & Eid, J. (2016). Sleep and fatigue among seafarers: The role of environmental stressors, duration at sea and psychological capital. *Safety and Health at Work*, 7(4), 363–371. https://doi.org/10.1016/j.shaw.2016.05.006

Iversen, R. T. B. (2012). The mental health of seafarers. *International Maritime Health*, 63(2), 78–89.

Jagosh, J., Pike, K., Henderson, S., & Calderón, M. (2017). *A realist review of merchant seafarers' welfare (2006 – 2016): Examining the changing context for directing charitable innovations.* A Report prepared by Southampton Solent University for the Maritime Charities Group (MCG).

Jepsen, J. R., Zhao, Z., & van Leeuwen. W. M. A. (2015). Seafarer fatigue: a review of risk factors, consequences for seafarers' health and safety and options for mitigation. *International Maritime Health*, 66(2), 106–117. https://doi.org/10.5603/IMH.2015.0024

Jeżewska, M., Leszczyńska, I., & Grubman-Nowak, M. (2013). Personality and temperamental features vs. quality of life of Polish seafarers. *International Maritime Health*, 64(2), 101–105.

Johnson, J. A. (2017). Big-Five model. In V. Zeigler-Hill & T. Shackelford (Eds), *Encyclopedia of Personality and Individual Differences*. Springer.

Judge T., & Klinger, R. (2008). Job satisfaction: Subjective well-being at work. In M. Eid & R. Larsen (Eds.), *The Science of Subjective Well-Being* (pp. 393–413). Guilford Publications.

Kaerlev, L., Hansen, J., Hansen, H. L., & Nielsen, P. S. (2005). Cancer incidence among Danish seafarers: A population based cohort study. *Occupational and Environmental Medicine*, 62(11), 761–765. http://dx.doi.org/10.1136/oem.2005.020818

Kanev, D.,Toncheva, S., Terziev, V., Narleva, K. (2017). *Specific aspects of motivation of seafarers*. Proceeding of 18th Annual General Assembly of the IAMU - Global Perspectives in MET: Towards Sustainable, Green and Integrated Maritime Transport, 1, ISBN: 978-954-8991-98-8.

Komšo, T., & Burić, I. (2016). *Dienerove skale subjektivne dobrobiti: Skala zadovoljstva životom, Skala prosperiteta i Skala pozitivnih i negativnih iskustava* [Dienerer's scales of subjective well-being: Satisfaction with Life Scale, Scale of Positive and Negative Experience, and Flourishing Scale]. Zbirka psihologijskih skala i upitnika, 8. University of Zadar.

Lipowski, M., Lipowska, M., Peplińska, A., & Jeżewska, M. (2014). Personality determinants of health behaviours of merchant navy officers. *International Maritime Health*, 65(3), 158–65. doi: 10.5603/IMH.2014.0030

MacLachlan, M., Kavanagh, B., & Kay, A. (2012). Maritime health: A review with suggestions for research. *International Maritime Health*, 63(1), 1–6.

McCrae, R. R., & Costa, P. T. (1987). Validation of the five-factor model of personality across instruments and observers. *Journal of Personality and Social Psychology*, 52(1), 81–90. https://doi.org/10.1037/0022-3514.52.1.81

McLaughlin, H. L. (2012). Seafarers and Seafaring. In W. K. Talley (Ed.), *The Blackwell Companion to Maritime Economics* (pp. 321–332). Blackwell Publishing.

McVeigh J., MacLachlan, M., Stilz, R., Cox, H, Doyle, N., Fraser, A., & Dyer, M. (2017). Positive psychology and well-being at sea. In M. MacLachlan (Ed), *Maritime Psychology: Research in Organizational and Health Behavior at Sea* (pp. 19–47). Springer.

McVeigh, J., & MacLachlan, M. (2019). 'A silver wave? Filipino shipmates' experience of merchant seafaring'. *Marine Policy*, 99, 283–297. https://doi.org/10.1016/j.marpol.2018.10.012

McVeigh, J., MacLachlan, M., Coyle, C., & Kavanagh, B. (2019a). Perceptions of well-being, resilience and stress amongst a sample of merchant seafarers and superintendents. *Maritime Studies*, 18(2), 139–158. https://doi.org/10.1007/s40152-018-0129-1

McVeigh, J., MacLachlan, M., Vallières, F., Hyland, P., Stilz, R., Cox, H., & Fraser, A. (2019b). Identifying predictors of stress and job satisfaction in a sample of merchant seafarers using structural equation modeling. *Frontiers in Psychology*, 10, 70. https://doi.org/10.3389/fpsyg.2019.00070

Mitroussi, K., & Notteboom, T. (2015). Getting the work done: motivation needs and processes for seafarers and dock workers. *WMU Journal of Maritime Affairs*, 14, 247–265. https://doi.org/10.1007/s13437-014-0064-y

Mlačić, B., & Goldberg, L. R. (2007). An analysis of a cross-cultural personality inventory: The IPIP Big-Five factor markers. *Journal of Personality Assessment*, 88(2), 168–77. https://doi.org/10.1080/00223890701267993

Nielsen, M. B., Bergheim, K., & Eid, J. (2013). Relationships between work environment factors and workers' well-being in the maritime industry. International Maritime Health, 64(2), 80–88.

Oldenburg, M. & Jensen, H.-J. (2019). Stress and strain among seafarers related to the occupational groups. *International Journal of Environmental Research and Public Health*, 16(7), 1153; https://doi.org/10.3390/ijerph16071153

Oldenburg, M. (2014). Risk of cardiovascular diseases in seafarers. *International Maritime Health*, 65(2), 53–57. doi: 10.5603/IMH.2014.0012

Oldenburg, M., Baur, X., & Schlaich, C. (2010). Cardiovascular diseases in the modern maritime industry. *International Maritime Health*, 62(3), 101–106.

Pauksztat, B. (2017). 'Only work and sleep': Seafarers' perceptions of job demands of short sea cargo shipping lines and their effects on work and life on board. *Maritime Policy & Management*, 44(7), 899–915. https://doi.org/10.1080/03088839.2017.1371347

Roberts, S. E. (2005). Work related mortality from gastrointestinal diseases and alcohol among seafarers employed in British merchant shipping from 1939 to 2002. *International Maritime Health*, 56(1–4), 29–47.

Roberts, S. E. (2008). Fatal work-related accidents in UK merchant shipping from 1919 to 2005. *Occupational Medicine*, 58(2), 129–137. https://doi.org/10.1093/occmed/kqm149

Roberts, S. E., & Marlow, P. B. (2005). Traumatic work related mortality among seafarers employed in British merchant shipping, 1976–2002. *Occupational and Environmental Medicine*, 62(3), 172–180. http://dx.doi.org/10.1136/oem.2003.012377

Ryan, R. M., & Deci, E. L. (2000). Self-determination theory and the facilitation of intrinsic motivation, social development, and well-being. *American Psychologist*, 55(1), 68–78. https://doi.org/10.1037/0003-066X.55.1.68

Ryan, R. M., & Deci, E. L. (2001). On happiness and human potentials: a review of research on hedonic and eudaimonic well-being. *Annual Review of Psychology*, 52(1), 141–66. https://doi.org/10.1146/annurev.psych.52.1.141

Siegler, I. C., & Brummett, B. H. (2000). Associations among NEO personality assessments and well-being at midlife: Facet-level analyses. *Psychology and Aging*, 15(4), 710–714. https://doi.org/10.1037/0882-7974.15.4.710

Sironi, E. (2019). Job satisfaction as a determinant of employees' optimal well-being in an instrumental variable approach. *Quality & Quantity*, 53, 1721–1742. https://doi.org/10.1007/s11135-019-00835-3

Slišković, A. (2017). Occupational stress in seafaring. In M. MacLachlan (Ed.) *Maritime Psychology: Research in Organizational and Health Behavior at Sea* (pp. 99–126). Springer.

Slišković, A., Galić, M., & Russo, A. (2021). Motivacijski čimbenici u odabiru pomorske karijere: Deskriptivno istraživanje na hrvatskim učenicima i studentima pomorstva [Motivational factors in choosing a maritime career: Descriptive research among Croatian students of secondary and higher maritime education], *Društvena istraživanja: Journal for General Social Issues*, 30(1), 93–113. https://doi.org/10.5559/di.30.1.05

Slišković, A., & Penezić Z. (2017). Lifestyle factors in Croatian seafarers as relating to health and stress on board. *WORK*, 56(3), 371–80. doi: 10.3233/WOR-172501

Slišković A., & Penezić Z. (2016). Testing the effects of different aspects of contract and on-board internet access on seafarers' satisfaction and health. *Archives of Industrial Hygiene and Toxicology*, 67(4), 351–361. https://doi.org/10.1515/aiht-2016-67-2785

Slišković, A. & Penezić, Z. (2015a). Occupational stressors, risk and health in the seafaring population. *Review of Psychology*, 22(1–2), 29–39.

Slišković, A., Penezić, Z. (2015b). Descriptive study of job satisfaction and job dissatisfaction in a sample of Croatian seafarers. *International Maritime Health,* 66(2), 97–105. doi: 10.5603/IMH.2015.0023

Soto, C. J., Kronauer, A., & Liang, J. K. (2016). Five-factor model of personality. In S. K. Whitbourne (Ed.), *Encyclopedia of adulthood and aging*, 2 (pp. 506–510). Wiley.

Strickhouser, J. E., Zell, E., & Krizan, Z. (2017). Does personality predict health and well-being? A metasynthesis. *Health Psychology*, 36(8), 797–810. https://doi.org/10.1037/hea0000475

Sulsky, L., & Smith, C. A. (2005). *Work stress*. Thomson Wadsworth.

Tremblay, M. A., Blanchard, C. M., Taylor, S., Pelletier, L. G., & Villeneuve, M. (2009). Work extrinsic and intrinsic motivation scale: Its value for organizational psychology research. *Canadian Journal of Behavioural Science*, 41(4), 213–226. https://doi.org/10.1037/a0018176

Tsai, C., & Liou, Y. (2017). Determinants of work performance of seafarers, *Maritime Business Review*, 2(1), 36–51. https://doi.org/10.1108/MABR-09-2016-0019

Vanhoutte, B. (2015). Hedonic and eudemonic wellbeing. In ESS ERIC (2015) *Measuring and reporting on Europeans' well-being: Findings from the European Social Survey.*

Yuen, K. F., Loh, H. S., Zhou, Q., Wong, Y. D. (2018). Determinants of job satisfaction and performance of seafarers. *Transportation Research Part A: Policy and Practice* 110, 1–12.

CHAPTER 9

A Study on the Sense of Relative Deprivation of Elderly Fishers from the Perspective of Ocean Sociology: The Example of Island S and G in Zhoushan City, China

Wen Zhang and Ya Wen

1 Introduction

The existing research on the elderly fishers in China mainly focuses on the support problems and social security of the elderly fishers. With the migration of population, many small fishing villages on islands have gradually become "old people's villages". Hongsen Tang focused on the situation and problems faced by the families of empty nest of elderly fishers. (Tang, 2007) Yanling Wang et al. analysed the deficiencies of old-age care for fishers in three aspects: first, the insufficiency of family support for the aged; second, the collective subsidy has tended to exist in name; third, the lack of community care. (Wang et al., 2009) Lili Chen believes that the implementation of international agreements and national policies has increased the number of fishers who have lost their sea. Coupled with the slow growth of fishers' income, the self-protection ability of fishers is weak. There are also many specific difficulties in building an ideal old-age security system for fishers. (Chen, 2009) In terms of the suggestions for elderly fishers' care, Chunfen Tong and Jingtian Li proposed that the elderly fishers' mutual aid should be combined with community care, institutional care and government help. (Tong and Li, 2016)

Different from the existing research on the elderly fishers, this paper mainly focuses on the subjective aspect of the problem, that is, the sense of relative deprivation, especially how the "three types of comparisons" deepen the elderly fishers' sense of relative deprivation, and what we can do to help them. This paper takes two islands in Zhoushan Archipelago in China as examples.

Known as "the city of thousand islands", Zhoushan archipelago in China is a typical area located by the sea. It has a long history of marine culture. In its long-term development, marine fishery is an important part of its economy. Island S and Island G are located in the north of Zhoushan Archipelago. They have unique marine fishery resources and are famous for fishing, aquaculture

 | DOI:10.1163/9789004518841_011

and fishery trade for a long time. Island S has been a fishing port town since the end of the 19th century. In addition to fishing, Island G has successfully cultivated mussels on a large scale, so it is also known as "mussel town". Island S covers an area of about 4.22 square kilometres. By the end of 2017, the total number of households in the town was 3,195, with a total registered population of 8,496 and a permanent resident population of 7,535. Among the registered population, 1,807 are over 65 years old. Island G covers an area of about five square kilometres. By the end of 2017, there were 3191 households in the township, with a total registered population of 8,159, a permanent resident population of 8,575, and a population of 1,964 elderly people over the age of 65. The two islands face each other across the sea, about 800 metres apart, and are now connected by a highway bridge.

When investigating the elderly fishers in Island S and Island G, a question similar to the "Easterlin Paradox" (Easterlin, 1974) has always puzzled us: "why do they still have a strong sense of relative deprivation despite the government's continuous policy measures to improve their lives in recent years?" Earlier, due to the household registration system, Chinese fishers and farmers were excluded from the old-age insurance. From the local social security department, we have learned that since 2012, fishers under the age of 60 can participate in old-age insurance. However, the problem is that elderly fishers over 60 still do not have old-age insurance. For the elderly fishers without insurance, the government has issued a kind of fishing age subsidy since 2015. According to the fishing years of the fishers, the monthly subsidy is calculated at ten yuan[1] per fishing year, and the maximum subsidy can be 400 yuan per month. Since the beginning of 2020, the local government further increased the payment of fishers' subsidy from 10 yuan per month to 16.7 yuan per month, with a maximum of 668 yuan per month. At present, the fishing age subsidy has become the most important source of income for the elderly fishers on Zhoushan archipelago.

In the questionnaire survey, we inquired about the degree of satisfaction to their old-age life of elderly fishers. The statistical results of 120 elderly fishers are shown in Table 9.1. Among them, 33 respondents answered "very satisfied" and "satisfied", accounting for 27.5%; 48 respondents answered "not very satisfied" and "very dissatisfied", accounting for 40%; Another 32.5% of the elderly fishers answered: "Just so so". This result can show that the elderly fishers have a strong sense of relative deprivation. When we try to understand

1 Yuan is the unit of currency in China. According to the current exchange rate, 1 yuan is almost equal to 0.1445 US dollars.

TABLE 9.1 The degree of satisfaction of elderly fishermen with their old-age lives

Degree of satisfaction	Samples (n)	Proportions (%)
Very Satisfied	6	5
Satisfied	27	22.5
Just so so	39	32.5
Not very satisfied	42	35
Very dissatisfied	6	5

them through interviews, we also find that they are dissatisfied and resentful on their old-age life.

In order to understand this seemingly contradictory phenomenon, on the one hand, we draw on ocean sociology to form the theoretical perspective and framework of this paper. On the other hand, we have also discovered a large number of historical and empirical facts through personal life history interviews, participation observation, questionnaire survey and other methods on Island S and Island G. The combination of theory and practice eventually helps us to solve this puzzle.

Ocean Sociology, according to the definition of Chinese historian Yang Guozhen, "is a discipline that focuses on the ocean century and ocean society, a special regional society in a specific historical period, studies the interaction between the ocean and human society, analyses the impact of marine development on modern society, and analyses a series of complex changes of human society caused by marine development." (Yang, 2000) According to Feng Cui, Ning'er Song and others, "The so-called ocean sociology refers to the application of the basic concepts, theories and methods of sociology to the practical activities of human in developing the ocean, their social roots and social impacts." (Cui, Song, Chen &Tang,2014, p. 15) The disciplinary system of ocean sociology is divided into five parts: the study of marine groups, organisations and communities; the study of marine social changes; the study of marine social problems, social conflicts and control; the sociological examination of important human activities on the sea; and the study of marine culture and history (Zhang, 2010, p. 11). Ocean sociology focuses on the marine social changes, and marine social problems brought about by marine development. The issue of relative deprivation of elderly fishers on the islands can be understood in this context.

In terms of research methods, the research team visited Island S and Island G in Zhoushan City, Zhejiang Province three times in May, July 2018 and February

2019. Mainly using the method of personal life history interviews, combined with a questionnaire survey and participant observation, the research team investigated the situation of 120 elderly fishers over 65 years old on the two islands. A sample of 120 elderly fishers was randomly collected. We conducted questionnaire surveys, participant observation and in-depth interviews with them in the streets, docks, communities and fishers' families. In addition, we also held discussions with local government officials and staff of relevant departments, visited fishing villages and gathered relevant information.

The basic information of the 120 elderly fishers we investigated is as follows. The fishers are generally old, 89 of them are over 65 years old, accounting for 74.17% of the total number, of which 43 are over 76 years old, accounting for 35.84% of the total. In terms of fishing years, they have been engaged in fishing for a long time. Seventy elderly fishers have been fishing for 41 years or more, accounting for 58.33%, and 22 for 31–40 years, accounting for 18.33%. The education level of the surveyed elderly fishers is generally low, with 41 illiterate and semi-illiterate, accounting for 34.17%; 63 with primary school education, accounting for 52.5%; and only 14 with junior school education, accounting for 11.67%; 2 with high school education or above accounted for 1.67%. Junior college education or above was zero.

2 Insufficient Social and Psychological Support

On the two islands, what we first found is that although the government has continuously introduced policies and measures to improve the lives of the elderly fishers, which has narrowed the distance between their economic income and their expectations, their social and psychological support is still obviously insufficient.

After the reform and opening up, the process of urbanisation in China has had a significant impact on the islands. Since the 1990s, Zhoushan has implemented the policy of "relocating small islands and constructing large islands". Young people migrated to cities, and the population of small islands has shown negative growth for many years. Mayor Chen of Island S introduced:

> Now, due to urbanisation, young people are moving to large areas, which also brings a lot of problems for the elderly. Island B used to be a village with thousands of people, but now it has become a small village with only a few hundred people. There are mainly old men and women; middle-aged women are called "little girls" jokingly. This is the case on many islands. The older generation has worked hard to train their children to

> be urban people. However, due to the high living costs in the city, many elderly people are still supporting their children when they grow up, and the return of children may not be expected. Some of these elderly people live with their children in the cities to help them with their children. Some are reluctant to go to big cities and prefer to stay on the island. They are used to living here. (Mayor Chen, interviewed on July 25, 2018)

Indeed, when we talked about children with the elderly, we found that most of their children did not work and live nearby. The nearer ones were in the county town or Zhoushan City, and the farther ones were in Ningbo, Hangzhou and Shanghai. According to the result of the questionnaire, only 28 older people (23.34%) lived with their children and spouses. 62 (51.67%) lived with their spouses, and 26 (21.67%) lived alone. "Living with their spouses" and "living alone" were 88, accounting for 73.34%. Therefore, most of the elderly fishers did not live with their children and grandchildren.

According to the current standard, when the population aged over 60 accounts for 10% of the total population in a country or region or the population over 65 accounts for 7%, it means that the country or region counts as an ageing society. According to the figures of Island S at the end of 2017, there were 1,807 elderly people over 65 years old, accounting for 21.27% of the total registered population (8,496); at the end of 2017, there were 1,964 elderly people over 65 years old on Island G, accounting for 24.07% of the total registered population (8,159). It can be seen that the ageing problem of the two islands is quite severe. Walking on the street, we can see that there are many old people and a few young people and children, yet the latter includes tourists from outside. Because many old fishers over the age of 65 do not adapt to the closed and fast-paced life in the city, they prefer to stay in their familiar environment and relatively open space on the island. It is worth noting that middle-aged

TABLE 9.2 The living conditions of the elderly fishermen

Living conditions	Samples (n)	Proportions (%)
Living alone	26	21.67
Living with spouses	62	51.67
Living with children	11	9.17
Living with spouses and children	17	14.17
Living with parents	10	0.83
Others	3	2.5

people aged at 40–50 are more adaptable to life outside, they say that most of them will not choose to stay on the island in the future. Therefore, some people describe these old fishers as "old people who will not be renewed" on the island.

Without vigorous young people and children, the old fishers left behind on the island have a simple and boring old-age life, which makes them feel more and more lonely. Without the support from young people, the old fishers are likely to lose their confidence and fall into the mire, when faced with difficulties. At the same time, the elderly fishers in the neighbourhood with similar experiences often talk about their unfortunate experiences together, which will actually magnify their negative emotions such as dissatisfaction and resentment, and lose the ability to see the problem from different perspectives and actively seek solutions. In the face of this situation, local government departments and social work institutions have not been able to provide adequate social support and services for the elderly fishers far away from their children and grandchildren.

In addition, when we use the questionnaire to investigate "the troubles and difficulties in the old-age life", many fishers not only have insufficient economic security and poor health but also strongly reflect that "they have not been treated fairly by society", which in fact shows that the elderly fishers are facing a big psychological dilemma. Through interviews, we have learned that the psychological dilemma of the elderly fishers is multi-faceted: there is a sense of marginalisation and oblivion shown by the word "old people who will not be renewed" on the islands, the sense of loss and abandonment because "youth has passed away" and "the past is no longer brilliant", a sense of imbalance and grievance when compared with other social groups, there is also a sense of betrayal resulting from not being treated justly by the state and society. However, these psychological dilemmas have not been paid enough attention and received enough psychological support.

3 "Three Types of Comparison" That Strengthen Relative Deprivation

By in-depth interview, we found that the elderly fishers do make a variety of "comparisons" in telling their personal life history, which may have influenced their perception and evaluation of their lives and then strengthened the sense of relative deprivation. We have summed up the three common types:

3.1 *Comparing with Their Own Past*

The old fishers on the islands now seem to be a group that has been marginalised and gradually forgotten in the process of modernisation, but they also had an extraordinary and brilliant past. When we recalled the past with them, they showed excitement, joy, and even pride from time to time, and took the trouble to describe the past to us again and again. The first thing they talked about was the local "fish season" and the fishing experience handed down from generation to generation:

> Old fishers said that Island S is located in the centre of the East China Sea fishing ground. Traditionally, the fishery resources are very rich. A set of fishery knowledge has been handed down from generation to generation, like when the fish are in what place, what fishing routes are and so on. Small yellow croaker is caught in spring, cuttlefish is caught in summer, large yellow croaker is caught in summer and autumn, hairtail fish is caught from autumn to winter. Each kind of fish is caught for more than two months. There is a difference between a big year and a small year of fishing, generally speaking, fish is more in the first year and less in the second year. Hairtail fish swims from north to south, and cuttlefish swims from south to north. Small yellow croaker and large yellow croaker goes to the north to lay eggs. (Uncle Wang, interviewed on May 20, 2018)

Many old fishers still remember the scenes of abundant fishery resources in the era of collectivisation. They recalled that, when they were young, they used to catch 40,000 or 50,000 jin[2] in a net. With good luck, it was possible to get more than 100,000 jin in one net. The docks on the island were full of fish. In 1976, many local fishers saw Ningbo fishing boats fishing large yellow croaker on the sea, which they would never forget. They described to us that there were so many fish that the net could not even be closed. Later, they heard that the harvest of Ningbo fishing boat was more than 40,000 loads. The old fishers said that at that time, the fish was sold to the state at a very low price. The large and small yellow croaker was only 0.14 and 0.15 yuan per jin.

Many old fishers also told us the story of "100,000 fishers coming to Island S" in the 1960s, which was a brilliant page in the history of Island S. At that time, when the winter fishing season came, fishers from Shanghai, Liaoning, Fujian, Ningbo, Hangzhou, Wenzhou and other places would come here to catch hairtail fish. During the whole month in winter, the streets were crowded with people. When it was windy, the ships returned and lined up in the port. People could even walk on the ships. The old fishers told us that the Guowei Hotel on the street used to be the headquarters of Shanghai, the building of Sizhoutang community was the headquarters of Ningbo, and the building opposite the

2 jin is a unit of weight commonly used in China. One jin is equal to 500 grams.

bank was the headquarters of Fujian Province. These buildings were built by the provincial governments that came to Island S to fish every year. During the winter fishing season, the night scenery on the street was very beautiful. The Town Committee would also play movies on the open square. Many fishers came from distant fishing villages to watch movies and participate in the lively and happy atmosphere.

Old fishers' youth bloomed in the prosperous fishery at that time. In 1977, at the age of 27, Uncle Ge was trained as "the youngest captain of Island S", which was a big honour for him. There was a little pride on his face when he talked to us about it. Among the seemingly ordinary old fishers we met, there were many well-known captains, "model workers" and "active members", who had made outstanding contributions to the national fishery construction. Uncle Wu shared with us some information in the era of collectivisation:

> At that time, the policy was that "the more you catch, the better, the more honours you will get." "Fishing during the day and fishing at night". If you caught a lot of fish, the town, the county and even the province would praise you as a "model worker." At that time, the slogan of catching fish was "go out early and return late, and frequently cast the net". Fishing more meant thinking well, and the more, the better. Some good captains who could catch more than 10,000 loads a year, were honoured as "Ten thousand loads captain". (Uncle Wu, interviewed on July27, 2018)

Some fishers missed the era after the reform and opening up. They said that, at that time, they really relied on their ability to live, and their strength was of great use. As long as you had the ability, everyone could be the leader of the ship. They were also young at that time, they could fish to earn money and help their families live a good life, so it was the happiest time.

Fishing, though glorious and fulfilling, was also an extremely hard and dangerous job. As the saying goes, "there are three kinds of hardships in the world: forging iron, grinding tofu and fishing". The labour intensity and danger of fishing are well known. Compared with the present, when the old fishers were young, the equipment on board was more backward, the conditions were more difficult, and the risks were greater:

> In the 1960s and 1970s, fishing vessels with 60 horsepower were out in the farther sea area, and in the near coastal area were our fishers' manual ship. There were four people on the 40 horsepower ship, cooking with a small stove. When the wind and waves were too big to cook, they ate cold rice and drank little water. A little fresh water on the ship was used

for cooking. When the wind was strong, you could not sleep for ten days. There was no weather forecast at that time, you did not know when the wind would come, so it was dangerous. The proverb says that fishing villages were "ten coffins and nine empty", and fishers always fished with "one foot in the coffin and one foot out." In 1957, there was a major accident in Lvsi fishing ground due to strong wind, and many people died. There was a lot of sand in Lvsi Sea, and the ship was easy to run aground. When the wind came, it overturned.

At that time, there were always dangerous situations at night because of the wind. If you were lucky, you could get help if there was another ship nearby. But there were few ships nearby, so there were many empty tombs here. Because the ship was very important, the crew knew their own ship like the palm of their hands. They were clear with every problem of it. (Uncle Li, interviewed on July 26, 2018)

Time has passed, and circumstances have changed. With the rapid decline of marine fishery resources, the wild large yellow croaker, which came "100,000 jin in one net" several decades ago, is now hard to find. The market price is more than 1,000 yuan per kilogram. And the young men who once fought and dedicated themselves to the fishing industry are now old. Recalling the extraordinary past, they are sad at heart. The glory of the past highlights the present bleakness and desolation. In the interviews, old fishers often said that the state did not care about them, which was unfair to them. They worked hard when they were young, but didn't get enough protection when they got old, so they feel betrayed, angry and dissatisfied.

3.2 *Comparing with the Younger Generation of Fishers*

Due to the progress of the times and the changes of the system, there are great differences in the situation of fishers of different ages. First of all, the most obvious difference is reflected in the treatments of old-age insurance. As mentioned above, the local social security policy is that fishers under the age of 60 (at the time of April 1, 2012) can participate in the insurance. This policy solves the problem of old-age insurance for younger fishers, who can enjoy a monthly pension of several thousand yuan after retirement, but many old fishers are rejected because they are over age. As we mentioned earlier, Uncle Ge was trained as "the youngest captain of Island S" at the age of 27. However, when he participated in the old-age insurance, he had "a little bit less luck":

Uncle Ge is a year late. He was born in 1951 and was 61 years old in 2012. Later, uncle Ge complained to the leaders who had trained him to be the

> captain, "You trained me as a captain before, but now I have no insurance." Now. he receives the government's fishing age subsidy every month. His fishing age is 28 years, and he gets 280 yuan a month.

Uncle Ge helplessly said that when he was young, he wanted to take part in insurance but could not participate because no policy existed. However, now, such a policy comes, but he cannot take part because he is over age. This is really a "trick of life"! Uncle Ge is a "little brother" among his friends, and many old fishers in their 70s and 80s are farther away from this age line.

In fact, not only in terms of the old-age insurance but also in many other aspects, the situation of the old and the young fishers is very different. Old fishers said that, in their times, the captain's and the crew's share were the same (both one share), the relationship between them was equal and being a captain did not make anyone rich. But now, the captain gets 2 or 3 shares (2/1/1/1/1; 3/1/1/1). Therefore, there is a big gap between the rich and the poor or between the captain and ordinary fishers. The younger Captain Wu confirmed:

> When Wu was 22 years old, he was trained as a captain. He thinks that being the leader of a ship needs: 1. Technology; 2. An economic foundation (ship owned by himself). The better these two conditions are, the faster you will develop. Now, people in their 40s are still making money when they are captains. If they do well, they can make 300,000 or 400,000 yuan a year. The captains are proud of being rich. He can hire people and let them do some odd jobs (picking up fish, cooking, etc.) and forbid them to do the main things like steering.

In addition to share income, now, the captain can own "horsepower index",[3] which is valuable. Old fishers said that when they were young, the horsepower index was not for sale. If a ship was obsolete and did not use the horsepower index, it would be returned to the brigade, and the brigade would give it to the following ships for free. But now, the horsepower index can be bought and sold. Due to the national policy of controlling the increase of ships, the horsepower index is becoming more and more valuable. If the captain quits fishing, he or she can get a lot of money by selling the horsepower index.

In addition, the policy of diesel subsidy implemented by the state since 2006 has brought a large amount of new income to the captains and shareholders.

3 In order to protect fishery resources and prevent the blind development of marine fishing capacity, the state controls the total horsepower of fishing vessels. A captain has to get the "horsepower index" first, if he wants to run a fishing vessel.

Diesel subsidies are now issued according to the horsepower index of a ship. After getting the money, shareholders will divide it according to their shares. It is said that the captains in the era of diesel subsidy really made money, but these old fishers had already retired at that time.

Compared with the younger generation of fishers, the old fishers' heart is bitter. During the interview, an old fisherman said: "the older generation contributed to the state, while the younger generation enjoys happiness from the state. It is important to have a good attitude." There is a deep sense of helplessness, grievance and imbalance in his speech.

3.3 *Comparing with Other Occupational Groups*

In addition to comparing themselves with their past and younger generation of fishers, old fishers also compared themselves with other occupational groups. This type of comparison, while not completely factual, is to strengthen their "sense of relative deprivation" further.

Some old fishers compare themselves to government officials. Those officials are supposed to serve the front-line personnel, but now they can get 4,000 or 5,000 yuan per month after retirement, while the old fishers only have a few hundred yuan of subsidies. Some old fishers think that the life of farmers is better than theirs. Farmers have land. If the land is expropriated, the farmer can be included in social insurance. What makes them particularly aggrieved is that those outsiders who come to set up small shops and do small businesses here can participate in social insurance and enjoy pension, but they cannot. Some fishers complained that their monthly subsidies of several hundred yuan were lower than the relief fund, etc.

It should be noted that the distinction between urban and rural areas, between different occupational groups and between local people and outsiders is becoming smaller and smaller, which is the embodiment of the increasing progress of China's social security policy. The reason why the old fishers cannot participate in the insurance is that they are over age (according to the current policy), not because of their occupation or region.

4 Marine Social Change and the Relative Deprivation of Old Fishers

C. Wright Mills, an American sociologist, once put forward the concept of "sociological imagination", which links "individual's life destiny" with "social structure in history" (Mills, 2004, p. 4). The individual is the epitome of the times. In this paper, from the perspective of ocean sociology, we also find that the relative deprivation of elderly fishers is not purely personal, nor just synchronic. It is closely related to marine social change.

Since the middle of the 20th century, humans have increased the intensity of marine development, which has brought about the rapid development of marine economy and the adjustment of marine industrial structures. The modern economic system with the core of marine resources exploitation and processing industry and coastal tourism service industry has gradually replaced the traditional marine economic system with the main contents of fishing, salt drying and maritime transportation. Marine development has also led to dramatic changes in the marine environment and society, including population and intergenerational changes, environmental degradation and changes in production and lifestyle, changes in marine social organisations and marine communities. There is a certain degree of disharmony and imbalance between marine development and social development (Cui & Tang, 2014). For example, in the interviews with fishers, we heard that the fishery resources in the East China Sea, such as large yellow croaker, were once rich and then depleted, while the fishers who were once in a blaze of glory were gradually marginalised and fell into the dark. We also heard about the changes in the fishery system and management methods in different periods and the psychological gap of elderly fishers. From the perspective of ocean sociology, we can find the social and historical reasons behind the relative deprivation of the elderly fishers. Today, when embracing the "ocean century" and enjoying the benefits and convenience brought by marine development to the whole society, we should not forget these elderly fishers who have made painstaking contributions to the national fishery development. We should pay more attention to their living conditions in their later years and do something for them as far as we can.

On the policy level, in order to reduce the relative deprivation of the elderly fishers, the legislature and the relevant government departments should actively promote the early introduction of relevant policies on the old-age social security for fishers, especially the issue of elderly fishers' participation in old-age insurance and increasing fishing age subsidy, so as to reduce the distance between the reality and the elderly fishers' expectation. At the same time, the government should pay attention to promoting the development of elderly service projects through government purchase, so as to provide adequate social and psychological support for the elderly fishers.

On the practical level, we should vigorously develop the social case, group and community work services for the elderly fishers, deeply understand their history and life, affirm their contributions and give recognition, and help them establish a positive attitude. This should belong to the category of "marine social work" proposed by some scholars (Deng, 2019). During the period that we stayed on the islands, members of our research group also tried to carry out a "reminiscence group", which helps the elderly fishers to face and reorganise their life experiences through the purposeful and guided therapeutic reminiscence of the past. This group has ultimately brought a lot of positive effects on the emotions, self-image and cognition of the elderly fishers.

Around the question raised at the beginning of the paper, we have conducted a study from the perspective of ocean sociology, and pointed out the close relationship between the drastic changes of marine society and the relative deprivation of the elderly fishers on the islands. In order to alleviate the uncoordinated and unbalanced relationship between marine development and social development, and to maintain the harmony and stability of marine society and realise justice, we still have a long way to go.

References

Chen, Lili (2009). On the Construction of Social Insurance System for Fishers: Based on the Survey of Zhoushan Fishing Area. *Journal of Zhejiang Wanli University*, 4, 28–34. (陈莉莉(2009). 论适合渔民需要的社会养老保险制度的建构——基于舟山渔区的调查.浙江万里学院学报,4, 28–34.)

Cui, Feng, Song, Ning'er, Chen, Tao & Guojian Tang (2014). *The Construction of Ocean Sociology, Basic Conception and Systematic Framework*. Beijing: Social Sciences Academic Press. (崔凤、宋宁而、陈涛、唐国建(2014). 海洋社会学的建构——基本概念与体系框架. 北京：社会科学文献出版社.)

Cui, Feng & Guojian Tang (2014). *Strategies of Coordinated Development between Ocean and Society*. Beijing: Ocean Press. (崔凤、唐国建(2014). 海洋与社会协调发展战略. 北京：海洋出版社.)

Deng, Qiongfei (2019). Marine Social Work: New Vision of Social Work Research. *Social and Public Welfare*, 8, 73–76. (邓琼飞(2019). 海洋社会工作——社会工作研究的一种新视野. 社会与公益,8, 73–76)

Easterlin, R. A. (1974). Does economic growth improve the human lot? Some empirical evidence. In P. A. David & M.W. Reder (Eds.). *Nations and Households in Economic Growth*. (pp. 89–125). New York: Academic Press.

Tang, Hongsen (2007). On the Social Care of Zhoushan Empty Nest Families. *Journal of Zhejiang Ocean University*, 3, 45–48. (唐洪森(2007).谈舟山空巢孤寡老人家庭的社会关爱.浙江海洋学院学报,3,45–48.)

Tong, C., Jingtian L. (2016). Research on the Support Mode of Chinese Elderly Fishers under the Background of Aging. *Journal of Guangdong Ocean University*, 2, 55–60. (同春芬、李静恬(2016).老龄化背景下我国渔民养老方式探究.广东海洋大学学报,2, 55–60.)

Wang, Yanling et al. (2009). Social Security Measures for Chinese Fishers Based on the Risk-taking Status of Marine Fishers. *Journal of Dalian Maritime University*, 5, 34–39.

(王艳玲等(2009). 基于海洋渔民风险承担状况的中国渔民社会保障措施. 大连海事大学学报, 5, 34–39.)

Wright Mills, C. (2001). *Sociological Imagination*, Chen, Qiang & Yongqiang Zhang (Trans.). Beijing: SDX Joint Publishing Company. (C·赖特·米尔斯(2001). 社会学的想象力. 陈强、张永强译. 北京：生活·读书·新知三联书店.)

Yang, Guozhen (2000). Conceptional Conformity of Maritime Studies as Subjects of Humanities and Social Science. *Journal of Xiamen University*, 1, 95–100. (杨国桢 (2000). 论海洋人文社会科学的概念磨合，厦门大学学报(哲学社会科学版), 1, 95–100.)

Zhang, Kaicheng (2010). *An Introduction to Ocean Sociology*. Beijing: Ocean Press. (张开城(2010). 海洋社会学概论. 北京：海洋出版社.)

CHAPTER 10

Families of Seamen in the Period of Political Changes and Today – Homelessness Issues

Roland Dobrzeniecki-Łukasiewicz

1 Introduction

The profile of the port town in Poland before the transformations of 1989 was structured by multiculturalism, frequently referred to as a window to the world, just as the Internet can be called nowadays. They were places where various social norms, cultures and skin colours were mixed and where one could take a breath of fresh air from the big world. Everything that was either unknown or only heard of in other towns was absorbed here and sensed on a daily basis by communing with the foreign ship's crews or directly – as the marine economy staff having contact with stories and items brought from abroad by the sailors and fishers. The world of port towns was completely different from the one in central Poland, different not only in terms of knowledge about other countries and cultures but also mentally different, shaped by material testimonies from abroad. Nowadays, it may sound awkward (particularly to the young generation not experienced with real socialism), but they reflect the reality we faced before 1989.

Poland's systemic transformation began in February 1989 and encompassed society, the economy, the state system and political life. It practically started with policy changes, which affected other elements of social reality. Thus, the systemic transformation led to a market economy and a democratic system. Polish transformation was revolutionary in nature and, as in the case of most countries of the former socialist bloc countries, was not entirely effortless. However, it has led to a relatively smooth transition to a system created under new norms, rules and institutions of a democratic nature. There has been a change from the principle of unified state power to the principle of separation of powers. Human and civil rights and freedoms have been developed in line with European standards. Legal guarantees of their compliance have been established. The monopoly of the communist party towards political pluralism was abolished. There has been a transition from a state based on the principle of socialist rule of law to the legal state, and finally from the principle of the sovereignty of the working people of towns and villages to the principle

 | DOI:10.1163/9789004518841_012

of national sovereignty. Relevant in the context of this study is the transition from a planned economy (artificially formed for the purposes of the policy of real socialism, in other words, the process of transition from a planned economy to a market economy) opening the way to a developed service sector, new forms of ownership and legal regulations allowing a variety of possibilities to undertake economic activities (Arak et al., 2019). The transformations of the market and parliamentary economy are slowly gaining ground also in the social consciousness, although some of its elements are unacceptable from the point of view of everyday life. The consequence of the lack of activation skills in the new socio-economic conditions were and are, inter alia, problems with employment, proper functioning in the new socio-economic realities, coping with the need to organize life individually and independently.These problems caused, among other things, a lowering of the standard of living and entering the sphere of marginalisation, exclusion and, as a consequence, often homelessness. The reform taking place at all levels of life requires a different social consciousness, which had to overcome awareness barriers, shape attitudes of social, professional and political activity leading to the formation of entrepreneurship and elimination of helplessness of individuals and social groups. However, eliminating the often ossified attitude of waiting for state paternalism, which was a kind of natural state shaped by decades of political coercion, was not easy and many individuals did not find themselves in the new reality. This applies not only to those living in Polish port cities, but also to residents of Pegeer (State Farms - very popular in communist Poland). Since 1989 we have been talking about the state becoming a real space for citizens' lives, about the actual empowerment of society within the new structures of state functioning. Polish society forced and succumbed to the changes taking place (Skorowski, 2014, p. 78).

2 Family in a Port Town

Sociology is one of the most important disciplines documenting and diagnosing changes in the quality of human life, particularly in the period of intense socioeconomic changes. From a sociological point of view, seas are the exploration of a specific environment, which, according to Yan Yunxiang, is a kind of litmus test of all kinds of changes taking place in the social space (Yunxiang, 2003). Observing the condition of the family in the context of intentionally introduced elements shaping it (such as 500 plus program in Poland), it is an equally important element, as well as activities not included in the scope of family model modification, but that can indirectly affect it. In the nineties of the last century, we participated in radical changes in a socioeconomic reality, also, or even primarily – at the microstructural level. These are new determinants of life, consumption, work, mentality models. A series of rapid changes in social systems was accompanied by the changes taking place in the models of family life. The aims of family life can be manifested in various ways. It is then obvious that changes in the sphere of values and goals of the family are an image strongly correlated with the functioning of the family inside, as well as the changes taking place in its environment, its condition and ability to last and develop.

Sociological analyses indicate the peculiar impact of the sea and sea-related economy, which is a temporary process of influencing social reality (Janiszewski, 1988, p. 5–14). In the environment of a port town, dependent on the maritime economy, the families of seafarers functioned as a distinctive link and a beneficiary of the two worlds characterised by freedom (heard and felt through stories and material items) and the one, where the life of real socialism in Poland took place. A special feature of these families was the work of one of the spouses on a sea-going vessel. William I. Thomas and Florian Znaniecki, who, while examining peasant families in a wide sociological context, evidenced a family structure, processes, its disorganisation, factors of its reorganisation and the adaptation of families to new living conditions, have already described research on the family functioning in such special conditions (Thomas, Znaniecki, 1967, p. 97–123).

3 Research Methodology

There were practically two bases for undertaking the subject of research in the field of marine sociology. The first is my own academic experience under the supervision of Professor Ludwik Janiszewski, who was my first doctoral thesis supervisor, and the second is the fact of many years of living in a port city in Poland, direct contact with seafarers and their families and their problems with the new reality after 1989. It can be said that personal participation in social change has been included in the scientific framework of the theory of marine sociology.

Maritime sociology, created by Ludwik Janiszewski and other employees of the University of Szczecin, developed the subject and methodological scope of the sub-discipline. Thus, the work of the University can be counted among the founders of marine sociology. We date the foundations for the new sub-discipline to 1963. It was in this year when systematic empirical research started, containing characteristic research tools and techniques, and their verification in the studied environment, also as a participating observer. This was a kind of an impulse to carry out the observation of the seafarers' environment and their families in a similar way. Personally, as a student of the Maritime School Complex I experienced work at sea, which I could later put into the framework of scientific studies. The idea thus created of a sub-discipline of sociology usually referred to as "marine sociology", i. e. the sociology of the sea, is today the basis for the world's analyses in the field of this specific human activity in specific social and economic conditions. It collected facts about the natural and social reality of seafaring people (Wozniak, 1988, p. 295).

Research in maritime sociology has clearly highlighted the specific characteristics of maritime occupations and cultural and family functioning in port cities. The years of transition I mention in the study also show the very significant importance of the time before 1989 and the systemic changes that shaped the specificity of the work of seafarers and, at the same time, showed their unnatural shape in the communist social and economic realities. Research in this area has shown not only the category of "seafarers" directly working at sea, but also the whole environment performing social and service functions in the specific environment of a Polish port city. Research on the changes in the quality of life of seafarers and maritime economy staff was a consequence of dialogue with the families that participated in the 1989 changes. An additional factor was interviews with several homeless people, who experienced working in the maritime industry in Świnoujście. Their homelessness was, in their opinion, a consequence of changes that took place at that time.

As a result, a short interview sheet was developed, the content of which was used in this study. The interviews were general conversations, mainly focused on collecting the opinions of the surveyed group on the changes that took place in their lives in the years of socioeconomic transformations in 1989. As a consequence of the several dozen years that have passed since 1989, there were very few families to talk to and the results included in this study are a kind of testimony of those days.

Testimony cannot in any way be predestined for scientific generalisations, but it presents the reality the families had to struggle with those days. The research was conducted in the port city of Świnoujście in the summer (July-August 2019). Many families formerly associated with the sea and sea work have gone to different places in Poland and abroad. I talked to, inter alia, families who moved to Warsaw or Silesia to earn their living and the sailors became miners (this range and extreme characteristics of the professions was horrifying to the sailors themselves).

The information included in the next chapter comes from interviews with 30 families (husband and wife) and 16 employees of companies related to the maritime economy (including three homeless people). An interview with the only woman who worked on deep-sea ships is particularly noteworthy. This case is special due to the fact that it is the only example of a female sailor in a male-dominated world and at the same time, the only testimony of the impact of such a characteristic work on the family life. The results of this interview are listed in this analysis.

4 Families of Seafarers and Fishers in the Transition Period

Following the statement of Arkadiusz Kołodziej, who in their work entitled '*The Concept of Marinization by Ludwik Janiszewski - To Understand the Influence of the Sea*' referred to sea-related human activities, including socio-cultural factor modifying social reality by creating marine elements in its area. This factor is composed of different economic, political, scientific and cultural activities. Kołodziej refers to Ludwik Janiszewski's work and his concept of marinisation, mainly focused on the influence of the professional sea-related activity on social reality (Kołodziej, 2019, p. 164–173).

R. Woźniak's definition states that "the subject of research in marine sociology are primarily the phenomena and processes of the formation, development and decline of various social communities, whose life and work co-determine the nature and intensity of the tasks of the efficiency of society and the state" (Woźniak, 1971). Ludwik Janiszewski referred to maritime sociology in a similar way, claiming that "the research subject of maritime sociology are various communities, institutions and social processes related to the basic directions and forms of human activity at sea". Janiszewski emphasised that marine sociology is "a detailed sociological discipline that studies collective, institutional and spontaneous forms of diverse, mostly economic, but not exclusively, human activity at sea, under the influence of the sea or for the benefit of the sea, with particular emphasis on the conditions and social consequences of this activity". Is it not a fact that in the context of the transformations of the aforementioned 1989, what is striking in both approaches is the reference to transformations and creative processes in the social environment of seafarers' work. These definitions, in my opinion, run significantly ahead of time to the moment when social and economic transformations have dramatically changed the face of "seafarers" and their working and living environment. It is impossible not to get the impression that these words have the character of "prophecies". The basis of individual analyses of the environment of seafarers and their families was also caused, as Robert Woźniak wrote, by the scientific resurgence of maritime sociology after 1989 related to the revolt of the masses and the changes that had so significantly affected the social organism (Woźniak, Woźniak, 2013, p. 69).

In the issues covered by this study, Janiszewski's concept is of great significance in the context of economic and political influence – related to the changes –, as well as the social element, being an unintentional beneficiary of these changes. Unintentional, as against the demonstrated will to change (everyone longed freedom, access to the world, a change to a democratic system), but no one expected the consequences of introducing systemic changes into the sphere of the internal functioning of families. Thus, the families of sailors and seafarers experienced the transformations of 1989 doubly. The situation of the sailors' families before 1989 was usually the following: a person working at sea (usually a man) supported the family using two sources of income. The first was a fixed salary (relatively low in comparison to other earnings), paid monthly by the employer, e.g. Przedsiębiorstwo Połowów (Eng. fishing company) in zloty. The second part was usually dollars paid as an addition to the salary for an abroad job – a foreign currency allowance (similar to business trip remuneration). A sailor's salary was not high. Hence, today, many sailors have low pensions, but foreign currency allowances were a goldmine, and even converted by the Polish authorities into so-called Baltona vouchers, became a source of their prosperity.[1] In economic realities, the second, dollar part of the salary was a huge income when converted into zloty, which made sailors' families benefiting from these goods extremely wealthy.[2] However, since the foreign currencies did not count into the retirement pension, the retirement pensions after leaving the workplace were rather small, not allowing a normal life. There was a certain regularity in the interviews – the majority of the families lived from day to day as if the world were to be the same all the time, so they spent money whenever possible. One of the families mentioned that exotic fruit was rotting on their tables (early 1980's), while others

1 Baltona, a chain of stores in Poland during the PRL period, was supplying ships in Polish and foreign seaports, diplomatic missions, and LOT Polish Airlines planes. Generally, it is associated with luxury products that could be bought with convertible currencies - dollars or sailor's vouchers. The 1980s, before the change of the economic system in Poland, saw the boom in Baltona, which trademark was a smiling sailor.

2 In 1980, a dollar was 180 zloty, and a year later – PLN 300. The introduced reforms caused the dollar to go up to 600 zloty. In the summer of 1989, it was 3 000 zloty and in autumn reached 14 000 zloty. The salary at that time was between 5 000 zloty to 20 000 zloty. If the foreign currency allowance for seafarer ranged from a few hundred to almost 2 000 dollars, the amount of monthly earnings was insurmountable, even if you only earned for six months per year. For example, the value of an apartment sold in 1988 was 600 dollars. I recall buying it by a seafarer for one foreign currency allowance.

were lining up for basic items. Some of them mentioned they did not spend a lot of money at all and lived a modest life, saving money for later, with the idea of starting a business or adding to their retirement pension. If they kept foreign currencies too long until valorisation in the nineties, they were unfortunately incredibly lossy. There is a popular anecdote among these people that the political transformation caused the value of the house to drop to the value of a hen running around the yard. Obviously, the possibilities to spend money were limited due to market conditions, but those more resourceful were able to invest their money. Unfortunately, there were only a few. When organising the research material, one should first of all base on the studies by Ludwik Janiszewski, who concluded that the time seafarers spent with their wives and children, was a moment of regaining mental balance (Janiszewski 1976: 138). Thus, the household of a port town marriage was really specific, deviating from standard families in Poland, due to the nature of their contacts and the social roles played by individual family members. The sailors, working away from home for six months in a quasi-total institution, treated their homes as a haven of peace and a place to rest.[3]

I took the notion of total institution by referring to the term "sea-ship" from Erving Goffman's concept of total institution. A seagoing vessel is, to my mind, an institution that exemplifies the term while obviously having its own distinct characteristics. The term total institution is used to analyse institutions where entire communities are treated in a bureaucratic manner while being physically isolated from the normal course of life activities. They are required to perform multiple tasks such as sleeping, working, resting within the same institution. Additionally, on a marine vessel, there is complete isolation from the home environment. This is why I advocate an approach to the ship as a total institution, and this is the term I will use, not least because, according to Goffman's theory, " every institution tends to constrain its members [...] the constraining or total character is often symbolised by physical barriers preventing contact with the outside world" (Goffman, 2006, p. 316).

In the case of a seagoing vessel, total institution is a very capacious, universal concept and refers to phenomena occurring in the lives of seafarers. An example was a paper with the telling title, "The seagoing vessel as a total institution". Of course, it should be mentioned that Janiszewski stressed the ambiguity of the term, acknowledging that it cannot be applied in the same sense to a sea-going ship, a prison, a concentration camp, or any other institution, since various tasks, goals, values, and social norms are realised in them (Janiszewski, 1992).

3 I advocate a scientific attitude that treats the ship as a total institution.

Based on my own observations of the seafarers' environment, I need to emphasise that the time of their schedule was distributed periodically in the systematic work. As a result, both spouses and even children needed to take a break from each other after a six-month stay at home together. When the husband left, the longing and waiting for his return intensified, and so every six months. The situation of seafarers on tramp steamers was different. There were times when a ship did not arrive in the country for a few months or even a year. There were shifts on the deep-sea fishing vessels, but they took place every six or eight months. These ships fished in distant waters, and there was no chance that they would appear in the country. However, this is a completely different work and family profile.

It should be emphasised that families associated with working at sea, concentrated in port cities, had a completely different quality of life and experienced the economic transformations taking place in Poland in a completely different way. They also looked at what was happening around them completely differently. However, this does not change the fact (as my research shows) that they experienced these changes strongly.

The marriages and families of seafarers have undergone significant changes, particularly as regards a traditional model, where the man works away from home, and the woman takes care of the hearth of the home. In the case of seafarers' families, this situation was caused by socio-political and economic changes. The first element of the changes was everyday life in general, here considered as the characteristic of the quality of life. The sailor, and thus his family, were the masters of the world in the communist times. The children wore clothes inaccessible to common people, the wife smelled of expensive perfume, and the house was full of top-shelf goods from Pewex and Baltona. It needs emphasising that the whole town benefited from the sea work because seafarers were engaged in barter trade. The port town lived in the lap of second-hand luxury, unavailable to the citizens from outside the port town enclave. Among the imported treasures were exotic fruits, coffee, fragrant soaps and shampoos with appealing labels, soda etc. These goods were accompanied by purchases from Pewex and Baltona and frequently reached commonly accessible barter trade markets. Denim or nylon coats, bought in foreign ports, were sold in wholesale lots in Turzyn, one of the most popular markets in Szczecin, and in Poland in general. Many people at that time dreamt of wearing original, branded clothes, a Wrangler denim jacket, having the latest world music records, a calculator or a watch. These products were unavailable in the country, or available in minimal quantities only in Pewex or Baltona, or on the black market. Seafarers also could take their families on board with them, where they had the opportunity to visit and shop in the

West. Seafarers' families had no financial problems - unless we consider those related to the acquired wealth that had to be hidden from the tax authorities. In such cases, even fabricated divorces came into play. However, I do not personally know a lot of families who were able to gather significant property; the majority of them lived as if the world were to remain the same. The changes following the transition caused not only the shutdown of maritime economy companies but also a change in the level of life of the seafarers family and the whole community of a port town. In terms of the analysis of these changes, an attempt is made to find a value of the family environment individualism, which was brought up by Paul Betts (Betts 2010). In reference to this analysis, it can be stated that each seafarer's family felt the process of change very distinctively and operated according to an individual management plan.

Another specific element of the changes were mutual family relations and the roles played in them. A typical seafarer's family was a working man and a woman taking care of the house and children. The division of roles was clear for all parties. The wife was responsible for all domestic duties for a few months of the year and was a full-time father and mother in one. In general, the life of such a family was completely different from that of others – nowadays, this profile is similar in terms of domestic duties division and the husband's work away from home for a few months. However, the financial conditions of those days allowed for the wife not to work or to undertake jobs that did not require education or professional experience. The sailor's wife had to cope on her own and get things such as fixing the sink, washing machine or power plug done. She could not ask her husband for advice and had to decide on her own. She had to take care of children and could not share these responsibilities with her husband. Children were also raised a bit differently when the father was not around – but this is a topic for another discussion. In the mentioned case of a female sailor, the family did not make it and the husband left to another woman. The family was a woman with one child. However, she did not quit the job as one providing stability and certainty of livelihood. Nevertheless, it happened at the expense of raising the child, who was raised by the grandmother. In this case, the family roles and the emotional level were disrupted. In the era of transformations, these roles were reconstructed when seafarers returned home and had no job. At that time, it usually appeared that a full-time marital life diverged from the previous reality. Suddenly, the husband was still at home and asserted his rights as to household management; there was no temporality of stay – which was often a chance to take the same time apart. Moreover, the children turned out to be different than they seemed to be during short stays ashore.

Previously, introducing own rules was acceptable because of its temporary nature, but now is a constant element of married life. In mutual relations, the wife's work was also impactful on the domestic conditions and on her, thus her husband's behaviour (Maintier, Joulain, Floch 2011: 242–250). The first conflicts began, accompanied by the lack of professional and financial stability. Women professional activity contributed to the phenomena not observed previously or observed only to a small extent – the participation of husband and wife in its implementation in the aspects related to running a household, as well as performing gainful activities and earnings particularisation (Biedroń 2009: 49–50). It is noteworthy that women rather followed a combination strategy model, combining motherhood with professional activity (Jarmołowicz, Kalinowska 2008:154). Thus, they dealt better with the necessity to reorganise their lives, which significantly affected also further described homelessness. Professional activity of women and their earnings affected not only the balance of power in the family but also the transformation of relationships at home. They also had an influence on the offspring, towards which the care-related rules, standards and practices were changed. By starting jobs, women were forced to organise the home space and mutual relations in the new dimension of being mothers, wives and lovers, having less and less time and energy to equally dedicate it to non-home matters. In the families of seafarers at that time, support and mutual help were highly desirable in the new reality. Men were not always able to meet these requirements, as proved further in the text.

The division of roles in the seafarers' houses directly affected education – being another variable – of the seafarers' wives, their experience and professional activity. Nowadays, seafarers' wives usually work, as today seafaring does not guarantee such luxury as to let them stay home. Hence, they have less time to look after the house and children, but, as I mentioned earlier, the everyday life and the reality of port towns changed as well. In the transformation period, seafarers' wives were either uneducated or had only primary or vocational education. They functioned perfectly in the times of prosperity, engaged in trade or minor works. Seafarers had a characteristic education, as discussed in the next paragraph.

Wives had to get education quickly, what was not that easy those days, or use educational resources within the limits of their own and educational system' capabilities. Education had a significant influence on the change of lifestyle in the era of transformation. Due to the changes, wives had to find their place on the labour market, as well as their husbands who lost their jobs suddenly.

In the 1980s, maritime academies trained in several fields (based on the experience of Świnoujście). The most popular was the sailor (usually working on ships at a fish processing plant[4]), mechanical fitter (usually working in the

4 There were two (basic) types of fishing vessels in the sea fleet. The first type was a vessel that only catches and stores fish, which, after filling the holds, was transported to a shore-based

engine room of deep-sea ships) and a navigator technician who could work on a bridge or in the engine. Such a distinctive division allowed people with technical education to be hired in the shipyard or port. The worst situation applied to people whose education was related to the specificity of a port town and maritime economy (i.e. sailors). Most of them signed foreign contracts with shipowners of foreign flags. Seafarers' wives were often able to do nursing or cleaning, as well as retailing in suburban markets or selling. In the 1990s (until 2004), the so-called white fleet operated in Poland. These were ships under different flags, but managed by German owners. The white fleet allowed for shopping in duty-free shops during the cruise. Apart from tourists and tradespeople from outside Świnoujście, many employees of the former maritime industry and their families had the chance to benefit from the cruises. Goods purchased on duty-free ships, which were successfully smuggled bypassing customs offices, found buyers on the border market, where German customers used to shop most often. In the mid-90s, the border market was attended not only by many former employees of the maritime-related companies but also graduates of the maritime vocational schools concentrated in Świnoujście. Their job characteristic did not let them get another job, and the market was a really profitable place at that time. Numerous migration processes outside Świnoujście, searching for new jobs and education, were observed after years.

The changes in the maritime economy were reminiscent of what was happening in state collective farms – a sharp increase in unemployment, no opportunities on the professional market, no professional activity, degradation of the family and its level of life.

The aforementioned factors had a direct influence on the last of the selected variables, i.e. homelessness. Shutting down the maritime economy-related companies had an effect similar to closing state collective farms. When the maritime economy collapsed in the transition period, the situation of many families deteriorated. No job for the head of the family or both spouses, problems with retraining (sailors are a specific professional group – especially those working in fish production). As a consequence, from day to day, entire families found themselves on the brink of an existential, and often also mental breakdown. They often became homeless. People, whose work was particularly directed towards the maritime economy, ended up on the street. Retraining was a slow process, and many times, people with many years of experience at sea were unable to retrain; they did not have enough enthusiasm, skills or mental strength.

---

processing plant or other vessels specialised in the processing itself. The second type were vessels that combined the function of fishing and processing. This means that the vessel was engaged in catching and processing the caught fish at the same time.

Homelessness obviously was not an immediate aftermath of losing a job since the majority of seafarers had their own apartments obtained in the times of prosperity. Most, if not all, companies centred by the sea, cared for securing a place to live, obviously to the extent allowed by the regime. Whole housing cooperatives were established, gathering only seafarers. Specific architecture performed its function when one person worked at sea. When the family had to live together permanently, they lacked space and functionality. For example, in Szczecin and Świnoujście, a lot of new apartments were built, which did not exceed 20 square meters per apartment, which was sufficient for a single seafarer in between the contracts, but was not enough for an entire family. The so-called family studio flats of 30 square meters were enough for a family when the husband spent most of his time working away from home, but was a source of conflict in other cases. Thus, the aforementioned homelessness was a process of gradual submerging into everyday problems, which, when cumulated, led to homelessness. In conversations with homeless seafarers and those familiar with such cases, a picture of entering homelessness was presented for several reasons. One of them was the change of family functioning from temporary to permanent. This change entailed several problems, such as changes in mutual functioning, performing social roles, communication, performing housekeeping duties, administering and completing formalities related to house, school and work. Accumulation of these elements often caused misunderstandings and conflicts that led to divorce. Men who could not cope with loneliness often left and ended up on the street. Another process was the gradual degradation of entire families. Losing financial stability resulted in conflicts, mental problems, addictions and – as a consequence – losing the ability to maintain a house. In the end, families ended up in substitute accommodation, but they could not maintain them either and ended up on the street. Also in this case rather men stayed on the street, as women, who decided to leave, coped differently – usually sheltered by distant relatives, frequently in another part of Poland.

In terms of homelessness, Świnoujście is a very peculiar town, not only due to homeless people being its inhabitants but also because of immigration that has been taking place here for many years. At first, migration was caused by an opportunity to earn extra money on the aforementioned white fleet, then – benefiting from the advantages of a tourist resort, where people could effectively collect life resources.

Arkadiusz Kołodziej, to whom I referred earlier, asked whether work on a sea-going vessel affects the family life of seamen (Kołodziej, 2019), to which I have responded in a way with this study.

Confirmation and at the same time reference to the question of the mentioned author are the answers to the questions from the interview sheet. In these statements, one could sense not only regret and longing for the times before the social changes, but also a kind of anger, quoting: "Things used to be better, we had the support of the company. Everyone knew what they were supposed to do was set from the top", "changes to the new policy have only done badly. They wrecked so many workplaces where everyone had employment", "Then everything was stolen, wrecked and people were left in the lurch".

Other responses related to the need to make changes to one's life, quoting: "When the old man stopped working on the sea, he had to look for work at another plant and what was different in this town? (Świnoujście), he had to retrain, first as a stoker and locksmith in a school. Fortunately, he graduated from a vocational school where they taught locksmithing. Then he started looking for another job."

Regarding the search for another job, there were also positive opinions, quoting: "The situation improved when the old man got a proposal to sail on a foreign ship, and his friend arranged it for him. Then he started sailing again, but his salary was completely different than when he was sailing in the Odra (name of the company)"

The assessments of the quality of life in the pre-transformation period were also very interesting, as quoting: "Once, when my husband came, there was everything at home, it was a holiday, he brought a lot of things, money and we could buy for the children whatever they wanted. We went to Pewex and it was a real prestige.[5] Especially when we were living somewhere in Poland, where it was miserable". Our children, that is "children of Odra", were children from high society compared to kids from Poland. When they went to organised summer camps, other children often envied them. Their different clothes were evident, even the food at the colonies was different and the cooks were different. It was a completely different world, not what it is now".

Currently, some of the families of former maritime workers meet regularly and talk about the past. It was also a great time to collect information useful for this study. These memories reflect a kind of nostalgia, sometimes sadness and anger. Generally, however, one gets the impression that this generation has already learned their history lesson and is fit for the new reality. The situation

5 Pewex- A state-owned enterprise running foreign currency stores in the times of the Polish People's Republic. In them, you could buy, for currency, imported and domestic goods, unavailable in other stores. A synonym for luxury goods in the times of the Polish People's Republic, available only to seafarers.

is worse in the case of people experiencing homelessness, where, next to anger, there is a very strong sense of historic injustice and resentment towards other people, often co-workers, colleagues, who get along somehow and have not thought about the colleagues who have not succeeded in life.

Apart from a number of typical economic elements influencing the functioning of the seafarers' families, the material focuses on the functioning of the family as a social group, shaped by the characteristics of the place of residence and the work performed.

5 Summary

All transformations in socioeconomic or political space cause changes in the family. As I have proven in this study, these changes relate to the professional commitment of family members, the division of roles in marriage, the durability of the marital bond and fundamental functions of the family, as well as domestic activity of family members, relations between them and functions performed.

The changes of the family in Poland can be viewed in a dichotomous wa., On the one hand, they were revolutionary, and on the other – evolutionary. Taking the collected material into consideration, it should be acknowledged that the changes in the style and quality of life that took place at the end of the last century were of enormous importance for the families of seafarers and families related to the maritime economy. They had a dual nature as they both diametrically transformed the way of life and caused the family to evolve to the needs of a new socioeconomic situation. In my opinion, the political situation was of minor importance for such families. The revolution of changes affecting the evolution of actions has an impact on the functioning of individuals and entire families to this day. It was of particular significance for the families who first lost their jobs, then family stabilisation, often turned into addictions and as a consequence – lost their previous lives and ended up on the street. It cannot be denied that the majority of the seafarers' families were able to cope with such a drastic change of style and quality of life. However, it does not alter the fact that some of them have been ruined. Homeless people, who can be met in support centres to this day, usually indicate the reason for their homelessness as related to the 1980s changes. They often come back to those times, that gave them a sense of security and basically formed their entire world. New socioeconomic circumstances forced them to deal on their own, and this was often the biggest problem.

Bibliography

Arak, P., Czernicki, Ł. , Czerwiński, A., Kukołowicz, P., Kutwa, K., Maj, M. (2019). *Polska 1989–2019 Społeczeństwo, gospodarka, kultura, Polski Instytut Ekonomiczny* (p. 8–10). Warszawa

Betts, P. (2010). *Within Walls. Private Life in the German Democratic Republic.* Oxford University Press

Biedroń, M. (2009). Realizacja funkcji rodziny w kontekście globalnych przemian socjokulturowych. In Ładyżyński, A., (ed.) *Rodzina we współczesności.* (pp. 49–50). Wrocław

Goffman, E. (2006). Charakterystyka instytucji totalnych. In Jasińska-Kania, L.M., Nijakowski, J., Szacki, M., Ziółkowski, A. (eds.) *Współczesne teorie socjologiczne.* Warszawa: Wydawnictwo Naukowe Scholar 2006.

Jarmołowicz, W., Kalinowska, B., Praca i płaca kobiet na polskim i unijnym rynku pracy, In Jarmołowicz, W. (ed.). *Przemiany na współczesnym rynku pracy.* (p. 154). Poznań

Maintier, J. W. Ch., Joulain, M., Le Floch, N. (2011). To what extent do attitudes to work and the subjective components of non-work contribute to the life satisfaction of men and women in dual - earner couples? *Women's Studies International Forum* 34, 242–250

Janiszewski, L., (1988). Marynizacja. Przyczynek teoretyczny. *Roczniki Socjologii Morskiej* 4, 5–14

Janiszewski, L., (1988). Marynizacja. Przyczynek teoretyczny, Rocznik Socjologii Morskiej, Maritimization. Theoretical contribution. *Yearbook of Maritime Sociology* IV

Janiszewski, L. (n.d.) Ludzie morza i ich rodziny w procesie przemian [Sea people and their families in the process of change], MB Poligrafia, (pp 23–41). Szczecin

Janiszewski, L., Socjologia morska jako nauka. Maritime sociology as a science, Socjologia morska, t. 1, Ossolineum 1985, (1964); zob. A. Matejko, Socjologia ludzi morza, "Tygodnik Morski", nr 34

Janiszewski L., (1976). Rodziny marynarzy i rybaków. *Studium socjologiczne,* (pp 138). Warszawa, Poznań

Janiszewski L., (1992). *Statek morski jako instytucja totalna* Wydawnictwo Uniwersytetu Szczecińskiego, Szczecin

Kołodziej, A. (2019). The Concept of Marinization by Ludwik Janiszewski - To Understand the Influence of the Sea. To Understand the Influence of the Sea. *Cultural Interaction Studies of Sea Port Cities*, 20, 159–179

Skorowski, H., Polskie przemiany w perspektywie politologiczno-socjologicznej MAZOWSZE Studia Regionalne, Analizy i Studia nr 15/2014

Thomas, W. J., Znaniecki, F., (1976). *Chłop polski w Europie i Ameryce* [Polish peasant in Europe and America], Vol. 1, (pp. 97–123). Warsaw

Woźniak, R. (1971). Środowiska nautyczne w Polsce w świetle socjologii. *Nautologia*, no 2–4.

Woźniak. M., Woźniak R., (2013). Mniejszości narodowe w morskiej metropolii transgranicznej. *Edukacja Humanistyczna* 29(2), 69–94

Woźniak, R. B., (1988). Nowe zakresy badań socjologii morskiej w Polsce, Ruch Prawniczy, Ekonomiczny i Socjologiczny zeszyt 3—(pp. 295)

Yunxiang, Y., (2003). *Private Life under Socialism: Love, Intimacy, and Family Change in a Chinese Village, 1949–1999*. Stanford

Index

www.ingramcontent.com/pod-product-compliance
Lightning Source LLC
LaVergne TN
LVHW010625300926
849162LV00001B/71